The Illustrated General Craufurd and His Light Division

MAJOR-GENERAL ROBERT CRAUFURD
LEADER OF THE LIGHT DIVISION

The Illustrated
General Craufurd and
His Light Division

The Military Career of Wellington's Belligerent
General during the Peninsular War

Alexander H. Craufurd

With a Short Biography of General Craufurd
by John William Cole

LEONAUR

The Illustrated General Craufurd and His Light Division
The Military Career of Wellington's Belligerent General during the Peninsular War
By Alexander H. Craufurd
With a Short Biography of General Craufurd
by John William Cole

FIRST EDITION

Leonaur is an imprint of Oakpast Ltd

Copyright in this form © 2019 Oakpast Ltd

ISBN: 978-1-78282-816-7 (hardcover)
ISBN: 978-1-78282-817-4 (softcover)

http://www.leonaur.com

Publisher's Notes

Contents

To

THE OFFICERS, NON-COMMISSIONED OFFICERS, AND PRIVATES
OF THE
43RD LIGHT INFANTRY (1ST OXFORDSHIRE LIGHT INFANTRY),
FORMERLY THE SENIOR REGIMENT OF THE
GLORIOUS LIGHT DIVISION,
THIS VOLUME, WHICH CONTAINS SO MUCH
CONCERNING THE GREAT DEEDS OF
THEIR MILITARY ANCESTORS,
IS DEDICATED,
AS A TOKEN OF SINCERE REGARD AND AFFECTION,
BY THEIR OLD COMPANION AND FRIEND,
THE AUTHOR.

While memorials of the war in the Peninsula exist, the name of Robert Craufurd will be for ever identified with this noble body of troops, (i.e. the 43rd, the 52nd, and the 95th Rifles.) Cole's *Memoirs of British Generals Distinguished during the Peninsular War* vol. 1.

Marching Order   Review Order   Marching Order

PRIVATES, 1810 – 1813.

Preface

There are two passages in English military literature which make one marvel that nothing approaching to a real memoir of General Robert Craufurd has ever been written; the one is in the Duke of Wellington's Despatches, and the other in the *Early Military Life of Sir George Napier*. Writing to Craufurd on April 9, 1810, Wellington says to him:

> Since you have joined the army, I have always wished that you should command our outposts, for many reasons into which it is unnecessary to enter.

Sir George Napier says of his old leader, Robert Craufurd:

> Although he was a most unpopular man, every officer of the Light Division must acknowledge that, by his unwearied and active exertions of mind and body, that division was brought to a state of discipline and knowledge of the duties of light troops, which never was equalled by any division in the British Army, or surpassed by any division of the French Army.

In some ways it may seem unsuitable that a *civilian* should write concerning so great a military leader and so glorious a division. But, unfortunately, no soldier has directed his attention to the work here undertaken; and being General Craufurd's grandson and present representative, I have at all events a strong hereditary interest in the subject, and I have also the advantage of an intimate acquaintance with letters and papers relating to the general's private as well as his public life. It is very likely that this volume may contain some technical errors or inaccuracies; but these can easily be corrected, if the book should attain to a second edition.

Of course, whilst writing this work, I have very frequently consulted military friends when I was in doubt as to the technical expressions used in war. And the fact that in my former writings I have been accustomed to deal with far deeper problems, demanding the most precise and accurate thinking, may possibly be of some use to me in this work that I have now endeavoured to perform.

This volume, however, is intended to be essentially light reading. One of my main objects has been to gather together into a compact and portable form the many interesting and amusing anecdotes about the Light Division, which are at present scattered through a considerable number of scarce and inaccessible books. Thus, to preserve and render easily accessible to the public all these famous stories, has appeared to me nothing less than a duty owing to the most glorious of all British Divisions, and to its renowned leader.

The letters and the long paper by Sir John Moore have never hitherto been published, so far as I know. I have a very large collection of Wellington's autograph letters to Craufurd. Unfortunately, these have been published in Gurwood's edition of the duke's *Despatches*. But many of them are so interesting that I have freely used them to illustrate my subject, quoting from the original letters in my own possession. The letter from Wellington, which is marked private, is now made public for the first time, to the best of my knowledge. Of course, the reasons for keeping it private have long since passed away.

Though I am quite aware of the necessary imperfection of my knowledge of military technicalities, it will be observed that I speak with perfect assurance and confidence when my subject leads me to deal with the ways, thoughts, and feelings of private soldiers. For many years I have been in the habit of giving voluntary assistance to army chaplains, or acting chaplains, in their work, during a great portion of each year. For five successive winters periods of about six months each I believe that I passed almost more time with the men in hospital in Shorncliffe camp than any other minister of any denomination. During the greater part of four summers I have helped the chaplain to look after the men belonging to three different cavalry regiments at Piershill barracks, near Edinburgh.

Besides my five winters passed in helping at Shorncliffe, I have also spent three winters in helping the acting chaplain at Parkhurst barracks, in the Isle of Wight. During the first part of this time the 43rd Light Infantry were at Parkhurst, and during the later part another regiment representative of the old Light Division was there, *viz.* the 4th Battalion of the Rifle Brigade.

Ever since the 43rd Light Infantry came home from India, I have been accustomed to help to look after the men of that regiment with peculiar regard and affection. I am an honorary member for life of its officers' mess, and I am accustomed to talk to its men in the most outspoken and familiar manner. This book is written from the point of view of one who sympathizes fully as much with what are called "common soldiers," as he does with British officers. I always feel keen interest in the men. Their frankness, and, in many cases, the warmth of their feelings always draw me towards them. And when I am with them, I feel that I am in contact with the realities of life, and not with its conventionalities, with human nature as it truly exists, and not with unmeaning artificialities.

I have also found that my decidedly "broad" views on religion have caused me to come into far closer contact with the hearts and minds of the men than most ministers ever come. A well-known dignitary of the Church of England once said to me:

> Your work amongst soldiers always interests me, as bringing into contact natures in many respects singularly different, yet singularly near in some ways.

What the dean meant was this, that the men have no cut-and-dry religious formulas, because they seldom think on such subjects, and that I have no such formulas, because deep and prolonged thought has deprived me of them. And so, from widely different causes, the men and I are alike, "naked and not ashamed" in a spiritual sense. I firmly believe that the sympathetic and compassionate Christianity of Christ is admirably suited to meet the real wants of soldiers and of thinkers; but the narrower forms of religion are, as a matter of fact, about equally repulsive to both these totally different classes of human beings. (Experience has taught me that a strong sense of humour and a real love of jokes are an immense aid to all who seek to get at and influence the hearts of soldiers.)

My best thanks are due to my friend General W. Napier, for his kind permission to make free use of his most interesting and admirable work, *The Early Military Life of Sir George Napier*, (republished by Leonaur as *George Napier of the 52nd*.) Nowhere else in the English language do we find so vividly and well expressed the feelings cherished towards their men by really great British officers; nowhere else can we find such genuine appreciation of the many fine qualities so often displayed by the English private soldier, and such a deep sense of the claims which he has on the consideration, kindness and often on the affection of those placed over him. The mind and heart of Sir George Napier were penetrated with the kindly sagacity of Sir John Moore; and if our present officers would learn of that noblest of all our leaders, (Moore), we should hear no more of mutinous conduct in our regiments.

CHAPTER 1

Earlier Life

Considering the comparative smallness of its population, Scotland may justly claim to have contributed very largely and generously to the successes and undying glories of Britain's most dangerous, most brilliantly picturesque, and most important war the long war waged against the French in the earlier years of this century. Besides the services of Sir Ralph Abercromby in Egypt, and besides the invaluable aid of the well-known Scottish regiments, the northern part of our kingdom gave to the army engaged in the Peninsular War Sir David Baird and Graham Lord Lynedoch, and also Sir John Hope, as well as many other illustrious soldiers. And to the famous Light Division itself, which is commonly considered almost entirely English, Scotland supplied its three most dominant and characteristic names, those of Moore, Craufurd, and Napier.

And amongst other Scottish names renowned throughout this same division were those of Sir James Shaw Kennedy, the most trusted and confidential of all the officers of General Craufurd, and of the brilliant young Charles Macleod, Colonel of the 43rd, and of William Campbell, brigade-major, an officer whose singular gallantry and nobleness of character endeared him to his general, and to William Napier, and to the whole British Army. The heroic Sydney Beckwith, Colonel of the 95th Rifles, was also, I believe, connected with Scotland in some way.

Robert Craufurd, like his friend and leader Sir John Moore, was descended from an old Ayrshire family. He was the third son of Alexander Craufurd, of Newark Castle, in the county of Ayr. The Craufurds of Newark were directly descended from those of Thirdpart, in the same county; and the family of Thirdpart were cadets of the house of Craufurd of Auchenames, who were the representatives of the old

13

Craufurds of Loudoun, a famous Ayrshire family which gave a mother to the Scottish patriot, William Wallace.

From this old stock young Robert Craufurd doubtless inherited a good deal of his constitutional pugnacity; for in earlier days in Ayrshire the Craufurds, together with their kinsmen the Campbells, were engaged in almost incessant family fights and quarrels with their neighbours and hereditary enemies the Kennedies.

Lawlessness and considerable disregard for conventional propriety and religious decorum, seem also in some measure to have been inherited from his progenitors by the future leader of the Light Division. For his ancestor in the time of King Charles I., the Rev. George Craufurd, minister of West Kilbride, seems to have been deposed "for worldly-mindedness, and for selling a horse on the Sabbath day." Possibly this latent impiety of the race may have been at work in the mind of the leader of the Light Division when, during his operations on the Coa, the whole army being sorely straitened for money:

> Craufurd, unable to feed his division, gave the reins to his fiery temper and seized some church plate, to purchase corn, a rash act which he was forced to redress; yet it convinced the priests that the distress was not feigned, and they procured some supplies.

Robert Craufurd's father sold the estate of Newark and settled in England. He was an intimate friend of "Old Q," the celebrated Duke of Queensberry. Though a man of considerable ability, he seems to have rather wasted his talents, leading the life of a man about town. From him his famous soldier son inherited a very violent temper as well as a great tendency to fits of depression and mental gloom. Alexander Craufurd (the father) married a Miss Crokatt, daughter of James Crokatt of Luxborough, in the county of Essex. The Crokatts also were people with Scotch connections. Alexander Craufurd was created a baronet in March, 1781.

Alexander's brother, Quentin Craufurd, was a very well-known man. In early life he went out to India, where he made a very large fortune. On returning home he settled in Paris, where he became an intimate friend of the unfortunate queen, Marie Antoinette, whom he assisted to escape on one occasion. He was a man of considerable talents, and an author of some reputation.

The two elder brothers of Robert Craufurd were both active men, occupying prominent positions in life. The eldest, James (afterwards Sir James), was British Resident at Hamburg from 1798 to 1803, and afterwards Minister Plenipotentiary at Copenhagen.

The next brother, Charles, was a far more remarkable man, an ardent soldier, endowed with great clearness and acuteness of judgment, who might have achieved much distinction if he had not been desperately wounded whilst serving with the Austrian Army. He and his more celebrated younger brother, Robert were firm and close friends. Together they translated one of the most famous German treatises on the art of war. As General Charles Craufurd's opinions will often be quoted in this memoir, it may be well to give here the following particulars concerning him, for some of which I am much indebted to an article in the *Dictionary of National Biography*, edited by Mr. Leslie Stephen.

Lieutenant General Sir Charles Craufurd, G.C.B., entered the army as a Cornet in the 1st Dragoon Guards, on December 15, 1778. He was promoted Lieutenant in 1781, and Captain into the 2nd Dragoon Guards in 1785. In that year he was appointed equerry to the Duke of York, whose intimate friend he became. He accompanied the Duke of York to the Netherlands as *aide-de-camp*, and was attached to the Austrian headquarters as representative of the English commander-in-chief. With the Austrian staff he was present at all the earlier battles of the war, was promoted for his services to the rank of Major in May, 1793, and Lieutenant-Colonel in February, 1794. In the middle of 1794 he left the Austrian headquarters, and was appointed Deputy-Adjutant-General to the English Army. In this capacity he specially distinguished himself by one daring charge, when, with but two squadrons of dragoons, he took three guns and one thousand prisoners.

In 1795 he was again sent on a special mission to the Austrian headquarters. He was an acute observer, and his reports are most valuable documents; they are preserved in the Record Office. In 1796, he was so severely wounded that he was invalided home, and henceforth his active services were lost to the army. But he still continued to give valuable advice to his more famous brother Robert, and exerted all his political and military influence in his favour. He was promoted Colonel on January 26, 1797, and Major-General on September 25, 1803. He married the widow of Thomas, third Duke of Newcastle, on February 7, 1800, on which same day his brother Robert was also married. Owing to his marriage General Charles Craufurd acquired considerable political influence during the minority of the young Duke of Newcastle. He entered the House of Commons as M.P. for East Retford in October, 1806, and resigned his seat in 1812. He was made Colonel of the 2nd Dragoon Guards in 1807, and promoted Lieutenant-General in 1810. He was made a G.C.B. on May 27, 1820, and he died in 1821.

Sir Charles Craufurd was a most intimate friend of General Charles Stewart, afterwards Marquis of Londonderry, from whom a most interesting and touching letter concerning General Robert Craufurd's death will be found in this volume.

Returning now to the subject of this memoir, I regret to say that I have been unable to ascertain where my grandfather, Robert Craufurd, received his earlier education. He was born on May 5, 1764, and entered the army at the early age of fifteen, and served four years as a subaltern in the 25th Regiment. Having been promoted to a company at the age of nineteen, he attended the reviews at Potsdam, together with his brother Charles. I have in my possession about six little notes addressed to the brothers Craufurd by the king, Frederick the Great, giving them permission to assist at the manoeuvres of the Prussian troops. These little notes are written in French by a secretary, and signed by the king himself. Young Craufurd visited the principal theatres of war on the continent, where, besides learning the German language well, he devoted his time to the prosecution of military studies, and pursued them with close application and unremitting ardour, so that he acquired a large knowledge of military tactics and of history.

Young Craufurd was promoted Captain into the 75th Regiment in 1783. On his return from the continent he was desirous of some active employment on foreign service, and consequently we find him employed in India under Lord Cornwallis. He served with the 75th Regiment through the war waged against Tippoo Sultan in 1790, 1791, and 1792, and distinguished himself wherever an occasion offered, for a time obtaining the command of his regiment as senior captain. Returning to England in 1794, he went to assist his elder brother, Colonel Charles Craufurd, who was then English representative at the Austrian headquarters. His elder brother being severely wounded, Robert Craufurd had the superintendence of the mission entrusted to him, and acquired much reputation in carrying it out. Returning to England, he was promoted Lieutenant-Colonel in December, 1797.

In 1798, an invasion of Ireland being apprehended, he was appointed Deputy-Quartermaster-General in that country. His services during the suppression of the Irish insurrection were warmly recognised by his former commander, Lord Cornwallis, and also by General Lake, more especially those rendered in the operations against. Gen-

FIRST HUSSARS.

SECOND HUSSARS.

eral Humbert and the French corps.

In 1799 he was again employed on a military mission to the Austrian armies during their campaign in Switzerland. Afterwards he served on the staff of the Duke of York in the expedition to Holland; and during that unfortunate campaign he secured the entire approbation of his commander, and added to his rapidly growing reputation.

During his whole life my grandfather seems to have been liable to fits of depression and disgust, during which he talked of retiring into private life. But he never could have endured a life of inactivity. And, well knowing this, his brother Charles gave him wise advice, as in the following letter, written in the year 1801. I have omitted the less interesting portions of the letter.

Clumber, January 11, 1801.

My Dearest Brother,

I am extremely anxious to hear about your health, which I have not done for some time. I most sincerely hope it is better; and with the recovery of that, depend upon it your spirits will recover. For I am convinced that your own manliness, fortitude, and resignation will prevent the disappointments you have hitherto met with from dwelling upon your mind; and certainly, it must be a very great satisfaction to you that your character for uncommon abilities, superior knowledge, and extraordinary intrepidity and firmness, is so universally established. Such a character as yours, no doubt, creates much jealousy, as that of every very superior person does. And you have always found that, in their struggles in this world, many of the first-rate men, and those who have rendered the greatest services to their country, have been treated with ingratitude and neglected.

But standing on so very broad a foundation of reputation as you do, and in possession of such transcendent abilities and superior knowledge and experience, surely you have a very good prospect before you. The great thing is to hold in contempt any adverse circumstances that may happen in this life, and never to despond, not to dwell upon the past, but eagerly to look forward to the future. And you may rely upon it that whatever aberrations you may reproach yourself with, they will never be placed to the account against so excellent a nature as yours.

I am extremely anxious to do away your idea of giving up everything and retiring quite from the busy scene of life; for I am

OFFICER OF THE 95TH RIFLES

RIFLEMAN OF THE 95TH RIFLES

RIFLEMAN FIRING PRONE

convinced that, when your health began to return, you would most sincerely repent it. I sincerely hope you will not allow such a determination to fix itself. The idea arises merely from that temper of mind which an illness that preys much upon the spirits throws a person into.

You will have seen in the papers that the place of Master and Lieutenant-General of the Ordnance in Ireland are abolished. But I think it may be of the greatest consequence to cultivate your connection with Lord Castlereagh; he may be of essential service to you in some other way. As to your situation in Ireland, so far from giving it up, I would write to him on the subject of insuring your succeeding to Cradock with the rank of colonel as was before intended in case of Cradock's removal or death. The latter may happen any day, as he is upon service; and the intrigues are so great, and people's merit and services so often forgotten, that really you owe it to yourself to prepare against this as much as possible. As you have only the rank of lieutenant-colonel, you know it would have required, at the time when your services were fresh in their memory, his exertion to get you made quartermaster-general; and, of course, according to constant experience, his exertion will be the more necessary now.

This certainly ought not to be the case, but it always is; and therefore, one must guard against it. He has much in his power, I do assure you; and as he interested himself so warmly about you before, I do not see why he should not do so again. Certainly, it was but justice this; and it will be great injustice now if the same disposition is not persevered in; and if he really wishes to serve you, he can easily do it, as your character stands so very high in every respect. Lord Camden, too, who you said was very hearty towards you on that occasion, may be of most essential assistance to you. These collateral circumstances should really be attended to; for a man's merit alone, however great, constantly meets with disappointment, if they are neglected.

Now that the Austrians will certainly be forced to make peace, do you think it would be worthwhile to persevere in your intention of raising a foreign regiment for the East Indian service? Perhaps upon the disbanding of some of their free corps, it might easily be done, if approved at home.

The duchess joins me in kindest love to you and your party,

BRITISH LIGHT INFANTRY

A PORTUGUESE CAÇADORE

I remain ever,

My dearest Bob,

Your most affectionate Brother,

C. Craufurd.

At the time when he received this letter, Robert Craufurd was a married man. On February 7, 1800, he had married Mary Frances, daughter of Henry Holland, Esquire, of Hans Place, Chelsea. Towards his wife he ever displayed unbounded affection; and in after years, when actively engaged in the Peninsular War, it was his enforced separation from his wife that caused him to go home for some months on leave, contrary to the wishes of Lord Wellington, and also made him often talk of retiring altogether from the army. But he was in reality ardently devoted to his profession and to his own famous Light Division, and he never actually intended leaving the army for long during the war.

Still, his way of talking as to his wishes misled many as to his intentions; and Colonel Charles Macleod of the 43rd has declared that the general meant to retire altogether after the capture of Ciudad Rodrigo. But General Charles Stewart afterwards Lord Londonderry who remained with Craufurd like a brother during his last illness, knew better than to think anything of the kind, and endeavoured to cheer the suffering leader by talking of future operations. Lord Wellington also at first only expected to be deprived of General Craufurd's services for a time, as is evident from his letter on the subject to the authorities at home.

Robert Craufurd sat in Parliament for a time as M.P. for East Retford, but resigned his seat in order to go on foreign service. As regards political and military interest, his most staunch and effectively useful friend was Mr. Windham, for some time the Minister for War.

CHAPTER 2

The Expedition to Buenos Ayres

Robert Craufurd was promoted colonel on October 30, 1805. He was consequently quite a junior colonel when Mr. Windham entrusted to him the command of a large force intended to conduct important operations towards the end of the year 1806. My information concerning this expedition is chiefly gathered from a book published in London in the year 1808, and called "*An Authentic Narrative of the Proceedings of the Expedition under the command of Brigadier-General Craufurd, until its arrival at Monte Video, with an Account of the Operations against Buenos Ayres under the command of General Whitelocke, by an Officer of the Expedition.*" No name is given by the author of this interesting narrative; but he declares his perfect willingness to give his name if it should be thought necessary.

The little army consisted of two squadrons of the 6th Dragoon Guards, the 5th, 36th, 45th, and 88th Regiments of Infantry, and also five companies of the Rifle Corps, and two companies of the Royal Artillery, making altogether about four thousand two hundred men. (The designation "The Rifle Corps" meant, in those days, the 95th Rifles, and not the 60th Rifles.) Alison tells us that it was originally intended to effect the conquest of Chili. The expedition started from Falmouth, on November 12, 1806.

To command this little army, Colonel Robert Craufurd had been nominated through the interest of Mr. Windham, the War Minister of the day. The unprecedented circumstance of a colonel (and nearly the junior of his rank) being appointed to a command fit for a lieutenant-general, excited much opposition to Mr. Windham's nomination, and loud murmurs on the part of those officers of superior rank who remained unemployed;

FRANCE

Sebastian
Bayonne
Fuenterrabia
Durango
Roncevalles
Pyrenees
Mts.
Vitoria Pampeluna
Figueras
Calahorra
Gerona
yos
Tudela
Ebro R.
Saragossa
Lerida
Barcelona
ro
Mts
Siguenza
s of Somo Sierra
Tortosa
Tarragona
DRID
40
Ucles
Majorca
ana
cid
I
N
Murviedro
na R.
Valencia
Iviza
orena
s de la
olina
Castella
Alicante
Murcia
C. Palos
Cartagena
anada
C. Gata

Map of the
SPANISH CAMPAIGN.

English Miles

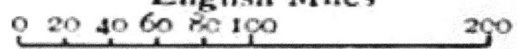

0 20 40 60 80 100   200

but the firmness of the Secretary of the War Department succeeded; and Colonel Craufurd raised to the rank of Brigadier on the occasion afterwards proved himself, as far as he came into action, in every respect worthy of the high opinion entertained of his talents and qualifications by his patron. He had a large staff attached to his command, and every appearance denoted it to be independent of any other. It would have been a happy circumstance for this little army, had it not afterwards fallen under the authority of any other person.

The expedition went to the Cape of Good Hope; and whilst there Craufurd's plans were entirely altered by his receiving the following letter of instructions from Mr. Windham.

Downing Street, January 2, 1807.

My Dear Sir,

Though I have often reproached myself for not having before written to you, I am very sorry to have occasion for retrieving my fault, such as is now presented to me.

In a dispatch of Lord Strangford's received this morning from Lisbon, and dated the 20th instant, mention is made that a vessel had just arrived from the Brazils (the *Sirpio*, a Portuguese ship) which gave an account that on November 2 a Spanish schooner had come to Paramoca, leaky and dismantled, having dispatches on board with the news of the recapture of Buenos Ayres, after a severe contest in which many were killed on both sides, and all the remaining English taken prisoners.

Though there is a hope that this news may not be true, measures must be taken as if it was; and the first step is to send a vessel after Admiral Murray with the dispatches which are now preparing for you and Sir Samuel Auchmuty, and of which the object is to attempt, by a combination of your joint forces, to recover what the intelligence alluded to would describe as lost. The supposition made is that Auchmuty, who did not sail from here till October 9, will not have reached his destination till after the disaster had taken place, and that proceeding probably in that case to the Cape, as finding himself unequal to repair what had happened, he will be there by the time the vessel leaving this (or some other sent by Admiral Murray) shall have arrived at the Cape likewise.

The instructions to him will then be that, if he does not con-

CONQUEST OF BUENOS AYRES

ceive the recovery of what is lost altogether hopeless, he will proceed to join you at the rendezvous which shall be fixed between you and Admiral Murray, and which will probably be either the Plata or Rio Janeiro. The latter seems to be preferable on account of the length of time which you may have to wait for his arrival, and which may require for the troops more refreshments than the Plata will afford you. Should Rio Janeiro be chosen, you will of course have to inquire, upon your arrival there, whether Auchmuty may not be still in the Plata prosecuting his operations, so as never to have received the instructions forwarded to him from you. In short, a meeting is to be concerted between him and you for the recovery, if possible, of what may be lost, except in the single case above alluded to, of his being so much of opinion that success is impracticable, as to make him take the decision of remaining at the Cape; in which case he will forward a vessel to you, signifying that you are no longer to expect him.

The whole of this we have been obliged to write in such a hurry that it has been difficult to make the instructions as full and as explicit as could be wished; but, knowing the general ideas, you will supply what is wanting for the particular cases. Though it has been thought right in one part to leave you a discretion, I mean as to acting without waiting for General Auchmuty, yet I have wished to put such a guard as may not leave you exposed to too much responsibility, which, with the enmity felt here both against you and me, ought to be made as little as possible. The case of Auchmuty's determining not to return or to make the attempt, and of your finding that anything could be done by you separately, is so little likely that no provision has been made for it. With most sincere wishes for your success and welfare, let me beg you to believe me ever, with great regard,

Your very faithful friend and servant,

W. Windham.

Accordingly, Craufurd and his little army go to Monte Video. They are there placed under the notorious General Whitelocke, together with the forces under Sir Samuel Auchmuty, the Government having meanwhile thought proper to send out a new commander-in-chief.

On May 10, 1807, the *Thisbe* frigate arrived at Monte Video, bringing out Whitelocke; and MajorGeneral Gower came with him as second in command.

From Monte Video the joint forces go to attack Buenos Ayres. Whitelocke, in a letter to Mr. Windham, states that he was joined at Monte Video on June 15, 1807, by the forces under Brigadier-General Craufurd.

It is unnecessary for me to give anything like a detailed account of the memorable and disastrous attack on Buenos Ayres, the most melancholy and disgraceful chapter in English military history. Whitelocke appears to have had almost every possible disqualification for such an enterprise, including a timidity and cowardice happily unique in the long annals of British commanders.

In this expedition Craufurd commanded the Light Brigade which formed the advanced guard of the army. His command originally consisted of eight companies of Light Infantry, a detachment of recruits (about seventy) of the 71st Regiment, and eight companies of the 95th or Rifle Corps. But from the day of his landing at the Ensinada until the junction of the two divisions of the army before Buenos Ayres, four companies were taken away from his Brigade and attached to the division of the army under the commander-in-chief in person. The invading army amounted altogether to nearly eight thousand men.

When the troops under Major-General Gower arrived near Buenos Ayres, the Spaniards commenced hostilities; but Craufurd, at the head of his light troops, made a vigorous charge, drove back the enemy in utter confusion and captured nine guns and a howitzer. The writer of the account from which I chiefly derive my information (himself an eye-witness) was perfectly certain that Buenos Ayres could have been taken straight off, if Craufurd had been supported "after the dispersion of three thousand of their best troops, at the entrance of their streets, threw confusion and dismay among the Spaniards in the town." This writer greatly blames General Gower for checking so extremely promising an attack.

> But General Gower would not authorise the attempt which, by all the information we afterwards received, would have been crowned with success, with but little, if any, loss. Our vexation, when ordered to retire, may therefore be easily conceived.

Craufurd himself confirmed this view by his evidence given at the trial of Whitelocke. He said:

I trust the court will here allow me to say that, from all I heard since, I am convinced that, if the main division under General Whitelocke had been as near as I thought it might have been, we certainly should have taken the town with ease; I had very strong doubts whether we might not have taken it with General Gower's corps.

Writing in October, 1810, to his brother Robert, General Charles Craufurd more than confirms this view, and by the most indisputable evidence. He says:

The duke told me, when here a few days ago, that he read lately in one of the papers an account of Whitelocke's affair at Buenos Ayres *by the second in command* to Liniers, in which it was asserted that if you had been allowed to advance into the town that evening, after defeating Liniers, as you proposed to do, you would certainly have taken the place.

And thus, the future leader of the audacious Light Division would have saved England from its greatest military disgrace and ignominy. One cannot help wondering how the home authorities ever came to place confidence in the dull and spiritless Whitelocke.

Even when the commander-in-chief arrived at the scene of action, he still delayed the attack, and so gave the inhabitants ample time for preparation for the defence. Most unfortunately, Whitelocke, in attacking the town:

Divided his troops into small detachments, and sent them in unloaded and unprovided with anything like proper and sufficient means for forcing barricades or other impediments in the streets.

The plan for taking the town was execrably bad in every way and ludicrously inadequate. There was no connection or communication between the different portions of the army, and when each portion had taken up the position assigned to it, there were no further orders from the commander, and no possibility of asking for any. General Craufurd with his light troops occupied the place that he was ordered to occupy, and there waited for further orders, but none were forthcoming. As he said at the trial of Whitelocke, he certainly did not expect to be abandoned to his fate, as he was.

The inhabitants shot down our men from the tops of their houses without any possibility of retaliation. Each house was turned into a little fortress. Ditches were dug in the streets, and heavy cannon used against our forces as they advanced. Sir Samuel Auchmuty effected all that he possibly could under such circumstances; but the terrible drawback was that our forces were so separated as to be unable to communicate with each other, still more unable to support each other.

Craufurd's forces, as might have been expected, were entirely unsuccessful; and at length he took possession of the convent of St. Domingo as a refuge for his men. But the enemy surrounded this on all sides, and:

> The surrounding enemy, to the number of six thousand, bringing up cannon to force the wooden gates, Craufurd, judging from the cessation of firing, that those next him had not been successful, with a bitter pang of heart, surrendered at four o'clock in the afternoon.

For some of these and other particulars I am much indebted to a very interesting work, *Cole's Distinguished Peninsular Generals*. Cole tells us that, even after Craufurd's surrender, Whitelocke still possessed five thousand effective soldiers and two strong posts in the town, and his communication with the fleet was uninterrupted. Yet he made no attempt to retrieve the disasters, but on:

> Liniers offering to give up all his prisoners captured on the day preceding, together with the 71st Regiment, and others taken with General Beresford, if Whitelocke desisted from any further attack on Buenos Ayres, surrendered Monte Video at the end of two months, and withdrew his Majesty's forces from the River Plata.

This spiritless fool accepted the hard terms, and made peace, thereby for ever basely staining the glorious annals of England's military history.

It is small wonder that our country was enraged at such unnecessary ignominy, and brought the commander-in-chief to trial for his pusillanimous feebleness. The officer who was an eye-witness of the heart-rending events informs us that:

> Above seventy officers and one thousand men were killed or badly wounded; one hundred and twenty officers and fifteen hundred rank and file were taken prisoners; and fifteen hundred stands of excellent arms fell into the hands of the Spaniards.

Well might Charles Napier say that Whitelocke ought to be shot,

BUENOS AIRES, MONTEVIDEO

AND VICINITY.

Scale of Miles.

0   10   20   30   40   50

One Inch = 32 Miles.

nia Suiza

U R U G U A Y

Florida

FLORIDA

Colonia Valdensa

olla

Rosario

Rosario

Cufre

Arroyo

Arroyo Davon

San José

S. Andres

SAN JOSÉ

Arroyo Peralta

Santa Lucia

H.

Pta. Sauce

Lucia

José

Can *lones*

illeria

Suares

CANELONES

Pta. Jesus Maria

Piedras

13

Penarob

Pta. Espinillo

MONTEVIDEO

L.S.

Nuevo Paris

Panela Rock

El Cerro

Matas Union

P L A T A

Pta. Yeguas

Aguada

Lobos o del Cerro

MONTEVIDEO

L.H.

Pta. Brava

30

13

Pta. Atalaya

Magdalena

L.S.

RS.

and that *"the blood of hundreds is on his head."*

Deep and furious were the disgust and anger of the future heroes of the Peninsular War. Craufurd, and his coadjutor, the brave and able Pack, and the gallant soldiers of the 95th Rifles, destined to earn undying glory in after years under happier circumstances, were peculiarly incensed against their discreditable leader. One of Craufurd's own men, "Rifleman Harris," writes thus in his interesting *Recollections*, (republished by Leonaur as *The Compleat Rifleman Harris*):

> This was the first time of our seeing that officer (Whitelocke). The next meeting was at Buenos Ayres; and during the confusion of that day one of us received an order from the fiery Craufurd to shoot the traitor dead if we could see him in the battle, many others of the Rifles receiving the same order from that fine and chivalrous officer. The unfortunate issue of the Buenos Ayres affair is matter of history, and I have nothing to say about it; but I well remember the impression that it made upon us all at the time, and that Sir John Moore was present at Whitelocke's court-martial; General Craufurd and, I think, General Auchmuty, Captain Elder of the Rifles, Captain Dickson, and one of our privates being witnesses. We were at Hythe at the time, and I recollect our officers going off to appear against Whitelocke.
>
> So enraged was Craufurd against him, that I heard say he strove hard to have him shot. Whitelocke's father, I also heard, was at his son's trial, and cried like an infant during the proceedings. Whitelocke's sword was broken over his head, I was told; and for months afterwards, when our men took their glass, they used to give as a toast, 'Success to *grey hairs*, but bad luck to *White locks*' Indeed, that toast was drunk in all the public-houses for many a day.

Before he surrendered, Craufurd consulted all his officers; only one questioned the necessity for a surrender; and upon Craufurd offering to put himself at their head and endeavour to force their way out, this one dissentient officer declined to be in any way responsible for such an attempt.

The future leader of the Light Division seems to have been extremely anxious that his own conduct at Buenos Ayres should form the subject of a regular inquiry; but this was deemed entirely unnecessary, the court-martial being satisfied that the failure was altogether caused by the cowardly incapacity of Whitelocke. At this trial Colonel Pack, afterwards destined to serve with Craufurd in so many brilliant exploits in the Peninsular War, gives evidence in favour of his indignant leader. He says:

> General Craufurd seemed perfectly ready to sacrifice his own life, but thought he was called upon to interpose to save the lives of those under him.

And he calls him "an officer whom I must ever respect and admire, though unfortunate." With all his fiery rashness, Robert Craufurd cared far too much for his men to permit him to sacrifice their lives unnecessarily.

But this unfortunate affair embittered his mind to the very end of his career, and much increased his constitutional tendency to melancholy brooding. And, no doubt, he had reasonable grounds for grief and anger when he reflected how very differently this South American expedition would have ended if he and Sir Samuel Auchmuty had been left alone, as at first intended, without the heavy burden of Whitelocke's superintending incapacity.

It is difficult indeed to believe that even the most carping of critics could ever have seriously questioned the undaunted courage of one whom William Napier habitually designated "the fiery Robert Craufurd." Still, much military criticism emanates from men entirely ignorant both of the art of war and of the generals conducting it. And so, it is likely enough that the disgrace of this wretched affair may, in the popular judgment, have somewhat stained the rapidly rising reputation of this intrepid leader. Even Charles Napier, when blaming some operations of Craufurd during the Peninsular War, apparently indulged in a meaningless sneer against his general for this business, though it is difficult to understand how Craufurd could have acted more advantageously when serving under Whitelocke.

But I suppose the world is pretty well agreed in thinking that many of Charles Napier's earlier judgments (for instance, his censures of Wellington) were hasty, violent, and unjust. In his later life the grand old hero of Meanee found out by bitterest personal experience how easy it is to misrepresent even the best actions, and how seldom actual justice is done to any born leader of men.

But however, this may be, Busaco and Ciudad Rodrigo were Craufurd's best reply to all unjust critics. The officer who stood alone, with his *aide-de-camp* only, on the crest of the glacis at Ciudad Rodrigo, in advance of his division, and in advance even of the "forlorn hope," and there sacrificed his life from his ardent zeal to see that Lord Wellington's orders were thoroughly carried out, certainly had small need of a certificate as to bravery even from Charles Napier.

General Craufurd, and apparently many other officers engaged in the expedition to Buenos Ayres, were under the impression that Whitelocke was a traitor as well as a timid and vacillating fool; but I have failed to find in the account of the court-martial any solid evidence in support of this impression.

Besides embittering the mind of my grandfather, his services under Whitelocke had, I think, an injurious effect on him in another way. I believe that the fact that he then and there saw plainly manifested and "writ large" the deplorable results of timidity, helped to increase unduly his own natural tendency to brilliant audacity, which Wellington occasionally had to check. Very possibly Robert Craufurd would never have fought unadvisedly beside the Coa River, if he had not in earlier years been thoroughly sickened with the disgraceful outcome of yielding vacillation. To go to school under Whitelocke was a bad training for General Craufurd, and he really needed an Arthur Wellesley to efface from his vivid intellect the erroneous ideas left in it by this earlier education. Wellington wisely directed and utilised that extraordinary quickness of perception and amazing rapidity of movement which General Gower could only thwart and General Whitelocke only paralyze.

CHAPTER 3

Sir John Moore on Some Changes in the Army

The hero of Corunna was constitutionally conservative; and this disposition made him look with much distrust on the changes which Mr. Windham, the Minister for War, introduced into the British Army. Alison, in his *History of Europe*, tells us that the changes effected by Windham, and especially his allowing soldiers to enlist for a limited period instead of for life, were attended with the very best results; but Moore disliked many of these innovations.

Craufurd, on the other hand, was always of an innovating disposition, as he afterwards showed by proposing many changes to his commander in the Peninsular War, some of which Lord Wellington adopted. His intimate friendship with Mr. Windham also made my grandfather the more inclined to view his proposals favourably. But Craufurd was also a friend of Sir John Moore; and this induced him to submit to Moore's judgment a paper of his own on the proposed alterations. And it was in answer to this paper that Moore addressed to Craufurd the following letter and detailed criticism which, to the best of my knowledge, are now made public for the first time.

Private.

Thursday.

My Dear Craufurd,

I return the paper you left with me. I have added upon a separate paper such observations as occurred to me. The fault of the proposed arrangement is that it is complicated.

I own I cannot bring my mind to approve of the limited service; the more I reflect on it, the more I dread its effects. I doubt if a single man will be induced by it to come into the army who would not have enlisted at any rate. And I wish that for the present Mr. Windham had been satisfied with raising the pay of the non-commissioned officers, bettering the Chelsea pensioners, and giving the soldier a right, at the expiration of twenty-one years, to his discharge, and to a shilling pension, and even more in cases where the Board thought it requisite; so that the old soldier, who could not work, should never be seen but in a comfortable situation.

I remain,

Yours faithfully,

John Moore.

OBSERVATIONS ON A PAPER SENT BY COLONEL CRAUFURD.

The numbers refer to similar numbers in the colonel's paper.

2. I cannot reconcile myself to the intention of discharging men in time of war. In the militia it was proved not to answer; but in the line the inconveniences are tenfold. But if it is adopted, the power of extending the service for six months must, when troops are abroad, be given to the military commander in peace as well as in war. The military commander may be enjoined and when once it is the law, there is no reason to doubt his obedience to it to send the soldiers, whose periods are expired, home by the first opportunity; but until such opportunity offers, there seems a necessity that the men, who are to continue to receive military pay and allowances, should continue for the time soldiers, and be subject to military discipline. Men of this description left loose upon the public in foreign garrisons, with money in their pockets, would commit every disorder. It is even for their own sakes that they should be under control.

And I see no reason why, during the short time they are thus detained, they should receive the additional pay, which is intended as a reward to the soldier who re-enlists. Should such men be put for a moment in every respect on a footing with the soldier who continues to serve his country?

The addition of a shilling a day, if paid to him at the time, would encourage irregularity, and lead him to acts which it would be impossible not to punish.

3. Some expedient must be fallen upon to prevent the men, whose periods are expired when in America and the West In-

dies, from going into the States, or from settling with the plant-ers. To this they will receive such encouragement that, if means are not taken to prevent it, no man will ever re-enlist when in those stations.

4. The additional penny and twopence proposed to be added to the soldier's pay, at the end of the first and second periods, is too trifling a sum to induce men, in the first instance, to enter the service. The pay of the soldier is already ample, perhaps too much so, and no addition can be made to it without hurting the service.

As an inducement to recruits, this addition will have no effect; and upon soldiers to continue, after the expiration of their pe-riods, it will have very little. It is by a bounty that the latter will be tempted; and as the bad consequences of a bounty are more transitory, it will injure the service less.

After twenty-one years' service many men will be found able and willing to serve; and as soldiers of this description are in-valuable, they should be encouraged to continue with their regiments. It is to such men, if any, that I should be inclined to give additional pay, and I should not think threepence a day too much. I would give them no bounty, and make the periods after twenty-one only for three years.

The pay of the non-commissioned officers was not raised, some years ago, in the same proportion with that of the men. It is by making their situation comfortable that a portion of the more respectable part of the population may be tempted into the army. The sergeants should have two shillings a day, the cor-porals one and sixpence. The pay of the sergeant-majors and quarter-master-sergeants should be raised. I believe it is now half-a-crown; it might be three shillings or three and sixpence. Upon re-enlisting, non-commissioned officers may have the same bounty as the privates; and sergeants who had served fourteen years, and had been non-commissioned officers seven years, might receive an addition of threepence or sixpence a day. To corporals it may not be necessary to give any increase; if they have real merit, they will be promoted, and it is useful to excite their emulation.

5. I see no necessity of any intermediate rank or class between the private and the corporals; and I shall always disapprove of

the powers of selection to rank or emolument in a regiment being vested in other hands than those of the colonel or commanding officer. This class is a refinement taken from some of the foreign services, neither necessary nor in the spirit of ours. We had better content ourselves, as heretofore, with plain sergeants and corporals, make their situations comfortable, and increase their number, if necessary, and leave to commanding officers who have modes of gratifying and distinguishing deserving old soldiers.

6. Men discharged at any period of their service for wounds, infirmities, etc., to receive sixpence per day, or ninepence, or a shilling as a pension, or to be put into a veteran battalion, at the option of the commander-in-chief or the Chelsea Board.

This certainty of being taken care of is a great encouragement to men to enter and afterwards to continue in the service. I cannot, therefore, think that a man at the end of fourteen years' service, who is still young and without ailment, if he refuses to re-enlist, is entitled from his service to any pension. Men of this description are most valuable; every encouragement should be given to them to continue in the service, and no temptation to withdraw from it. If they withdraw, they should forfeit all the advantages of their former service. If they re-enlist, at the end of twenty-one years they get the shilling pension; but to place men of this kind in veteran battalions is to mix with the weak and infirm the very best soldiers in the service. It would be better far to form privileged corps of them, give them superior advantages, and make them the elite of the army.

It is thought, from the returns which have lately been called for, that a very small proportion of our soldiery ever attain fourteen years' service. The returns of the present army may lead to this conclusion; but it must be recollected that we are now only recovering from the effects of a very destructful St. Domingo and West India war, which, together with the great augmentation made recently to the army, renders the number of old soldiers at this moment proportionally small. A great part of our force at the end of the last war was for limited service, and was disbanded at the peace.

7. A soldier who at any period of his service is disbanded, at a peace, from reduction of establishment, if he registers, which is,

I apprehend, a declaration of his wish to remain or to re-enter the service, upon re-entering it is but just that he should get credit for his former service, and be entitled to all its advantages. But the service of the line should be held so high that no service of any other kind should be substituted for it, nor any person entitled to the rewards it holds out by other than actual service in the line.

8. The veteran battalions being composed of men discharged from the regiments of the line as unfit for active service, but deemed by the commander-in-chief fit for garrison and home duties, if after twenty-one years they are able and still willing to continue in them, may receive the additional threepence a day, as is proposed to similar men in the Line.

9. Instead of what is here proposed, which will act as a bribe to non-commissioned officers to retire from the service, whom it is most desirable to retain, I should propose a rate of Chelsea to be established for sergeants and corporals, to which such alone were entitled who had served seven years in their respective ranks, and were discharged with good characters. To this might be added, for cases of superior merit, an increase in the pay and in the number of letter men.

(*Note:*—Letter men were those of the pensioners at Chelsea who had a letter from the king to the commissioners authorising them to increase their pensions.)

J. Moore, Lieut.-General.

Having already explained the principle upon which I found the propriety of increasing the pay of the field officers and captains of the army much beyond that of the subalterns, the following rates are submitted—

		PRESENT PAY.			PROPOSED PAY.		
		s.	d.		£	s.	d.
Lieut-Colonels	.. ..	15	11	.. ..	1	0	0
Majors	.. .. ..	14	1	.. ..		17	0
Captains	.. .. ..	9	5	.. ..		14	0
Lieutenants	.. ..	5	8	.. ..		7	0
Ensigns	.. .. ..	4	8	.. ..		5	0
Adjutants	.. ..	8	0	.. ..		9	0
Quartermasters	.. ..	5	8	.. ..		7	0

The field officers, adjutants, and quartermasters to have, besides, forage for the horses they are obliged to keep by regulation; and if not all the above regimental officers, at least from the captains inclusive down, to be exempt from the Income Tax. (Some of the proposals here criticised by Moore originated with Mr. Windham, and were not Craufurd's own ideas.)

J. M.

CHAPTER 4

The Retreat to Vigo

In October, 1808, Craufurd sailed from Falmouth with Sir David Baird, for the Peninsula, and apparently even then had command of the Light Brigade of the corps which Baird was ordered to take to the assistance of Sir John Moore. But there was some difficulty as to giving Craufurd this command, or allowing him to retain it, as will be seen from the following unpublished letter addressed by Sir John Moore to him after his arrival.

> Salamanca, November 13, 1808.
>
> My Dear Colonel,
> I had the pleasure of your letter of the 3rd. I hope you do not doubt my wish to oblige you. I feel how unpleasant it would be to descend from a rank once held, and I should have much satisfaction in relieving you from that, as any other thing that was disagreeable to you; but you are notified to me, not as brigadier, but as colonel upon the staff. Not only so, but it has been added that, as this may be disagreeable to you, to descend from a rank you once held, it has been signified to you that, if you choose it, you have the duke's permission to return to England. I should be most sorry, were you to accept this alternative, and I hope to give you a command you will like. But I cannot give you a rank the duke does not choose to give you, and which, at any rate, exceeds my power.
> As to the arrangement you propose of brigades and divisions, I need only say it is so contrary to what I think proper for the army, that I need trouble you no further on that score. The army will be organised, when united, in the manner which is thought best generally for the service, without regard to the

43

regiments coming from Corunna or Lisbon; and the plan you propose would be unjust to other officers.

I hope you will see all this as it is meant, and that you will believe that no one regards or esteems you higher than, my dear Craufurd,

> Yours faithfully,
>
> John Moore.

The difficulty here mentioned by Moore seems to have been got over in some way; for Craufurd retained the rank of brigadier, and had command of the Light Brigade, numbering about three thousand men. Until separated from the main body of Moore's army, Craufurd, after the junction of the forces, and the beginning of the retreat, was given the charge of the rear guard, a post requiring extraordinary quickness and readiness.

Baird's forces united with those of Sir John Moore at Mayorga, on December 20. After this they at first advanced; but before long Moore received intelligence which made it absolutely necessary to retreat as rapidly as possible; otherwise he would have been surrounded. Even as things were, his retreat was exceedingly dangerous.

During the earlier days of this retreat, Craufurd's duty was to check the advance of the enemy as much as possible, in order that the rest of the army might be able to retire.

The circumstances under which Moore began his enforced retrograde movement were eminently disagreeable. Quartermaster Surtees, of the 95th Rifles, says:

> Winter had now completely set in, the face of the country being covered with deep snow; the weather was unusually severe. Our prospect, therefore, was by no means a pleasant one. To commence a retreat in front of a greatly superior force, and with the probability that other French armies might be before us, and intercept our retreat upon the sea, which was distant from us nearly two hundred and fifty miles, with the country in our rear already exhausted of everything that could contribute to our support, and with such excessively bad weather, rendered it as unpleasant a situation as troops could well be placed in. Added to which, our commissariat was by no means so efficient in those days as they have latterly become; and our troops in general, being young and unaccustomed to privation, it was but too obvious that, should the retreat continue long, many would

44

be the disasters attending it. On Christmas Day, our brigade, as the rear of the infantry, commenced its uncomfortable retreat. (*Surtees of the Rifles by William Surtees* is also published by Leonaur.)

At this time Craufurd's Brigade performed efficient service at the bridge of Castro Gonzalo:

The commander-in-chief approached the bridge of Castro Gonzalo early in the morning of December 26; but the stores were a long time passing, a dense fog intercepted the view, and so nicely timed was the march, that the scouts of the imperial horsemen were already infesting the flank of the column, and even carried off some of the baggage. The left bank of the river commanded the bridge, and General Robert Craufurd remained with a brigade of infantry and two guns to protect the passage; for the cavalry was still watching Soult, who was now pressing forward in pursuit. (*Napier*).

This bridge of Castro Gonzalo was much menaced by the light cavalry of the imperial guard, who rode close up to the bridge, captured some women and baggage, and endeavoured to surprise the post. And on this occasion, as Napier relates, two private soldiers of the 43rd, John Walton and Richard Jackson displayed something of that extraordinary discipline and marvellous courage which afterwards made their regiment one of the very greatest in the world.

Napier tells us:

On the 27th, the cavalry and the stragglers being all over the river, Craufurd commenced destroying the bridge amidst torrents of rain and snow; half the troops worked; the other half kept the enemy at bay from the heights on the left bank; for the cavalry scouts of the imperial guard were spread over the plain. At ten o'clock at night a large party, following some waggons, again endeavoured to pass the piquets and gallop down to the bridge; that failing, a few dismounted, and extending to the right and left, commenced a skirmishing fire, whilst others remained ready to charge, if the position of the troops, which they expected to ascertain by this scheme, should offer an opportunity. They failed, and this anxiety to interrupt the work induced Craufurd to destroy two arches instead of one, and blow up the connecting buttress. The masonry was so solid that it was not until twelve o'clock in the night of the 28th that all preparations were completed, when the troops descended the heights on the left bank, and passing very silently by single files, and over planks laid across the broken arches, gained the other side without loss.

This was a bold and perilous measure, as the enemy might have attacked during it; but its success was perfect. And Craufurd then marched to Benevente, where the cavalry and the reserve still remained.

On December 31, Moore's forces were divided. Quartermaster Surtees, of the 95th Rifles, informs us thus:

Till now our brigade had formed the rear of the infantry, there being some cavalry in rear of us; but it was now determined that ours and the Light German Brigade under Brigadier-General Charles Alten, should strike off from the great road (to Corunna) and take the route for Orense and Vigo. This was done, I understand, with a view to secure a passage across the Minho at the former place, should Sir John with the main army be compelled to retreat in that direction, and probably with the view also of drawing off a part of the enemy's overwhelming force from the pursuit of that body, and to induce them to follow us into the mountains. Notwithstanding this, they continued to pursue Sir John on the great road, whilst they left us free altogether.

So now Robert Craufurd was left alone in independent command of that Light Brigade which afterwards acquired such undying distinction under him. His regiments now were the 2nd battalion of the 95th Rifles, a battalion of the 43rd, and also one of the 52nd.

During this terribly trying and rapid retreat the general took note of many defects in our way of marching, and gathered many wise hints and suggestions which he afterwards collected together in his famous *Standing Orders for the Light Division*, a work by which he left his mark permanently on the British Army.

On January 1, 1809, began their march by a most difficult road through the mountains, which were then covered with snow. Food was extremely scarce, and during the next few days want and fatigue compelled many to fall out, some of whom, no doubt, perished in the snow on the bleak mountains; others fell into the hands of the enemy, and some few rejoined their regiments after having obtained some little refreshment from the natives.

The little army reached Orense on January 7, having previously pushed on, by double forced marches, a few hundred men, to take possession of the bridge over the Minho at this place. There they remained for a day, and obtained provisions for the men, who were literally starving. Their condition at this time was wretched, as their shoes were nearly all worn out, and many were travelling with bare feet. But their minds were now more at ease in one respect, in that they had 'secured the passage of the Minho, and thus prevented the enemy from getting in before them; for strong fears had been felt that the French would have detached a corps from their main body to seize this pass, and thus cut off their retreat to Vigo.

On the 9th they left Orense, and in a few days more reached Vigo, and were put on board the vessels destined to take them home. But before starting they waited some days in order to give stragglers a chance of coming in. From Vigo they then went home to England.

I will now proceed to give some extracts from the *Recollections of Rifleman Harris,* (now republished as *The Compleat Rifleman Harris*), a private in the battalion of the 95th Rifles serving under General Craufurd in this retreat. The book is both scarce and very amusing; and it is full of stories about the general, to whom this private soldier was extremely devoted. I make no apology for offering to the public so many expressions of the thoughts and feelings of what the world calls a "common soldier;" for I know well, from prolonged and most friendly intercourse with the men, how keen an observer and how just a judge the private soldier often is of those who exercise command over him; and I confess that in my opinion it is usually the fault of the officers themselves when they are permanently disliked by their men.

The book from which I am about to quote is a book of anecdotes, and not a history, and consequently it is not arranged in any precise chronological order.

Concerning the officers of those days Harris writes:

The officers too are commented upon and closely observed. The men are very proud of those who are brave in the field, and kind and considerate to the soldiers under them. An act of kindness done by an officer has often during the battle been the cause of his life being saved.

They are a strange set, the English, and so determined and unconquerable, that they *will* have their way if they can. Indeed,

47

THE REAR-GUARD ON RETREAT

SIR JOHN MOORE FATALLY WOUNDED, 16TH JANUARY, 1809

it requires one who has authority in his face, as well as at his back, to make them respect and obey him. They see too often, in the instance of sergeant-majors, that command does not suit ignorant and coarse-minded men, and that tyranny is too much used in the brief authority which they have. A soldier, I am convinced, is driven often to insubordination by being worried by these little minded men for the veriest trifles, about which the gentleman never thinks of tormenting him. The moment the seventy of the discipline of our army is relaxed, in my opinion, farewell to its efficiency; but for our men to be tormented about trifles (as I have seen at times) is often very injurious to a whole corps.

It might be well, even in these days, if the above remarks of this brave rifleman were read, marked, learnt, and inwardly digested by many.

This narrative begins *before* Craufurd's Light Brigade was separated from the main army under Sir John Moore. During this earlier period Harris received, through Quartermaster Surtees, a very peremptory order to exercise his skill. He said:

Now, Harris, keep your eyes open, and mind what you are about here. General Craufurd orders you instantly to set to work, and sew up every one of these barrels in the hides lying before you. You are to sew the skins with the hair outwards, and be quick about it, for the general swears that if the job is not finished in half-an-hour, he will hang you.

The latter part of this order was anything but pleasant; and whether the general ever really gave it, I never had an opportunity of ascertaining. I only know that I give the words as they were given me; and, well knowing the stuff Craufurd was made of, I received the candle from the hands of Surtees, and bidding the men get needles and waxed thread from their knapsacks, as the quartermaster withdrew, I instantly prepared to set about the job.

After the retreat began, Harris writes concerning his leader:

As we passed the walls of the convent, I observed our general (Craufurd) as he sat upon his horse, looking at us on the march, and remarked the peculiar sternness of his features; he did not like to see us going rearwards at all; and many of us judged there must be something wrong by his severe look and scowling eye.

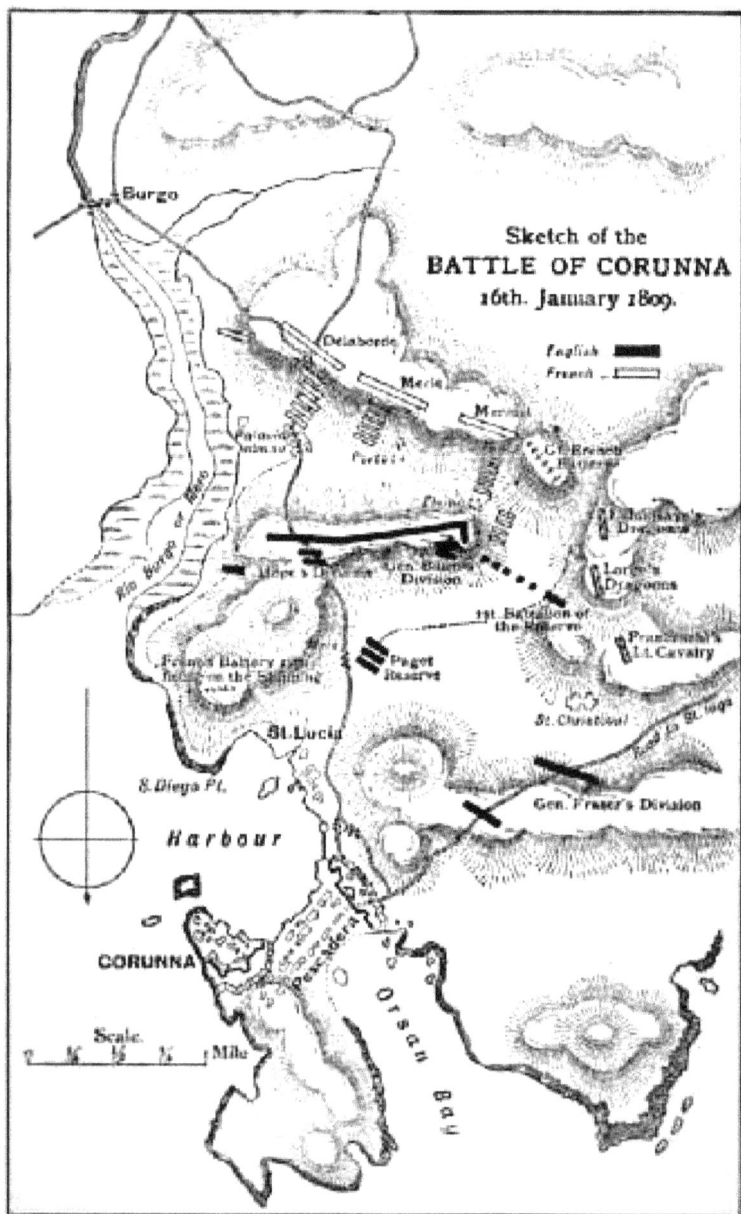

Sketch of the
BATTLE OF CORUNNA
16th. January 1809.

English ████
French ░░░░

Burgo

Delaborde

Merle

Mermet

G. l. French
Infantry

Paldando
Infantry

Portier

Plessis

Hope's Division

Gen. Baird's
Division

Lahoussaye's
Dragoons

Lorge's
Dragoons

French Battery sun
fire from the Shipping

Paget
Reserve

1st. Battalion of
the Reserve

Franceschi's
Lt. Cavalry

St. Lucia

St. Christoval

Road to St. Iago

S. Diego Pt.

Gen. Fraser's Division

Harbour

CORUNNA

Scale.
0 ¼ ½ ¾ Mile

Orean Bay

'Keep your ranks there, men,' he said, spurring his horse towards some riflemen who were avoiding a small rivulet. 'Keep your ranks, and move on, *no straggling* from the main body.'

Their sufferings from fatigue and want of food were now very great, and the men began to wonder if they were ever to be halted again.

Many, even at this period, would have straggled from the ranks and perished, had not Craufurd held them together with a firm rein. One such bold and stern commander in the East, during a memorable disaster, and that devoted army had reached its refuge unbroken! Thus, we staggered on, night and day, for about four days, before we discovered the reason of this continued forced march.

An Irish rifleman then asks one of his officers where they were being taken to, and the officer replies: "*to England, if we can get there.*"

The men soon began to murmur at not being permitted to turn and stand at bay, cursing the French, and swearing they would rather die ten thousand deaths, with their rifles in their hands in opposition, than endure the present toil. They also heard at this time sounds of fighting between the French and our main army under Moore; and this made their present position all the more tantalizing. Harris remarks:

Craufurd seemed to sniff the sound of battle from afar with peculiar feelings. He halted us for a few minutes occasionally, when the distant clamour became more distinct; and his face turned towards the sound, and seemed to light up and become less stern. It was then indeed, that every poor fellow clutched his weapon more firmly, and wished for a sight of the enemy.

About this time the French were very near. Craufurd ordered his riflemen to conceal themselves amongst the hills. And Harris and a bold comrade climbed to the very top of a mountain, to have a good look at the enemy. They here came into very close quarters indeed with some of the French. And:—

About a quarter of an hour after this, as we still lay in the gully, I heard some person clambering up behind us, and upon turning quickly round, I found it was General Craufurd. The general was wrapped in his great coat, and, like ourselves, had been

51

for many hours drenched to the skin, for the rain was coming down furiously. He carried in his hand a canteen full of rum and a small cup, with which he was occasionally endeavouring to refresh some of the men. He offered me a drink, as he passed, and then proceeded onwards along the ridge. After he had emptied his canteen, he came past us again, and himself gave us instructions as to our future proceedings.

Though he was so extremely strict as to discipline, it is plain that Craufurd really cared for his men, and did all he could to help them. The keen eyes of young William Napier soon perceived this; for when writing home to his mother on November 10, 1808, he observes:

I like our general, Craufurd, much; he is very attentive to the men.

And later on, in this harassing retreat our rifleman tells us:

Our men, spite of the vigilance of the general, seemed many of them resolved to stray into the open country, rather than traverse the road before them. The coming night favoured their designs, and many were, before morning, lost to us through their own wilfulness.

On this occasion even, the faithful Harris straggles away and is lost, and sticks fast in a morass, together with a comrade. But by-and-by some lights seem to approach them.

The lights, we now discovered, were furnished by bundles of straw and dried twigs, tied on the ends of long poles, and dipped in tar. They were borne in the hands of several Spanish peasants, from a village near at hand, whom Craufurd had thus sent to our rescue. He had discovered, on reaching and halting in this village, the number of men that had strayed from the main body, and immediately ordering the torches I have mentioned to be prepared, he collected together a party of Spanish peasants, and obliged them to go out into the open country, and seek for his men, as I have said; by which means he saved on that night many from death.

The wilfulness and folly of his men often caused General Craufurd to treat them severely: but they never made him in any way indifferent to them or neglectful of their welfare. Hence it came to pass that in this most trying retreat, the men identified themselves with their leader, and endured at his hands, punishments which in all probability they would not have endured, if inflicted on them by an ordinary general of the commonplace sort. The fiery temper of the commander was by no means entirely uncongenial to his followers these fierce riflemen would have cared little for a meek and mild general and his unfeigned solicitude for their comfort, combined with his good sense and keen appreciation of the humorous, secured to him much of the affection and loyalty of his men, as well as much of their admiration.

Concerning the great difficulties and trials of this retreat, Harris writes thus:

Being constantly in rear of the main body, the scenes of distress and misery I witnessed were dreadful to contemplate, particularly amongst the women and children, who were lagging and falling behind, their husbands and fathers being in the main body in our front. We now came to the edge of a deep ravine, the descent so steep and precipitous that it was impossible to keep our feet in getting down, and we were sometimes obliged to sit and slide along on our backs; whilst before us rose a ridge of mountains quite as steep and difficult of ascent. There was, however, no pause in our exertions; but, slinging our rifles round our necks, down the hill we went; whilst mules, with the baggage on their backs, weaned and urged beyond their strength, were seen rolling from top to bottom, many of them breaking their necks with the fall, and the baggage crushed, smashed, and abandoned."

After the snow commenced, the hills became so slippery (being in many parts covered with ice) that several of our men frequently slipped and fell; and being unable to rise, gave themselves up to despair, and died. There was now no endeavour to assist one another after a fall; it was everyone for himself, and God for us all!

I remember, among other matters, that we were joined, if I may so term it, by a young recruit, when such an addition was anything but wished for during the disasters of the hour. One of the men's wives, who was struggling forward in the ranks with us, presenting a ghastly picture of illness, misery, and fatigue, being very large in the family-way, towards evening stepped from amongst the crowd, and lay herself down amidst the snow, a little out of the main road. Her husband remained with her;

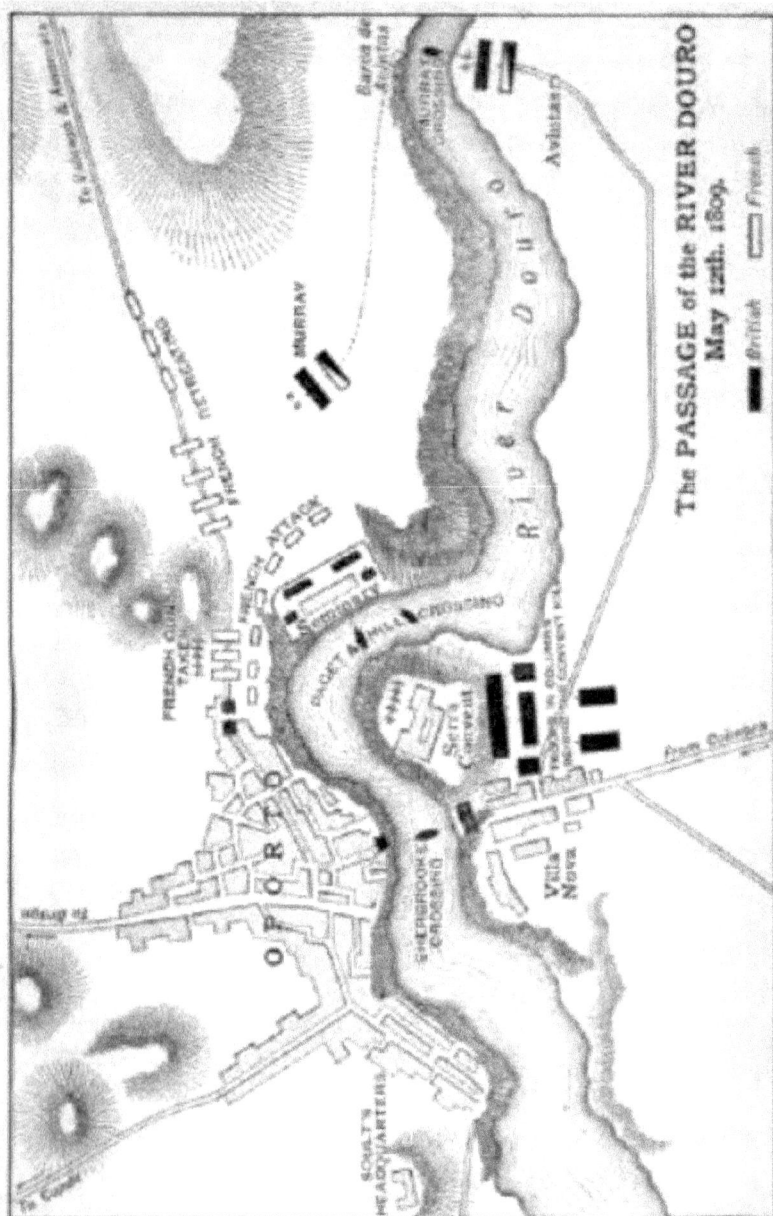

The PASSAGE of the RIVER DOURO
May 12th. 1809.

British ▬ French ▭

and I heard one or two hasty observations amongst our men, that they had taken possession of their last resting-place. The enemy, indeed, were not far behind at this time, the night was coming down, and their chance seemed in truth but a bad one. To remain behind the column of march in such weather was to perish; and we accordingly soon forgot all about them. To my surprise, however, some little time afterwards I, being myself then in the rear of our party, again saw the woman. She was hurrying with her husband after us, and in her arms, she carried the babe she had just given birth to. Her husband and herself between them managed to carry that infant to the end of the retreat, where we embarked. God tempers the wind, it is said, to the shorn lamb; and many years afterwards I saw that boy a strong and healthy lad.

The shoes and boots of our party were now mostly either destroyed or useless to us from foul roads and long miles, and many of the men were entirely barefooted, with knapsacks and accoutrements altogether in a dilapidated state. The officers were also, for the most part, in as miserable a plight. They were pallid, way-worn, their feet bleeding, and their faces overgrown with beards of many days' growth. Many of the poor fellows, now near sinking with fatigue, reeled as if in a state of drunkenness, and altogether I thought we looked the ghosts of our former selves. Still, we held on resolutely; our officers behaved nobly; and Craufurd was not to be daunted by long miles, fatigue, or foul weather. Many a man in that retreat caught courage from his stern eye and gallant bearing. Indeed, I do not think the world ever saw a more perfect soldier than General Craufurd.

When about a couple of miles from this village, Craufurd again halted us for about a quarter of an hour. It appeared to me that, with returning daylight, he wished to have a good look at us this morning; for he mingled amongst the men as we stood leaning upon our rifles, gazing earnestly in our faces as he passed, in order to judge of our plight by our countenances. He himself appeared anxious, but full of fire and spirit, occasionally giving directions to the different officers, and then speaking words of encouragement to the men. It is my pride now to remember that General Craufurd seldom omitted a word in passing to myself. On this occasion he stopped in the midst, and addressed a few words to me, and glancing down at my feet, observed, 'What! no shoes, Harris; I see, eh?'

'None, sir,' I replied; 'they have been gone many days back.'

He smiled, and passing on, spoke to another man, and so on through the whole body.

Craufurd was, I remember, terribly severe during this retreat if he caught anything like pilfering amongst the men. As we stood, however, during this short halt, a very tempting turnip-field was close on the side of us, and several of the men were so ravenous that, although he was in our very ranks, they stepped into the field and helped themselves to the turnips, devouring them like famishing wolves. He either did not or would not observe the delinquency this time, and soon afterwards gave the word, and we moved on once more.

About this period, I remember another sight which I shall not to my dying day forget; and it causes me a sore heart, even now, as I remember it. Soon after our halt beside the turnip-field, the screams of a child near me caught my ear, and drew my attention to one of our women, who was endeavouring to drag along a little boy of about seven or eight years old. The poor child was apparently completely exhausted, and his legs failing under him. The mother had occasionally, up to this time, been assisted by some of the men taking it in turn to help the little fellow on; but now all further appeal was vain. No man had more strength than was necessary for the support of his own carcase, and the mother could no longer raise the child in her arms, as her reeling pace too plainly showed. Still, however, she continued to drag the child along with her.

It was a pitiable sight, and wonderful to behold the efforts the poor woman made to keep the boy amongst us. At last the little fellow had not even strength to cry, but, with mouth wide open, stumbled onwards until both sank down to rise no more. . . . Poor creatures! they must have bitterly regretted not having accepted the offer which was made to them to embark at Lisbon for England, instead of accompanying their husbands into Spain. The women, however, I have often observed, are most persevering in such cases, and are not to be persuaded that their presence is often a source of anxiety to the corps they belong to.

"Rifleman Harris" was extremely devoted to his general, concern-

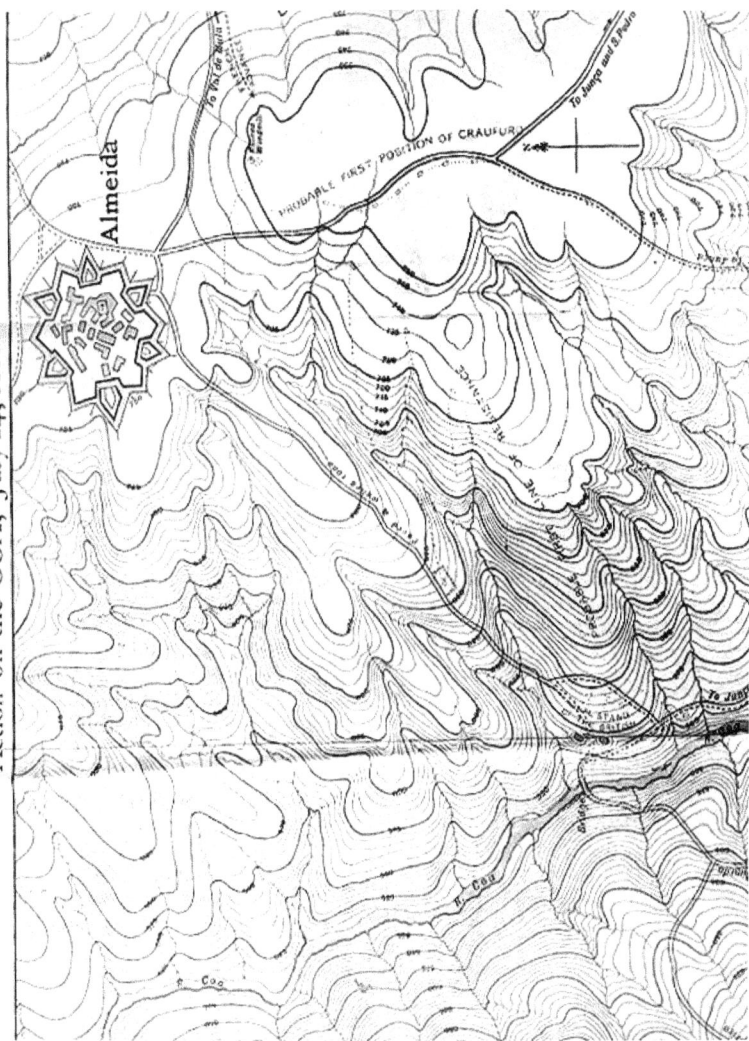

Aktion on the COA, July 24, 1810

Almeida

PROBABLE FIRST POSITION OF CRAUFURD

To Vte de Boira

To Juego and S.Pedro

To Junta

ing whom he writes at considerable length and tells several interesting anecdotes.

He says:

I do not think I ever admired any man who wore the British uniform more than I did General Craufurd. I could fill a book with descriptions of him; for I frequently had my eye on him in the hurry of action. It was gratifying, too, to me to think that he did not altogether think ill of me, since he has often addressed me kindly when, from adverse circumstances, you might have thought that he had scarcely spirits to cheer up the men under him. The Rifles liked him; but they also feared him, for he could be terrible when insubordination showed itself in the ranks. 'You think, because you are riflemen, you may do whatever you think proper;' said he, one day, to the miserable and savage-looking crew around him in the retreat to Corunna: 'but I'll teach you the difference before I have done with you.' I remember one evening, during the retreat, he detected two men straying away from the main body; it was in the early stage of that disastrous flight, and Craufurd knew well that he must do his utmost to keep the division together. He halted the brigade with a voice of thunder, ordered a drum-head court-martial on the instant, and they were sentenced to a hundred apiece. Whilst this hasty trial was taking place, Craufurd dismounting from his horse, stood in the midst, looking stern and angry as a worried bull-dog. He did not like retreating at all, that man. The three men nearest him as he stood were Jagger, Dan Howans, and myself. All were worn, dejected, and savage, though nothing to what we were after a few days more of the retreat. The whole brigade were in a grumbling and discontented mood; and Craufurd doubtless felt ill pleased with the aspect of affairs altogether.

'D—n his eyes,' muttered Howans, 'he had much better try to get us something to eat and drink than harass us in this way.'

No sooner had Howans disburdened his conscience of this growl, than Craufurd, who had overheard it, turning sharply round, seized the rifle out of Jagger's hand, and felled him to the earth with the butt-end.

'It was not I who spoke,' said Jagger, getting up and shaking his head. 'You shouldn't knock me about.'

'I heard you, sir,' said Craufurd, 'and I will bring you also to a court-martial.'

'I am the man who spoke,' said Howans.

'Very well,' returned Craufurd, 'then I'll try you, sir.'

And accordingly, when the other affair was disposed of, Howans' case came on. By the time the three men were tried, it was too dark to inflict the punishment. Howans, however, had got the complement of three hundred promised to him; so Craufurd gave the word to the brigade to move on. He marched all that night on foot; and when the morning dawned, I remember that, like the rest of us, his hair, beard, and eyebrows were covered with the frost, as if he had grown white with age. We were, indeed, all of us in the same condition. Scarcely had I time to notice the appearance of morning, before the general once more called a halt. We were then on the hills. Ordering a square to be formed, he spoke to the brigade, as well as I can remember, in these words, after having ordered the three before-named men of the 95th to be brought into the square.

'Although,' said he, 'I should obtain the good will neither of the officers nor of the men of the brigade here by so doing, I am resolved to punish these three men according to the sentence awarded, even though the French are at our heels. Begin with Daniel Howans.'

This was indeed no time to be lax in discipline, and the general knew it. The men, as I said, were some of them becoming careless and ruffianly in their demeanour; whilst others, again, I saw with the tears falling down their cheeks from the agony of their bleeding feet; and many were ill with dysentery from the effects of the bad food they had got hold of and devoured on the road. Our knapsacks, too, were a bitter enemy on this prolonged march. Many a man died, I am convinced, who would have borne up well to the end of the retreat, but for the infernal load we carried on our backs. My own knapsack was my bitterest enemy; I felt it press me to the earth almost at times, and more than once felt as if I should die under its deadly embrace. The knapsacks, in my opinion, should have been abandoned at the very commencement of the retrograde movement, as it would have been better to have lost them altogether, if by such loss we could have saved the poor fellows who, as it was, died strapped to them on the road.

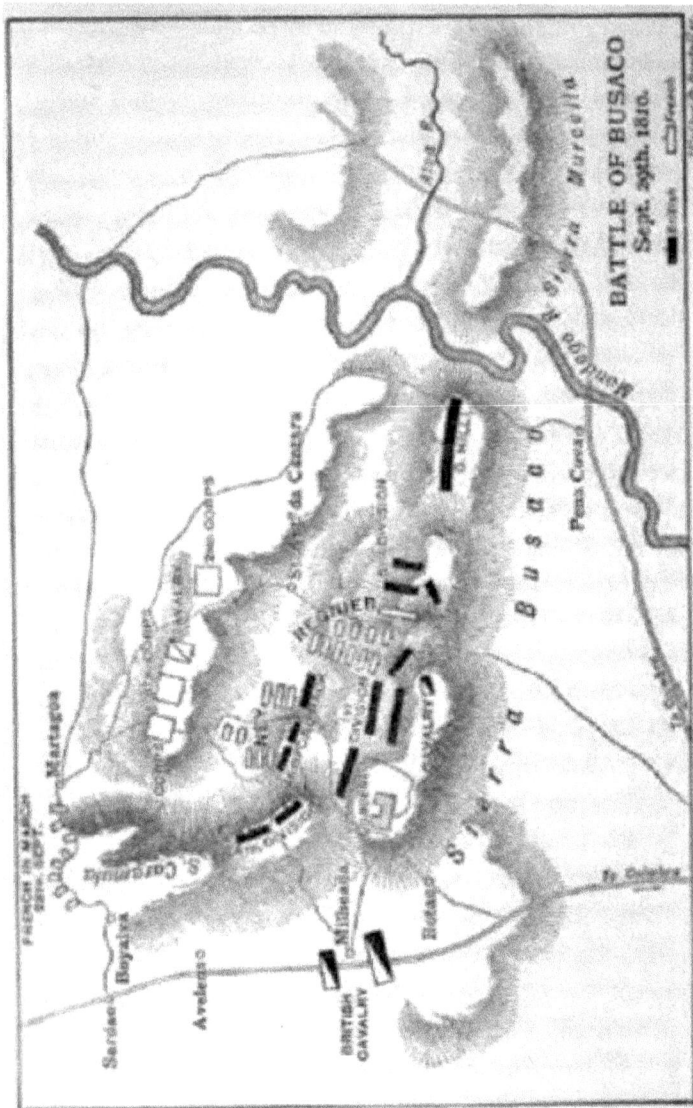

BATTLE OF BUSACO
Sept. 29th. 1810.

There was some difficulty in finding a place to tie Howans up, as the Light Brigade carried no halberts. However, they led him to a slender ash tree which grew near at hand.

'Don't trouble yourselves about tying me up,' said Howans, folding his arms; 'I'll take my punishment like a man.'

He did so without a murmur, receiving the whole three hundred. His wife, who was present with us, I remember, was a strong, hardy Irishwoman. When it was over, she stepped up and covered Howans with his grey great-coat. The general then gave the word to move on. I rather think he knew the enemy was too near to punish the other two delinquents just then; so, we proceeded out of the cornfield in which we had been halted, and toiled away upon the hills once more, Howans' wife carrying the jacket, knapsack, and pouch which the lacerated state of the man's back would not permit him to bear.

It could not have been, I should think, more than an hour after the punishment had been inflicted upon Howans, when the general again gave the word for the brigade to halt, and once more formed them into square. We had begun to suppose that he intended to allow the other two delinquents to escape, under the present difficulties and hardships of the retreat. He was not, however, one of the forgetful sort, when the discipline of the army under him made severity necessary.

'Bring out the two other men of the 95th,' said he, 'who were tried last night.'

The men were brought forth accordingly, and their lieutenant-colonel, Hamilton-Wade, at the same time stepped forth. He walked up to the general, and, lowering his sword, requested that he would forgive these men, as they were both of them good soldiers, and had fought in all the battles of Portugal.

'I order you, sir,' said the general, 'to do your duty. These men shall be punished.'

The lieutenant-colonel, therefore, recovering his sword, turned about, and fell back to the front of the Rifles. One of the men, upon this, I think it was Armstrong, immediately began to unstrap his knapsack, and prepare for the lash. Craufurd had turned about meanwhile, and walked up to one side of the square. Apparently, he suddenly relented a little, and again turning sharp round, returned towards the two prisoners. 'Stop,' said he; 'in consequence of the intercession of your lieutenant-colonel, I

GENERAL CRAUFURD AT THE BATTLE OF BUSACO

GENERAL CRAUFURD AT CIUDAD RODRIGO

will allow you thus much. You shall draw lots, and the winner shall escape; but one of the two I am determined to make an example of.'

The square was formed in a stubble-field, and the sergeant-major of the Rifles, immediately stooping down, plucked up two straws, and the men, coming forward, drew. I cannot be quite certain, but I think it was Armstrong who drew the longest straw, and won the safety of his hide; and his fellow gamester was in quick time tied to a tree, and the punishment commenced. A hundred was the sentence; but when the bugler had counted seventy-five, the general granted him a further indulgence, and ordered him to be taken down, and to join his company. The general, calling for his horse, now mounted for the first time for many hours; for he had not ridden all night, not indeed since the drum-head court-martial had taken place. Before he put the brigade in motion again, he gave us another short specimen of his eloquence, pretty much, I remember, after this style: 'I give you all notice that I will halt the brigade again the very first moment I perceive any man disobeying my orders, and try him by court-martial on the spot.'

Many who read this, especially in these peaceful times, may suppose this was a cruel and unnecessary severity under the dreadful and harassing circumstances of that retreat; but I who was there, and was besides a common soldier of the very regiment to which these men belonged, say it was *quite necessary.* No man but one formed of stuff like General Craufurd could have saved the brigade from perishing altogether; and, if he flogged two, he saved hundreds from death by his management. I detest the sight of the lash, but I am convinced the British Army can never go on without it. Late events have taught us the necessity of such measures.

On this subject our rifleman has happily not turned out a true prophet; but we must remember of what very rough and often criminal materials the army was composed in his days, so that soldiers then probably needed a very different kind of treatment from that which suits them in our days. For my own part, I am well convinced that Sir Charles Napier was right in holding that, *in time of peace,* flogging might well have been abandoned very many years before it actually was.

General Craufurd was always greatly disliked by the majority of his officers; but there is ample evidence that in the end he was much beloved by the men. The following story from this rifleman, Harris, well exemplifies the general's hostility to incompetent or ill-behaved officers in his division.

It was perhaps a couple of days after this had taken place that we came to a river. It was tolerably wide, but not very deep, which was just as well for us; for had it been deep as the dark regions, we must have somehow or other got through. The avenger was behind us, and Craufurd was along with us, and the two together kept us moving, whatever was in the road. Accordingly, into the stream went the Light Brigade, and Craufurd, as busy as a shepherd with his flock, riding in and out of the water, to keep his wearied band from being drowned as they crossed over. Presently he spied an officer, who, to save himself from being wet through, I suppose, and wearing a damp pair of breeches for the rest of the day, had mounted on the back of one of his men. The sight of such a piece of effeminacy was enough to raise the choler of the general, and in a very short time he was plunging and splashing through the water after them both.

'Put him down, sir, put him down; I desire you to put that officer down instantly!' And the soldier in an instant, I dare say nothing loath, dropping his burden like a hot potato into the stream, continued his progress through. 'Return back, sir,' said Craufurd to the officer, 'and go through the water like the others; I will not allow my officers to ride upon the men's backs through the rivers; all must take their share alike here.'

Wearied as we were, this affair caused all who saw it to shout almost with laughter, and was never forgotten by those who survived the retreat."

General Craufurd was, indeed, one of the few men who was apparently created for command during such dreadful scenes as we were familiar with in this retreat. He seemed an iron map; nothing daunted him; nothing turned him from his purpose. War was his very element, and toil and danger seemed to call forth only an increasing determination to surmount them. I was sometimes amused with his appearance and that of the men around us; for, the Rifles being always at his heels, he seemed to think them his familiars. If he stopped his horse, and halted

Battle of
FUENTES D'ONORE
5th. May, 1811.

■ Allies ☐ French

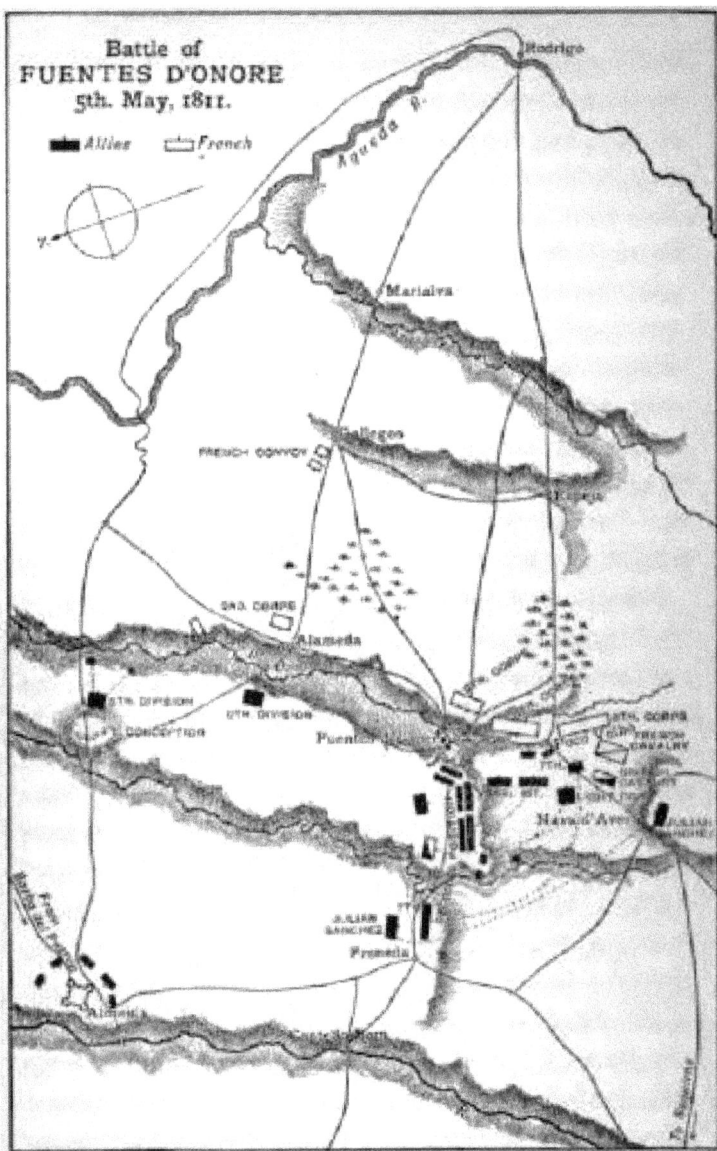

Agueda R.

Rodrigo

Marialva

Gallegos

FRENCH CONVOY

3RD. CORPS

Alameda

5TH. DIVISION

LT. CONCEPTION

6TH. DIVISION

Fuentes

CORPS

9TH. CORPS

FRENCH
CAVALRY

LIGHT DIV.

Nava d'Aver

JULIAN
SANCHEZ

J.ULIAN
SANCHEZ

Pozovelho

Almeda

Castello Bom

to deliver one of his stern reprimands, you would see half-a-dozen lean, unshaven, shoeless, and savage riflemen standing for the moment leaning upon their weapons, and scowling up in his face as he scolded; and when he dashed the spurs into his reeking horse, they would throw up their rifles upon their shoulders, and hobble after him again. He was sometimes to be seen in the front, then in the rear, and then you would fall in with him again in the midst, dismounted and marching on foot, that the men might see he took an equal share in the toils which they were enduring. He had a mortal dislike, I remember, to a commissary. Many a time have I heard him storming at the neglect of those gentry, when the men were starving for rations, and nothing but excuses forthcoming. 'Send the commissary to me!' he would roar. 'D—n him, I will hang him, if the provisions are not up this night.'

This last extract from "Rifleman Harris," is peculiarly interesting as throwing light on the vexed question whether it was Picton or Craufurd who threatened to hang the commissary, who thereupon went and complained to Lord Wellington.

It is evident that it was really Craufurd who used the threat. This opinion is confirmed by other evidence besides the testimony of Harris. Kincaid, who was for some time Adjutant of the 95th Rifles under Craufurd, ascribes the threat to his own general, and not to Picton; but he says that the threat was to put the commissary into the guardhouse. Sir William Napier, when criticising Robinson's *Life of General Picton*, (republished in *Picton* by Leonaur), in an appendix to his history of the Peninsular War, objects to this writer attributing to his hero (Picton) all the good stories concerning the war, with special reference to this story. From which one may justly infer that Napier considered that this famous anecdote had been erroneously attributed to Picton.

I have also very recently in October, 1890 received a few lines from General Whichcote, who joined the 52nd Regiment at the beginning of the year 1811; and he says that he remembers that it was Craufurd who threatened to hang the commissary, and that the incident occurred at a place called Alfayates.

The story is so well known that it is scarcely worthwhile, perhaps, to repeat it. Still it may be unknown to some of my readers. General Craufurd threatened to hang a commissary if the rations for his divi-

Second Siege of Ciudad Rodrigo, 1812

sion were not produced at a certain time. Whereupon the commissary went to Lord Wellington and complained greatly, and also asked his advice as to what he had better do. Apparently, Wellington, seemed sympathetic at first; for he said, "Did General Craufurd go so far as that? Did he actually say he would hang you?"

"Yes, my lord, he did," said the commissary.

To which Wellington then answered, "Then I should strongly advise you to get the rations ready; for if General Craufurd said he would hang you, by G—d, he'll do it."

Harris also writes further concerning his general:

Twice, I remember, he was in command of the Light Brigade. The second time he joined them he made, I heard, something like these remarks, after they had been some little time in Spain: 'When I commanded you before, I know full well that you disliked me, for you thought me severe. *This time I am glad to find there is a change in yourselves.*'

Towards the close of this retreat, as they were gradually and wearily and dejectedly crawling to Vigo, our rifleman again closely observes his trusted leader.

I remember to have again remarked Craufurd at this period of the retreat. He was no whit altered in his desire to keep the force together, I thought; but still active and vigilant as ever, he seemed to keep his eye upon those who were now most likely to hold out. I myself marched during many hours close beside him this day. He looked stern and pale, but the very picture of a warrior. I shall never forget Craufurd, if I live to a hundred years, I think. He was in everything a soldier.

Here I am very reluctantly compelled to say farewell to this brave, faithful, and intelligent private soldier, whose simple narrative is so full of interest. After this expedition, Harris served no more under his beloved leader. His health was utterly destroyed by the fatal Walcheren expedition, and he had to retire from the army altogether. But the old soldier's heart was always with the gallant 95th Rifles and their fiery general. And his deep pride in his old comrades was abundantly nourished and satisfied as he heard from afar of their marvellous discipline and steadfast valour in the Peninsular War. The grand march to Talavera, the fierce combat at the Coa, the brilliant action at Sabugal, the splendid victory of Busaco, the cool and unyielding intrepid-

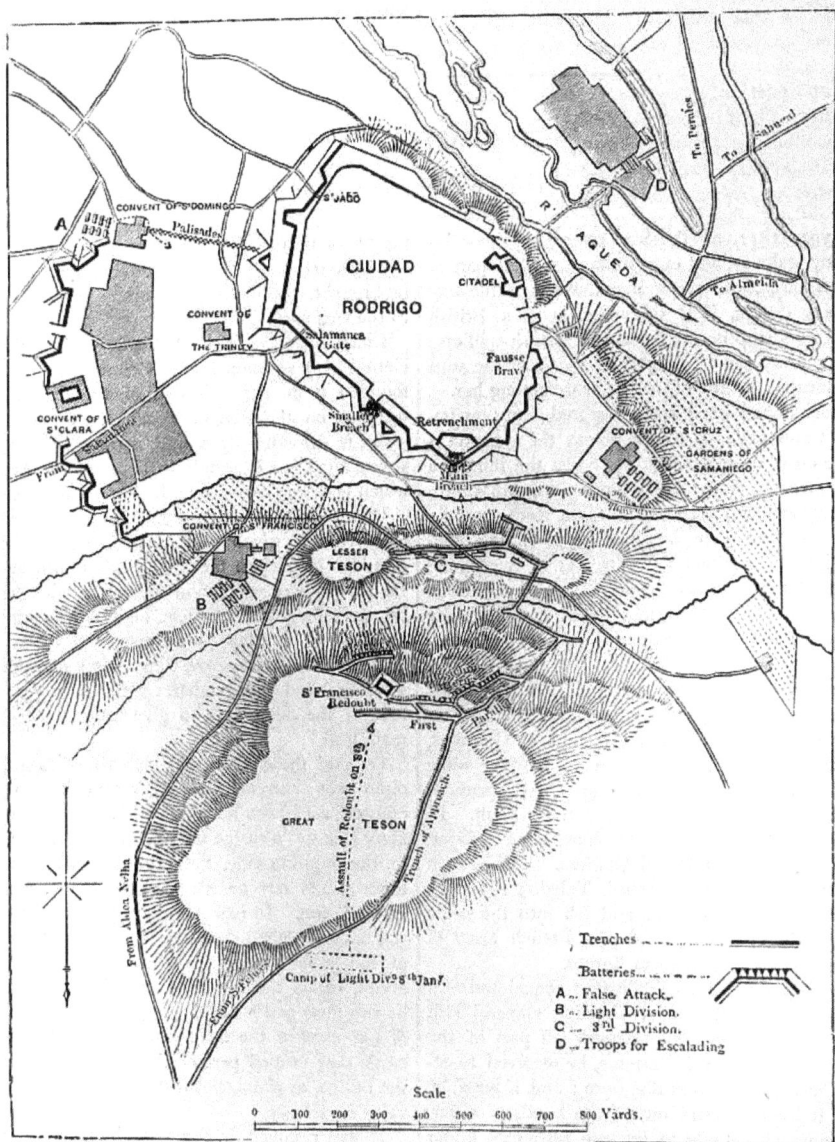

PLAN OF THE SECOND ASSAULT ON CIUDAD RODRIGO, 1812

ity displayed at Fuentes d'Onoro, the successful storming of Ciudad Rodrigo, must all have thrilled this soldier's heart with joy and pride for his old corps. And, doubtless, this most faithful private mourned as truly as any one belonging to the army, when he learnt that those qualities which, in the retreat to Vigo, he admired so fervently in his old general, had led to his premature death as he stood alone in advance of his whole division at Ciudad Rodrigo.

I am glad to say that in the rest of this volume I shall have the valuable aid of another of General Craufurd's riflemen, Edward Costello, a non-commissioned officer, whose book, *Adventures of a Soldier*, is certainly one of the most amusing and interesting of all the many works which have been written concerning the most brilliant of all our many wars. (Republished by Leonaur as *Rifleman Costello.*)

CHAPTER 5

Craufurd's Services under Wellington

Robert Craufurd did not remain very long in England after his return from Vigo. Orders were given to the 43rd, the 52nd, and the first battalion of the 95th Rifles, to prepare for service again, with the least possible delay, and to form a brigade under Brigadier-General Robert Craufurd, their destination being Portugal. On May 25, 1809, they embarked at Dover, and sailed immediately to the Downs, where they were detained several days by rough weather. They were again delayed by bad weather off the Isle of Wight, and finally passed the Needles on June 18. This delay in starting was decidedly unfortunate, for, had it not occurred, this splendid Brigade would almost certainly have been with Sir Arthur Wellesley at the Battle of Talavera.

They reached Lisbon on June 28, and were busily engaged till July 2, in purchasing horses, mules, packsaddles, and many other necessities for the coming campaign.

About this time the leader of this brigade received two letters of information one from Colonel Bathurst, and the other from General Charles Stewart, who was an intimate friend of Robert Craufurd, having served with him in the Austrian campaigns. I give both these letters, as it is interesting to know how far Craufurd was able to form any accurate conjecture as to the probability of Sir Arthur Wellesley giving battle to the enemy.

Private.

Castello Branco, July 1, 1809.

Dear Sir,

I am sincerely rejoiced that you are arrived, and I beg to congratulate you on having so fine a brigade.

Our latest accounts this day state that Joseph Bonaparte passed through Toledo, and has joined Victor with 5000 fresh troops; and it is said that Sebastiani has also moved by Toledo for the same purpose. If so, the enemy will have near 50,000 men at Talavera.

Cuesta has in consequence given orders to withdraw his army again behind the Tagus between Almaraz and Arzobispo. He has about 32,000 men. Venegas has about 14,000 or 15,000 in La Mancha.

Ney has abandoned Corunna and withdrawn to Lugo, and is said to be marching by Villa Franca and Astorga.

Soult, with from 8000 to 10,000 men, is on his way, I imagine, to Zamora.

Kellerman, etc., have retired from Asturias, and the forces, supposed to be near 10,000 men, are between Leon, Salamanca, and Valladolid.

Romana is at Orense, and has in all 15,000.

Blake has about 20,000 men, and is opposed to Suchet, who commands about 15,000 at Saragossa.

I have sent you this short statement for your private information, as I thought it might be satisfactory to you, and therefore beg you will excuse the haste with which I write.

We go towards Placentia tomorrow, and I have just sent off to request Cuesta to establish a bridge over the Tagus on this side the Tietar, to communicate with us.

> Believe me, with great esteem,
> > Dear Sir,
> > > Ever yours,

> > > > > F. Bathurst.

General Charles Stewart (afterwards Lord Londonderry) wrote as follows

> Zarza Mayor, July 3, 1809.

My Dear Robert,

I am much rejoiced to hear of your arrival on many accounts, and long to have some conversation with you. I sent orders to Lisbon that you might be furnished with all the general orders given out by the town major. Pray let me know up to what date you have received, and if any are wanting. The disembarkation returns of your brigade are arrived today; one woman only in the 95th. Happy regiment! Your friend Elder is the most pleas-

antly situated. How did you leave Charles? What is your specu-
lation about our old friends the Austrians? I long to be on the
Danube again; there is something in this country I am mortally
sick of, and my situation does not keep me in spirits. We have
no news in our part . . . . We move headquarters on the 5th to
Coria, and on the 7th to Placentia. God bless you. Hoping soon
to shake you by the hand,

      Believe me, ever yours most truly,

                         Charles Stewart.

The following long letter from Mr. Windham, for some time Minister for War, contains much interesting matter.

                    Beaconsfield, July 18, 1809.

Dear Sir,

Though I have long been full of an intention to write to you,
I might have remained possibly in that state for a considerable
time, if the additional drop to make me flow over had not just
been furnished by a gentleman, who wishes me to give him a
letter of introduction for his son. The gentleman in question
saw you, I think, at the York Hotel at Dover, and felt much
obliged by the leave you gave his son to pass some time with
him. His name is Norris, a physician settled in this neighbourhood, and universally esteemed as well for his conduct in his
profession as for his general worth and liberality.

Besides the profits of his profession, he has a competent private
fortune, a circumstance which I mention as showing that his
son, who is an only child, had no motive but liking for entering
the army, and may therefore be presumed to have some of the
qualities which may make him deserving of encouragement in
his profession. It was, in fact, entirely against the wishes of his
parents that he went into the army. His choice was fixed, and
fixed in circumstances affording a good presumption that it was
formed on right grounds. The object of my application is only
to recommend him to your notice, and to such favour as he
may be found deserving of, and as his situation (an Ensign in
the 52nd) may be capable of.

We know little for a good while past of your operations in the
Peninsula; nor are they in fact those which are of most importance; though it can never happen that operations can be indifferent in which credit is to be gained or lost by our troops, or

that I personally should not feel interested in those in which you may have a part. Our fate, and that of all Europe, is to be looked for from the banks of the Danube. But as the issue there may not be conclusive, nor the cause completely decided one way or the other, it is of great consequence that things should go well in other parts, so as to be ready in case the result at Vienna should be something short either of complete success or complete failure, I am, upon that principle, a great enemy to what we are now doing in sending forth an immense expedition, for no other object, as I apprehend, than of destroying the ships and naval preparations of the enemy in the Schelde.

With the notice that they must have had of our intention, and with the uncertainties attached to all such operations, there must be a great risk, notwithstanding the amount of force, of failure. But the object is, in my opinion, inadequate; and therefore, despairing of all effectual co-operation with the North of Germany, I should be of opinion for sending the whole of this armament to join what we have already in Spain, so as to make our success in that quarter complete.

Were the whole of the French force driven out of Spain, and the Spanish Government established throughout, it must be a very complete triumph of Bonaparte over the Austrians that could enable the French to get back into Spain, aided as the Spaniards might continue to be with the presence of our army. And if Bonaparte, instead of being successful, should fail against the Austrians, there is no part more advantageous than Spain from which operations could be begun against France itself; I mean with a view of profiting by the troubles which, in the state of things supposed, could hardly fail to arise in that kingdom.

Instead of this, we shall be risking forty thousand men (the risk not being less when the commander is a person so totally devoid of experience as Lord Chatham) for the mere respite to be obtained by the temporary destruction of ships and arsenals, without any credit to be gained for our exertions in the cause of Europe, and with little other motive than that of furnishing a topic of boast for the ministerial papers during the recess.

If there were any expedition (meaning any separate attempt) by which I would be at all tempted, it would be one which few would look to, and which could only be thought of with a view to distant consequences; I mean the capture of Belleisle, a place perfectly useless and unproductive in the first instance, but of inestimable value in case the exertion of the Austrian armies (the only external means that now remain) should succeed in *shaking* the power of Bonaparte, without being able to overthrow it. If the dominion of France is ever to be overturned, it must be, I believe, in part by internal causes. Till the battles of the 21st and 22nd of May, internal causes could *alone* be looked to; and if internal causes are the sources on which we are to depend, I know no way in which our endeavours can be made to co-operate so effectually as by the station which I am speaking of. No such idea, however, has, I take it for granted, ever entered anyone's mind, or would for a moment be listened to.

Though I do not urge your writing, knowing how much your time must be taken up, yet I must not be so careless about my own satisfaction as not to say how glad I shall be, if on any occasion you can tell me how you are going on, as well with respect to yourself personally as with respect to all that is doing and may be expected. Could Mrs. Windham be reconciled to my absence, I am far from being sure that I should not make you a visit, however little capable I am beginning to feel myself even of such fatigues as a mere residence at headquarters would expose me to. I am afraid, indeed, that such is my state at present; so, it is well, perhaps, that regard to Mrs. Windham's anxieties puts at once an end to the question. I should feel otherwise great advantage, as well as satisfaction, in getting some clinical lectures from you on the art of war during the course of a campaign. I am greatly inclined to the belief that your commander, with whom I hope you now are, will exhibit specimens of a very excellent praxis. I have a great idea that Sir Arthur possesses what may fairly be called military genius.

You will see, by the date of this, from what house I am writing. I am sitting in the very chair and leaning on the very desk from which those counsels issued which, one may fairly say, would have saved the world, had they been listened to, from half the calamities under which it is now suffering. What an example have we in this instance of the difference between man and man, as operating on the fate of nations! All such differences are now overlooked in the present temper of the country; and while the whole rage is for pulling the constitution to pieces, under the notion of looking for abuses, the conduct of campaigns and wars, and of the political counsels of the country, are considered as matters of no consequence. In military warfare, though the contention is for mutual destruction, there is at least the satisfaction of contending only against known and avowed enemies; and your friends, by those at least who are in command, may be made to do what shall be thought best. In political warfare the chief contention is with the folly, ignorance, perverseness, and interestedness of those whom you are endeavouring to serve. But the topic is too long to go on upon.

Ever, with great truth and regard,

Yours,

W. Windham.

P.S. Fine sport between Mr. Wardle and Mrs. Clark. The parliament is to be disgraced and the constitution to be pulled to pieces, because a majority of the House of Commons would not give full credit to the assertion of a witness whom Mr. Wardle now declares, in his own case, is not to be credited upon her oath!

I now return to the movements of General Craufurd and his brigade after reaching Lisbon. From a narrative by Colonel J. Leach, of the 95th Rifles, (*Rough Sketches of the Life of an Old Soldier* republished by Leonaur as *Captain of the 95th Rifles*) we learn that, instead of landing the brigade at Lisbon, and marching it to Santarem, it was determined to convey the regiments in boats to the village of Vallada, forty miles above the capital, and that the baggage-animals should be sent by land to Santarem. Accordingly, they went to Vallada.

Concerning this brigade Colonel Leach writes thus with natural pride:

The three regiments composing the Light Brigade having now landed, I may observe that unprejudiced persons, and those neither directly nor indirectly connected with it, have pronounced it the finest and most splendid brigade that ever took the field. I will venture to go so far as to assert that, if it has been equalled, it has never been surpassed in any army, whether the materials of which it was composed, its fine appointments and arms, its *esprit du corps*, its style of marching and manoeuvring, and in short, every requisite for a Light Brigade, be considered. Each regiment was nearly eleven hundred strong.

To this we may add that in each battalion there were many soldiers

76

who had seen a good deal of active service. Some of Craufurd's men had been with him in the terrible expedition to Buenos Ayres under General Whitelocke, and some had fought under Sir John Moore at Corunna.

From Vallada the brigade marched first to Santarem, where it halted some little time, waiting for the baggage-animals, ammunition, and commissariat arrangements. They then moved on to Abrantes.

Costello, in his book remarks:

> The excellent orders our brigadier issued for maintaining order and discipline on the line of march, on this occasion, though exceedingly unpopular at first, have since become justly celebrated in the service.

Craufurd was excessively strict during this march.

> But yet, with all this, strange as it may appear, Craufurd maintained a popularity among the men, who, on every other occasion, always found him to be their best friend.

The weather during this famous march was almost intolerably hot, and so, for the most part, the troops moved during the night or very early morning. After reaching Castello Branco, they encamp near Zarza Mayor on the 20th of July, and arrive at Coria on the 22nd. On the 24th, 25th, 26th, 27th, they continued their march under a burning sun. On the 28th they heard sounds of something like a distant cannonade; and this caused the leader of the Light Brigade to make his wonderful march, in order, if possible, to join Sir Arthur Wellesley before the fighting was over. Concerning this extraordinarily rapid movement Sir William Napier wrote:

> That day (July 29) Robert Craufurd reached the English camp, with the 43rd, 52nd, and 95th regiments, and immediately took charge of the outposts. These troops had been, after a march of twenty miles, hutted near Malpartida de Plasencia, when the alarm caused by the Spanish fugitives spread to that part. Craufurd, fearing for the army, allowed only a few hours' rest; and then, withdrawing about fifty of the weakest from the ranks, recommenced his march with a resolution not to halt until the field of battle was reached. As the brigade advanced, crowds of the runaways were met with, not all Spaniards, but all propagating the vilest falsehoods—'Sir Arthur Wellesley was killed,' 'The French were only a few miles distant'—nay, some, blinded

by their fears, pretended to point out the enemy's advanced posts on the nearest hills. Indignant at this shameful scene, the troops hastened rather than slackened their impetuous pace, and, leaving only seventeen stragglers behind, in twenty-six hours crossed the field of battle in a close and compact body, having in that time crossed over sixty-two English miles in the hottest season of the year, each man carrying from fifty to sixty pounds weight upon his shoulders. Had the historian Gibbon known of such a march, he would have spared his sneer about the delicacy of modern soldiers.

Even after this unprecedented march, the fine appearance and bearing of Craufurd's splendid brigade were such as to evoke the heartiest admiration of the victors of Talavera. On this occasion, as on so many others in after times, there was with the Light Brigade "a magnificent troop of Horse Artillery, under the command of Captain Ross."

Colonel Leach, of the 95th Rifles, was in this most renowned march, and tells us much of the frightful labour and suffering of the soldiers during it.

> Each soldier carried from sixty to eighty rounds of ammunition, a musket or a rifle, a great coat, and (if I recollect rightly) a blanket, a knapsack complete with shoes, shirts, etc., a canteen and haversack, bayonet, belts, etc. Such a load, carried so great a distance, would be considered a hard day's work for a horse...
> .. It must also be added that for some days before we had been very scantily supplied with provisions.

During the whole of this march the soldiers often suffered much from thirst, as one may gather from the following story of Colonel Leach:

> Having reached a pool of stagnant water near the road, in which cattle had been watered during the summer, and where they had constantly wallowed, a halt was ordered for an hour or two. Those who have never been in similar situations, may be inclined to doubt my veracity when I state that the whole brigade, officers and soldiers, rushed into this muddy water, and drank with an eagerness and avidity impossible to describe. The use of such an execrable beverage, except on extreme occasions like the one in question, when we had been the whole day without water, under a sun as oppressive as can be experienced

in Europe, might indeed be deemed extraordinary; but excessive thirst knows no law.

The accuracy of Sir William Napier's reckoning as to the exact length of this march has been questioned in recent years; but, even if we make some slight deduction from the number of miles, this amazingly rapid movement of the Light Brigade still remains unparalleled in the British Army, if we take into account the extremely disadvantageous and trying circumstances under which it was made. Colonel Leach makes the march fifty miles in twenty-four hours.

Had Craufurd only known that Sir Arthur Wellesley was likely to be engaged with the enemy, he might easily have been in time to join in the Battle of Talavera. But, not knowing this, he moved in a very gradual manner during the earlier part of the march, on account of the extreme heat. He was always very careful to spare his men unnecessary hardship.

Costello informs us that on the battlefield of Talavera they found the wounded and dying in a fearful condition.

The long grass, which had taken fire during the action, was still burning, and added dreadfully to the sufferings of the wounded and dying of both armies; their cries for assistance were horrifying, and hundreds might have been seen exerting the last remnant of their strength, crawling to places of safety.

Costello, like almost everyone else, formed a very unfavourable opinion of Wellesley's ally, the Spanish general, Cuesta, whom he calls:

That deformed-looking lump of pride, ignorance, and treachery. He was the most murderous-looking old man I ever saw.

General Craufurd was much pleased that his commander at once intrusted to him the charge of the outposts of the army. For this work he was, no doubt, pre-eminently fitted. Sir George Napier wrote of him:

His knowledge of outpost duty was never exceeded by any British general, and I much doubt if there are many in any other service who know more of that particular branch of the profession than he did.

Lord Wellington says to Craufurd in a letter dated April 9, 1810, and published in the duke's *Despatches*:

Since you have joined the army, I have always wished that you should command our outposts, for many reasons into which it is unnecessary to enter.

Successful though Wellesley had been at Talavera, his position was very soon again beset by perils; and these were much increased by the almost incredible stupidity and obstinacy of the fatuous Cuesta. The English commander was soon in considerable danger of being hemmed in by various French armies; and it became of the highest importance to secure a line of retreat. For this purpose, while the English Army moved towards Deleytoza, Craufurd's Brigade and six guns were directed to gain Almaraz, secure the boat-bridge, and oppose any attempt to seize the Puerto de Mirabete. This was done with the greatest rapidity, though the way was very rugged. Colonel J. Leach writes thus:

> To reach and to secure the bridge of Almaraz was, however, of such vast importance, that if only fifty men of the division had strength to accomplish it, push on they must. In reality we were not certain whether, on our arrival, we should not find Marshal Soult's army in possession of it; in which case, the situation not only of our division, but of the whole British Army would have been far from enviable.

However, all went well, and the Light Brigade became masters of this very important bridge. Before long the army fell back to the neighbourhood of Badajoz, whence there were safe communications with Lisbon.

It is melancholy to think what a fine and effective reinforcement Wellington might have received about this period, if a large English army had not been destined to waste its strength in the pestilential marshes of Walcheren.

Early in September, 1809, Craufurd's Brigade was stationed at Campo Mayor, where it remained for about three months, the headquarters of the army being at Badajoz.

Sir Arthur Wellesley wrote rather an interesting letter to the leader of the Light Brigade from Badajoz on September 4. In it he says:

> I halted at Merida for some days, in consequence of some letters I received from Lord Wellesley expressing a desire that I should remain within the Spanish frontier, at least for a time.

He also says to Craufurd:

I should put you in front on the other side, only that I think the movement we shall probably make next will be across the Tagus. The enemy appear to entertain a design to attack Ciudad Rodrigo. Soult proposes this operation in a letter to the king which we have intercepted; and I think it not improbable that they will attempt it. If they should attempt it, we must make an effort to prevent its success; and I know of none that would have the effect excepting a movement to that quarter. If, however, I should be mistaken, and the enemy should come this way, we could put you in front before the army could be collected.

It is perhaps worth noticing that Wellington always spelt the word enemy incorrectly; he invariably wrote it "ennemy." I have corrected the error in this volume, lest it should be attributed to my ignorance.

In this same letter, Sir Arthur Wellesley intimates that the army was then very flourishing so far as money was concerned:

I have given directions that your commissary may be supplied with money. His want of it hitherto is to be attributed entirely to the deputy-commissary-general, as there is more money with the army than we know what to do with; and we ought to pay in ready money for everything we receive.

On September 29, Lord Wellington addressed a long letter to General Craufurd on the subject of camp-kettles. He begins by saying that he has been for some time very anxious about the matter, and adds:

I am much obliged to you for your sentiments on the subject.

The leader of the Light Brigade advocated the use of tin kettles as being so much lighter and more portable. But Wellington foresaw various objections to their general use.

In deciding this question, much depends upon the care which the officers take of their men, and the degree of minute attention which they give to their wants. In a regiment well looked after it is certain that tin kettles would answer best, as the officers would oblige the soldiers to take care of them. . . . But in two thirds of the regiments of this army such care would not be taken; whether the regiments would have kettles or not would depend upon that most thoughtless of animals, the soldier himself; and I should very soon hear that there were none.

... Upon the whole, therefore, I prefer the iron kettle to the tin for general purposes; but I have no objection to try the latter in some of our best regiments, in order to see how the experiment would answer. I agree with you about the expediency of allowing the captains of companies to ride. The forage required for this purpose is no object, as forage for two or three hundred more mules or horses cannot be very difficult to procure. The objection, I think, is, the increased number of batmen and servants which will be taken out of the ranks, which becomes an object of the greatest consequence.

Lord Wellington went to Lisbon at the beginning of October, having determined to create those lines of Torres Vedras which afterwards proved such an invincible obstacle to the French. By the middle of November, he had returned to Badajoz. He does not appear to have confided to the divisional leaders of the army the highly important fact of his having created these most formidable lines. His reticence on this subject was probably injurious in some respects, by causing his subordinate generals inadvertently to thwart some of his wise schemes.

About December 12, General Craufurd's forces left Campo Mayor, and marched to Aronches, on their way to the north of Portugal. On January 4, 1810, they arrived at Pinhel, quite near to the river Coa, which was afterwards destined to be so closely associated with the almost unrivalled activity of the ubiquitous Light Division during four months of most perilous outpost work.

On January 3, 1810, Wellington writes from Coimbra to Craufurd:

We have a store of provisions in Almeida, from which you will draw what you require, if it should be necessary, but don't use it unless it is so. . . . I wish that you would desire Captain Campbell, and any other officers in your division who are capable of it, to examine the course of the Coa which runs by Almeida, and to report upon it; and if possible, let me have a plan of it; likewise, if the position of the enemy will allow of it, the course of the Agueda. . . . Hereafter I shall fix my headquarters at Vizeu, and will go forward and pay you a visit."

Colonel Leach tells us that General Craufurd remained some time at Pinhel with the 43rd and 52nd Regiments, whilst the battalion of the 95th Rifles, with some of the famous 1st German Hussars, were the only troops at first pushed across the Coa, to observe the enemy's outposts on the Agueda. These advanced troops crossed the Coa on

January 6, 1810.

On January 31, 1810, Wellington writes to General Craufurd:

I am going for a few days to look about me at Torres Vedras. . . . I don't think the enemy is likely to molest us at present; but I am desirous of maintaining the Coa, unless he should collect a very large force, and obviously intend to set seriously to work on the invasion of Portugal. If that should be the case, I don't propose to maintain the Coa, or that you should risk anything for that purpose; and I beg you to retire gradually to Celorico, where you will be joined by General Cole's Division. From Celorico I propose that you should retire gradually along the valley of the Mondego upon General Sherbrooke's Division and other troops which will be there. If you should quit the Coa, bring the hussars with you."

On February 4, Wellington writes to supplement this letter, and seems more inclined to maintain the Coa.

As my views, in the position which the army now occupy, are to take the offensive in case of the occurrence of certain events, I wish not to lose the possession of the Coa; and I am anxious, therefore, that you and General Cole should maintain your positions upon that river, unless you should find that the enemy collect a force in Castille which is so formidable as to manifest a serious intention of invading Portugal.

General Craufurd having written to inform his commander that Marshal Ney was moving towards Ciudad Rodrigo, Wellington writes again from Vizeu on February 18:

I don't understand Ney's movement, coupled as it was with a movement upon Badajoz from the south of Spain. The French are certainly not sufficiently strong for two sieges at the same time; and I much doubt whether they are in a state even to undertake one . . . In answer to your letter of the 1st, I have only to assure you that in every event I should have taken care to keep your command distinct, as I am convinced that you will be able to render most service in such a situation. You will have heard that General Stewart is gone to Cadiz; but General Picton is coming to the army, which will render necessary a new arrangement, and will oblige me to deprive you of Colonel Mackinnon's Brigade. But I will make up for you the best corps

LIEUTENANT-GENERAL SIR THOMAS PICTON

SIR ROWLAND HILL

I can, including your own brigade, of which you shall continue to have the separate command.

Accordingly, the following general order was issued by Lord Wellington, dated at Vizeu, February 22, 1810.

The 1st and 2nd battalions of Portuguese Chasseurs are attached to the brigade of Brigadier-General Craufurd, which is to be called the Light Division.

The 2nd Chasseurs seem afterwards to have been exchanged for the 3rd Chasseurs.

Notwithstanding this order of the commander-in-chief, many ignorant writers on the Peninsular War will persist in calling Craufurd's famous command the Light Brigade during its subsequent brilliant career, long after it had become a division. Considering that Craufurd's rank was then only that of a brigadier, his commander must undoubtedly have held a very high opinion of his abilities; for, before General Picton came out to the army, Craufurd had under his command, on the retreat from Talavera, several other English regiments besides his own favourite brigade. These regiments were now made part of General Picton's Division. Colonel Leach calls them "Colonel Donkin's Brigade," and says that they consisted of the 45th, a battalion of the 60th, and the 88th.

General Craufurd did not at first expect much from the Portuguese troops placed under his command; but they eventually proved very useful. Costello, in his book, expresses a very low and probably rather unfair opinion of these Portuguese. He says,

We were here joined by the 1st and 3rd Regiments of Portuguese Caçadores. These fellows I never had any opinion of from the very first moment I saw them. They were the dirtiest and noisiest brutes I ever came across. Historians of the day have given them great credit; but during the whole of the Peninsular War, or at least the time they were with us, I never knew them to perform one gallant act. On the line of march, they often reminded me of a band of strollers. They were very fond of gambling; and every halt we made was sure to find them squatted, and with the cards in their hands.

On the other hand, Costello greatly admired the German hussars, so long attached to the Light Division. He says;

MAJOR GENERAL SIR JOHN COLBORNE

ARTHUR WELLESLEY, 1ST DUKE OF WELLINGTON,

As cavalry they were the finest and most efficient, I ever saw in action; and I had many opportunities of judging, as some troops of them generally did duty with us during the war while on outpost duty their vigilance was most admirable.

About the middle of March, Craufurd began his more serious and important outpost work between the Coa and the Agueda Rivers. Lord Wellington wrote him a long letter on March 8. In it he says:

I am very much obliged to you for your letter of the 6th, which I received last night. The fact is that the line of cantonments which we took up, principally with a view to the accommodation of the troops during the winter, and their subsistence on a point on which it was likely that it might be desirable to assemble the army, will not answer our purpose of assembling on the Coa, if eventually that should be deemed an object. Neither does our position, as at present occupied, suit the existing organisation of the army. For these reasons, I have long intended to alter our dispositions, as soon as the season would permit the troops to occupy the smaller villages on the Coa, and as I should be able to bring up the Portuguese light troops of your division to the front.

Since we took up the position which we now occupy, our outposts have come in contact with those of the French; and although there is some distance between the two, still the arrangement of our outposts must be made on a better principle, and the whole of them must be in the hands of one person, who must be yourself. I propose, therefore, as soon as the weather will allow of an alteration of the disposition of the advanced corps, that your division, with the hussars which will be put under your orders, should occupy the whole line of the outposts, and, with this, the Portuguese corps shall be brought up to the front as soon as the state of the weather will allow them to march.

I am desirous of being able to assemble the army upon the Coa, if it should be necessary; at the same time, I am perfectly aware that if the enemy should collect in any large numbers in Estremadura, we should be too forward for our communications with General Hill even here, and much more so upon the Coa. But till they will collect in Estremadura, and till we shall see more clearly than I can at present what reinforcements they have received, and what military object they have in view, and particularly in the existing disposition of the army, I am averse to withdrawing from a position so favourable as the Coa affords, to enable us to collect our army and prevent the execution of any design upon Ciudad Rodrigo. I wish you, then, to consider of the parts to be occupied in front of and upon the Coa, to enable me to effect that object. The left should probably be at Castello Roderigo; and I believe you must have a post of observation as far as Alfayates on the right. However, you must be a better judge of the details of this question than I can be; and I wish you to consider of it, in order to be able immediately to carry the plan into execution when I shall send to you.

I intend that the divisions of General Cole and General Picton should support you on the Coa without waiting for orders from me, if it should be necessary; and they shall be directed accordingly.

This letter clearly shows that Wellington had great confidence in Craufurd; and it was to a certain extent evoked by the not unnatural jealousy of Generals Cole and Picton at having a brigadier thus placed over them and assigned a more important command, notwithstanding the fact that he was their junior.

For the rest of Craufurd's operations between the Coa and the Agueda, up to the day of the memorable battle, the most ample and reliable information is to be found in a diary of General Sir James Shaw Kennedy, who was *aide-de-camp* to the leader of the Light Division, and his most confidential officer. That this officer was thoroughly able to judge correctly of these remarkable operations, is sufficiently proved by the fact that Sir William Napier, writing in the year 1852, speaks of him as having displayed "great intelligence, great zeal, and undaunted courage on very many occasions." And Napier adds:

He is, perhaps, with the exception of Lord Seaton, the very ablest officer in the service. (See the *Life of Sir William Napier*, by H. A. Bruce.)

In a letter on outpost duties to Lord Frederick Fitzclarence, Sir James Shaw Kennedy explains clearly the main object of Craufurd's operations between the Rivers Coa and Agueda:

The objects to be gained by the Light Division holding as long as possible the whole of the country on the left bank of the

Agueda up to the bridges and fords over that river, were to encourage the governor of Ciudad Rodrigo to make a stout defence, to keep open the communication with Almeida as long
as possible, and to command the resources of the country. These
were objects of great importance, as delay in taking these towns
was a formidable obstruction to the French Army, from its
obliging them to undertake the operation against Portugal at a
late season of the year; and was of immense value to Lord Wellington in allowing time for bringing to greater maturity his
defensive preparations. The object was great; but the operation
of holding a country so extensive as that between the Coa and
the Agueda by a single small Infantry Division of about 2500
strong, with one cavalry regiment 400 strong, (the 1st German
Hussars) and six light guns, the original force with which it was
undertaken, was unusually bold and hazardous, being done in
the face of Ney's corps supported by a powerful cavalry.

As the operation progressed, Craufurd's force was augmented to
3500 infantry, with occasional assistance of some squadrons of
the 16th Light Dragoons, and on the very last days of the operation by the whole of the 14th and 16th Light Dragoons; and
he was supported on his right by Carrera with 3000 Spaniards.
But although Craufurd's force was thus somewhat increased,
his operation became greatly more hazardous and difficult as it
progressed; for in the more advanced part of it he was opposed
to two entire corps of the French Army under Massena, and say
6000 cavalry."

This formidable task, however, General Craufurd undertook
when at such a distance from the rest of the army as to be
totally unsupported by any portion of it beyond the Coa. This
operation by General Craufurd was completely successful as
an advanced post and outpost operation. He held his ground
firmly to the last without any loss; and remained in sight of
Ciudad Rodrigo till the place was reduced to the last extremity,
after a noble and protracted defence, considering the defective
nature of its works; and he kept Almeida open and free from all
molestation, up to the day of its being invested by the whole of
Ney's corps supported by four or five thousand cavalry.

As an operation of an advanced corps, therefore, nothing could
have been more successful. The whole of General Craufurd's
force he brought back in perfect safety under the guns of

Almeida, and had nothing further to do but to cross the Coa at his leisure, and place his outposts on the left bank.

General Shaw Kennedy then proceeds to explain some of the reasons which made this case an exceptional one.

I place first among these the personal qualifications of General Craufurd. This extraordinary undertaking was in a great measure one of his own bringing about. He almost led the commander-in-chief into it by the enthusiastic zeal with which he entered upon it, and the activity and ability with which he carried it through. He by these means may be said at least to have caused the commander-in-chief to endure it; for no prudent commander-in-chief would have done so unless he had great confidence in the person conducting the operation.

Another peculiarity of this case was the great knowledge of outpost duties possessed by the 1st Hussars of the German Legion. General Craufurd, in fact, worked out the most difficult part of the outpost duty with them. He had the great advantage of speaking German fluently, and he arranged for the outpost duties of the different parts of the long line he had to guard, by his personal communications with the captains chiefly of that admirable corps, men who were all masters themselves of the subject. They knew his plan for each space that they covered, but not his general plan; and each worked out his part most admirably. The general communicated with them direct. He had the advantage of possessing, with great abilities and activity and energy, uncommon bodily strength, so that he could be on horseback almost any length of time.

These German hussars are universally acknowledged to have been the most efficient cavalry in our army at that period. Lord Wellington says to General Craufurd in one of his letters that he thinks that the work required by the leader of the Light Division will be better done by these men than by the 14th or 16th Light Dragoons. Between Craufurd and his German cavalry there was, as General Shaw Kennedy intimates, a very close sympathy and mutual comprehension. Nor did these his trusted and valued soldiers forget their wonderful leader after his death. Major William Campbell, writing to Craufurd's widow in the year 1814, says,:

Upon one occasion after my late return to Lord Wellington's

army, when I was surrounded by a considerable number of the officers of one of the German hussar regiments that had generally served under him, the commanding officer of the regiment, in expressing his regret to me that he (Craufurd) was no longer there to conduct them, said, with peculiar emphasis, that there was not an officer in the corps that would not willingly give his best horse an expression of more than ordinary strength in German if he was there again.

Kincaid, who was for some time Adjutant of the 95th Rifles, writes thus concerning these most efficient cavalry soldiers:

I have seen the day, however, that I would rather have dispensed with my dinner (however sharp set) than the services of one of those thoroughbred soldiers; for they were as singularly intelligent and useful on outpost duty, as they were effective and daring in the field. The 1st Regiment of Hussars were associated with our division throughout the war, and were deserved favourites. . . . The hussar was at all times identified with his horse; he shared his bed and board, and their movements were always regulated by the importance of their mission. If we saw a British dragoon at any time approaching at full speed, it excited no great curiosity among us; but whenever we saw one of the 1st Hussars coming on at a gallop, it was high time to gird on our swords and bundle up.

Their chief, too, was a perfect soldier, and worthy of being the leader of such a band; for he was to them what the gallant Beckwith was to us a father as well as a leader. He was one who never could be caught napping. They tell a good anecdote of him after the Battle of Toulouse, when the news arrived of the capture of Paris and of Bonaparte's abdication. A staff officer was sent to his outpost quarter to apprise him of the cessation of hostilities. It was late when the officer arrived; and, after hearing the news, the colonel proceeded to turn into bed as usual, 'all standing,' when the officer remarked with some surprise, 'Why, Colonel; you surely don't mean to sleep in your clothes tonight, when you know there is an armistice?' 'Air mistress or no air mistress,' replied the veteran, 'by Got, I sleeps in my breeches!'

Writing of an earlier period of the war, Kincaid also tells us of this fine and vigilant soldier that:

The chief of the German hussars, meeting our commandant one morning: 'Well, Colonel,' says the gallant German in broken English, 'how do you do?' 'Oh, tolerably well, thank you, considering that I am obliged to sleep with one eye open.' 'By Gott,' says the other, 'I never sleeps at all.'

For some time, the 14th and 16th Light Dragoons were attached to the Light Division; and it must not be thought that General Craufurd undervalued their merits. On the contrary, he was most anxious to have them under his command, and valued them greatly. Both he and Lord Wellington had an extremely high opinion of Colonel Talbot, of the 14th Light Dragoons, and greatly regretted his death. And on one important occasion, when the 16th Light Dragoons were in much danger of losing their reputation through ignorant gossip, Craufurd's remarks to Lord Wellington concerning them were the chief means by which their character was saved from unjust depreciation. Nor was Charles Lever, the novelist, wrong in supposing that the leader of the Light Division had a great regard and esteem for the 14th Light Dragoons, which he considered a very admirable regiment. But still, for outpost work, there was no cavalry equal to his German hussars.

Colonel Leach says:

In addition to the 1st German Hussars, and his division of infantry, the following troops were sent across the Coa during the spring to reinforce Brigadier-General Craufurd: a troop of Horse Artillery, commanded by Captain Ross, and the 14th and 16th Light Dragoons; the whole forming a command of which a lieutenant-general might have been ambitious.

Many were much displeased at this arrangement. Colonel Leach observes:

Jealousy, which rears its head in all communities and societies, I fear, is to be found in military as well as in civil life. Amongst a certain number (I hope a few only) of malcontents in the army, the very name of the Light Division or the outposts was sufficient to turn their ration wine into vinegar, and to spoil their appetite for that day's allowance of ration beef also. In good truth, general officers were to be found, whom I could name, that bore towards us no very good will, perhaps because it was not their lot to hold so prominent a command as that of our more fortunate and favoured brigadier.

Notwithstanding the surpassing excellence of the German hussars, and Craufurd's great knowledge of outpost work, the operations between the Coa and the Agueda would not have been possible, in face of such an overwhelming force of the enemy, except for some special circumstances. General Shaw Kennedy tells us that:

The people of the country were enthusiastically in our favour; the French could rely on nothing that they told them, and could only look upon them as most determined enemies. This prevented all enterprise on the part of the French. They kept in masses, and acted with the greatest caution. A party of guerillas, under Don Julian Sanchez, acted through the cantonments of the French army, and obtained information of their movements, as well as giving them annoyance.

At this critical period Craufurd's plans were all formed on the most precise calculations. His confidential *aide-de-camp* writes again:

When General Craufurd took up the line of the Agueda with the 1st German Hussars, he kept his infantry back entirely, with the exception of the infantry post of four companies of the Rifles at Barba del Puerco, upon the calculation of the time that would be required to retire the infantry to the Coa, after he received information from the cavalry posts of the enemy's advance. By this means he gained the great advantage of watching the enemy's movements, preserving the country from their foraging parties, and encouraging the defence of Rodrigo. If we are properly to understand the operations of General Craufurd, the calculation, as above stated, must never be lost sight of; for it was upon that calculation that he acted all along. The cause of hazarding the four companies at Barba del Puerco forms a separate consideration. It was formed upon the belief that the pass there was so difficult that four companies could defend it against any numbers, and that, if turned higher up the river, the hussars would give Colonel Beckwith warning in ample time to enable him to make a safe retreat.

It would only weary my readers, if I were to attempt to give anything like a full account of Craufurd's perilous and brilliant work during more than four months between the rivers Coa and Agueda. So, all I intend to do here is to notice a few of the more remarkable events, and to give interesting extracts from Wellington's correspondence with the leader of the Light Division at that critical period of the war. Sir William Napier says,

Craufurd having now four thousand men and six guns, about the middle of March lined the Agueda with his hussars, from Escalhon on his own left to Navas Frias on his right, a distance of twenty-five miles. His infantry occupied the villages between Almeida and the lower Agueda; the artillery entered Fort Conception, and the *Caçadores* were held in reserve. The French were then extended from San Felices back to Salamanca and Ledesma; and as they thus left the pass of Perales open, Carrera, who was at Coria, could also act in concert with Craufurd. The line of the Agueda was long; but from Navas Frias to the Douro it was rendered unfordable by heavy rains, and only four bridges crossed it on that extent. One was at Navas Frias, another a league below at Villar, one at Ciudad Rodrigo, and one at San Felices, called the Barba del Puerco.

The two first were distant, and the hussars being alert, the infantry were sure of time to concentrate around Almeida, before an enemy could from thence reach them. Ciudad Rodrigo commanded its own bridge. That of San Felices was near, and the French troops close to it; but the channel of the river was so profound that a few rifle companies seemed sufficient to bar the passage. This disposition was good while the Agueda was flooded; but that river was capricious, often falling many feet in a night without apparent cause. When fordable, Craufurd concentrated his division; yet to do so safely required from the troops a promptitude and intelligence the like of which have seldom been known. Seven minutes sufficed to get under arms in the night, a quarter of an hour, night or day, to gather them in order of battle at the alarm posts, with baggage loaded and assembled at a convenient distance in the rear; and this not upon a concerted signal and as a trial, but all times certain, and for months consecutively.

Scarcely had the line of the Agueda been taken, when General Ferey, a bold officer, desiring to create a fear of French enterprise, and thinking to surprise the division, collected six hundred Grenadiers close to the bridge of Barba del Puerco, where he waited until the moon rising behind him cast long shadows from the rocks, deepening the darkness in the chasm.

Then silently he passed the narrow bridge, and with incredible speed ascending the opposite side, bayonetted the sentries, and fell upon the piquet so fiercely that friends and enemies went fighting into the village of Barba del Puerco while the first shout was still echoing in the gulf below.

So sudden was the attack, so great the confusion, that the British companies could not form, and each soldier encountered the nearest enemy, fighting hand to hand, while their colonel, Sydney Beckwith, conspicuous by his lofty stature and daring actions, a man capable of rallying a whole army in flight, exhorting and shouting, urged all forward until the enemy was pushed over the edge of the ravine in retreat. This combat, fought on the 19th, showed that the French might be bearded while the Agueda was flooded. But the whole army was sorely straitened for money; and Craufurd, unable to feed his division, gave the reins to his fiery temper and seized some church plate to purchase corn, a rash act which he was forced to redress; yet it convinced the priests that the distress was not feigned, and they procured some supplies. (Napier's *War in the Peninsula*).

Colonel Beckwith was certainly one of the very best of General Craufurd's officers. Kincaid tells us the following story of him during this short but fierce combat:

The colonel, while urging the fight, observed a Frenchman within a yard or two taking deliberate aim at his head. Stooping suddenly down and picking up a stone, he immediately threw it at him, calling him at the same time a 'scoundrel,' and 'to get out of that.' It so far distracted the fellow's attention that while the gallant Beckwith's cap was blown to atoms, the head remained untouched.

Kincaid adds that this was:

The first and last night-attempt which the enemy ever made to surprise a British post in that army.

Lord Wellington thanked the heroic Beckwith and his men greatly for their admirable conduct in this combat, and General Craufurd issued an order highly complimentary to the Riflemen. Craufurd seems to have been peculiarly gratified with his men.

Concerning the general position about this period Kincaid (in his *Random Shots of a Rifleman* this is republished along with his *Adven-*

tures in the Rifle Brigade in *The Complete Kincaid of the Rifles* by Leonaur) expresses himself thus:

> The Light Division, and the cavalry attached to it, was at this period so far in advance of every other part of the army that their safety depended on themselves alone; for they were altogether beyond the reach of human aid. Their force consisted of about four thousand infantry, twelve hundred cavalry, and a brigade, (Kincaid has here inadvertently *greatly* over-estimated the amount of Craufurd's artillery) of horse artillery; and yet, trusting to his own admirable arrangements and the surprising discipline of his troops, did Craufurd with this small force maintain a position which was no position, for three months, within an hour's march of six thousand horsemen, and within two hours' march of sixty thousand infantry of a brave, experienced, and enterprising enemy, who was advancing in the confidence of certain victory.

In a letter dated March 20, Lord Wellington says to Craufurd:

> I hope that you will find the *Caçadores* better than you expect they will be. It is impossible to get Elder's corps for you; otherwise you may depend upon it that I should have been happy to make your division so much stronger.

Writing on March 23, Wellington remarks:

> I wish I could send you some money; but we are in the greatest distress, and what is worse, have no hopes of relief. . . . To this add that Government leaves me to my own inventions in this as well as in other respects.

On March 24, the commander-in-chief says, in a letter to Craufurd:

> I think you was quite right in occupying Barba del Puerco under the circumstances in which you did occupy that place, and equally so in withdrawing the troops from thence on the night of the 22nd, when there was a prospect that they would be attacked by a very superior force. . . . Do you keep any cavalry in Barba del Puerco? It might be useful to be as near the French posts as possible, in order to encourage and facilitate desertion.

And on March 26 he says:

By this time you will have been joined by the two battalions of *Caçadores*, and will be the best judge what to do with them.

Wellington had no great opinion of the veracity of Spanish generals, as is evident from a letter to Craufurd on March 30. He says:

I enclose a letter for General Carrera, in which I have requested him to communicate with you. I beg you to observe, however, that very little reliance can be placed on the report made to you by any Spanish general officer at the head of a body of troops. They generally exaggerate on one side or the other, and make no scruple of communicating supposed intelligence, in order to induce those to whom they communicate it to adopt a certain line of conduct.

A letter dated April 4, 1810, from Wellington to Craufurd contains much of general interest. He says:

The Austrian marriage is a terrible event, and must prevent any great movement on the continent for the present. Still, I don't despair of seeing at some time or other a check to the Bonaparte system. Recent transactions in Holland show that it is all hollow within, and that it is so inconsistent with the wishes, the interests, and even the existence of civilized society, that he cannot trust even his brothers to carry it into execution. If the Spaniards had acted with common prudence, we should be in a very different situation in the Peninsula; but I fear there are now no hopes.

In a letter written on April 15, the great commander says to his subordinate general:

Your feeling respecting your command is exactly what it ought to be, and what might be expected from you. As long as I could make up a division of the proper strength for the service, with your brigade and Portuguese troops and cavalry, nobody would have reason to complain. But the lieutenant-general and the senior major-general of the army, recently arrived, are without commands, and it would not answer to throw more English troops into your division, leaving them unemployed. You may depend upon it, however, that whatever may be the arrangement which I shall make, I should wish your brigade to be in the advanced guard.

In a letter written on April 20, Wellington had to check General Craufurd's excessive ardour for fighting. He writes thus:

> The consequence of the attack which you propose would be to commence a description of warfare upon our outposts, in which we should certainly sustain some loss of men, and I should be obliged to bring up the army to the front, than which nothing could be more inconvenient and eventually injurious to us. I don't know whether the state of tranquillity in which affairs have been for some time is advantageous to the French, but I know that it is highly so to us. The British Army is increasing in strength daily, and a continuance of the tranquillity in which we have been, for a short time longer, will add considerably to our numbers. The discipline and equipment of the Portuguese troops is improving daily. The equipment in particular, which is now very defective, will in a short time be complete, as all the articles for it are arrived from England. The sick of this army also are coming out of hospital.
>
> The arms for the militia have lately arrived, but some time must elapse before they can be transported to the points at which they can be issued to the different corps. . . . I am not insensible of the advantages which we should derive from the successful issue of an expedition such as you have proposed, particularly on the state of the war in Spain. But I think that the Spaniards begin to be sensible of the advantages which they derive from our position in this country, and are aware that circumstances do not allow us to interfere with more activity at present in the operations of the war. Upon the whole I prefer not to undertake this expedition.
>
> In answer to your letter of the 17th, I will only tell you that it has excited any feeling in my mind excepting anger. I have already told you that I shall regret exceedingly the existence of a necessity to place in other hands the command of our advanced guard; and I shall regret it particularly if it should deprive me of your assistance altogether. I expect Marshal Beresford here in a day or two, when I shall be able to make arrangements which may enable me to leave you in the command of your division, which I am very anxious to do.

Lord Wellington repeatedly had to complain of the conduct of the Spaniards. In a letter written to Craufurd on April 23, he says:

The Spaniards, I believe, think it necessary to our existence to assist and protect them; and I have more than once been obliged to remind different authorities with which I have been in communication, that their protection is their own concern, and that if they expect that we should assist them, they must give us every assistance of provisions and supplies which the country can afford.

It is quite plain that the English commander-in-chief was at this time anxious to preserve Ciudad Rodrigo from the French, if possible. For he writes to Craufurd thus on April 27:

I still doubt, however, the intention to make a serious attack upon Ciudad Rodrigo. I don't think the enemy is sufficiently strong for that operation without calling in Junot's corps; and I understand that the attack upon Astorga still continues.

However, interested as we are to preserve Ciudad Rodrigo, and particularly not to allow that place to fall into the enemy's hands without making an effort to save it, I should not have been justified if I had taken no notice of the movements made since the 23rd, connected with other recent preparations, notwithstanding the inconvenience which this movement is to us.

General Craufurd was always extremely anxious that the soldiers of his division, including the Portuguese troops, should be properly fed; and this anxiety sometimes caused him to make alterations in the commissariat arrangements without having first obtained the sanction of his commander. Accordingly, on May 5, Lord Wellington says in a letter to Craufurd:

Nothing can be more advantageous to me, or give me more satisfaction, than to receive the assistance of your opinion upon any subject. But you may depend upon it that there are few of the general arrangements of the army which have not been maturely considered by me; and that although some inconveniences may attend some of them, they are the smallest that, after full consideration, it was found would attend any arrangements of the subjects to which the arrangements relate. I therefore request that whenever you see reason to wish to make any alteration, you will let me know it, but not make the alteration without reference to me.

General Craufurd was an extremely sensitive person, and always felt acutely anything like censure from his commander, whom he very greatly admired. So, he appears to have taken his last rebuke too much to heart. And so, a few days later Wellington writes to soothe his feelings, saying:

> I am really concerned that you should believe that I had any such feeling as disapprobation towards you, in consequence of our little discussions upon commissariat concerns.

Napier tells us in his history that the River Agueda continued in flood until the end of May, and that, in consequence, Craufurd maintained his advanced position till that time.

> Then came advice from Andreas Herrasti that the French battery train was in motion; and on June 1, Ney, as we before said, descended from the hills with fifty thousand men, and threw his bridges over the Agueda. This concentration of the French on the Agueda enabled Wellington to draw down sixteen militia regiments from Braganza to the lower Douro, and he could now bring provisions up that river as far as Lamego. On the 8th four thousand French cavalry crossed the Agueda, and Craufurd concentrated his forces at Gallegos and Espeja.

Again, Napier tells us:

> On the 10th the Agueda became fordable in all parts; but Craufurd, seeing the enemy was raising redoubts to secure his lower bridge, and making other preparations for the siege, still maintained his dangerous position. He thus encouraged the garrison of Ciudad Rodrigo, and protected the villages between the Azava and the Coa from the enemy's foraging parties. . . . On the 25th the French batteries opened; their cavalry closed upon the Azava; and Craufurd withdrew his outposts.

Writing to the general of the Light Division on June 10, Wellington says concerning the besieged inhabitants of Ciudad Rodrigo:

> I am apprehensive that I shall not be able to do more for them than oblige the enemy to keep a large force collected in this quarter for the purpose of this enterprise. With an army one fourth inferior in numbers, a part of it being of a doubtful description, and at all events but just made, and with not more than one third of the enemy's cavalry, it would be an operation of some risk to leave our mountains and bring on a general ac-

tion in the plains; and would most probably accelerate the period of our evacuation of the Peninsula. However, I don't give over all thoughts of attempting their relief, at least by throwing in supplies, which possibly might be done without a general action. This must depend upon the position which Massena contrives to hold with the right of the army.

About this period Wellington was again afraid that he might be forced, against his own wishes, to deprive Craufurd of the command of his division. Accordingly, he wrote the following letter, which, to the best of my knowledge, is now published for the first time. It is interesting as affording a decided proof of Wellington's high opinion of Craufurd, and of his extreme reluctance to give into any other hands the command of the advanced guard of his army.

Private.

Celorico, June 20, 1810.

My Dear General,
You will have observed that I have hitherto been able to make arrangements in such a manner as to leave you in command of our advanced posts; but by a letter which I received last night from Cadiz, I find that General Ferguson is sent to that place, in order that General Stewart may join the army. This arrangement, at least the last part of it, had before now been proposed to me, and I had resisted it; but it is now effected in the usual manner in England. I mention this to you in order that you may not be surprised when you will hear of it. Possibly circumstances, such as those which have already occurred to preclude the necessity of my displacing you, and which I did not expect when we last corresponded upon this subject, may enable me again to avoid doing what will be very disagreeable to me, and, in my opinion, disadvantageous to the service. But I now apprise you of what may happen.

Ever yours most faithfully,

Wellington.

Again, as on former occasions, Wellington managed to keep Craufurd in command of his division; and until his death the division was never intrusted to other hands, except during the few months when General Craufurd was in England on his own private affairs.

At the beginning of July Ciudad Rodrigo still resisted; the French pushed their infantry on to the Azava; and Craufurd, placing his cav-

101

alry at Gallegos, concentrated his infantry in the wood of Alameda, two miles in rear. Napier tells us that:

> Craufurd, obstinately resolute, however, not to yield a foot of ground he could keep by art or force, disposed his troops in single ranks on the rising grounds in the evening of the 2nd, and using some horsemen to raise dust in the rear, made the infantry pass the heights slowly, as if a great army was advancing to succour the place. The artifice was successful; he gained two days.

But a little later on:

> Craufurd took a fresh post with his infantry and guns, in a wood near Fort Conception; his cavalry, reinforced by Julian Sanchez and Carrera's Divisions, were disposed higher up on the Duas Casas; and the French withdrew behind the Azava, leaving only a piquet at Gallegos.

Charles Napier, writing at the end of June, says that the Light Division ought not to stay in its perilous position. He remarks:

> We shall be attacked some morning, and lose many men, (see *The Life of Sir Charles Napier,* by his brother Sir William).

Yet Wellington, writing to Craufurd on *July* 16, says:

> I am desirous of holding the other side of the Coa a little longer.

And on July 5, Wellington seems to have thought that Craufurd might again occupy his former *more advanced* position, from which he had retired. He writes thus:

> If the enemy have drawn in again from Gallegos, I think it would be desirable that you should resume your position at Alameda, and place your piquets of cavalry on the Agueda, so as at all events to have a view of the place, encourage its continued resistance, and know what is going on. In that case I would throw the troops of General Picton's Division again into La Conception, and the 14th Dragoons should continue there. If you think you are better on this, side the Duas Casas, you might either keep the 14th Dragoons with you, or send a part or the whole of them to the rear, as you may think proper.

From a careful perusal of Wellington's letters to Craufurd at this critical period I have come to the conclusion that the commander-in-chief was far more anxious to delay the surrender of Ciudad Rodrigo than the Napiers thought he was, and also far more desirous to retain the power of helping it, if the movements of the French in other parts should permit him to do this. In short, Wellington was in favour of bolder measures than Charles Napier considered wise and practicable. And this fact in great measure accounts for General Craufurd's apparent rashness.

In a letter from Wellington to Craufurd on July 8, it is to be observed that the Commander, like his subordinate general, thought it probable that the French would not attack Almeida. This in great measure accounts for General Craufurd's lingering there too long, and not crossing the Coa earlier. Wellington writes thus:

> I agree with you in thinking that the enemy will not attack Almeida; and it is not improbable that, after Ciudad Rodrigo will have fallen, they will direct their march upon Castello Branco, and thus endeavour to cut in between General Hill and me; but I have in some degree provided for this movement.

On July 10 there occurred an event which caused no small amount of talk throughout the English Army, and which greatly vexed and annoyed the leader of the Light Division. The enemy's marauding parties had latterly become extremely troublesome, annoying the villages immediately in front of the British posts, and plundering them of anything which could be found. Lord Londonderry says also that they were in the habit of committing "acts of barbarity." General Craufurd determined to cut off the next of these marauding parties. Charles Napier, at that period of his life always desirous to revile his general, accuses Craufurd of cruelty for this; but Lord Londonderry evidently thought that the cruelty was on the side of the French. General Craufurd:

> Planted an ambuscade of nine squadrons, supporting it with artillery, five companies of Riflemen, and a battalion of *Caçadores*.

Unfortunately, this attempt was a failure. Sir William Napier attributes the failure to Craufurd's hot temper, owing to which:

> He pushed straight through a stone enclosure difficult to clear, and thus disordering his men, gave the enemy, two hundred strong, time to form square behind a rather steep rise of ground, and so far from the edge as to be unseen until the ascent was gained.

But Charles Napier's acrimonious censoriousness was not content to lay the blame on the hot temper of his general. He accuses Craufurd of "ignorance of cavalry." Perhaps many might think this a very "ignorant" accusation. Of course, the leader of the Light Division might be skilful or unskilful in handling cavalry; but he could scarcely be "ignorant" of it, considering his long service with the Austrian Army, and considering also the fact that he, together with his brother, General Charles Craufurd, had translated into English one of the chief German treatises on the art of war. Moreover, I have shown already that the colonel of the 1st German Hussars (the most efficient cavalry then serving in our army) and his officers had an extremely high opinion of Craufurd's prolonged work with them at the outposts. And I suppose that this celebrated colonel of hussars had a far better practical knowledge of cavalry than Charles Napier had at the time when, as a young and inexperienced soldier, he wrote this condemnation of his leader.

Lord Londonderry wrote thus concerning this affair:

The enemy's force did not exceed thirty cavalry and two hundred infantry; but they were advantageously posted in an open space, just beyond a narrow defile; and to reach them it was necessary to thread that defile in a long line. The consequence was that, though the hussars who led, formed up in succession as they got through, and charged their opponents with great gallantry, they effected nothing more than the dispersion of the handful of horse; for the infantry had time to form a square, and not all the efforts of our people could succeed it breaking it. The hussars rode bravely up to the bayonets, but were repulsed by a volley closely thrown in, which killed or wounded upwards of a dozen men. The remainder wheeled off, and pursuing the French cavalry, made way for a squadron of the 16th. These galloped forward, but also took to the left, and leaving the infantry uninjured, joined in pursuit of the cavalry.

When the last charge was made, the French square was without fire, every man having discharged his piece, and none having been able to load again; but when a third attempt was made, they were better prepared to receive it. It fell to the lot of Colonel Talbot of the 14th to lead this attack. It was made with daring intrepidity; but the enemy remained perfectly steady, and reserving their fire till the bridles of the horses touched their bayonets, gave it with such effect that Colonel Talbot, with several of his men, were killed on the spot. The rest drew off; upon which, General Craufurd despairing of success by the exertions of cavalry alone, despatched an orderly to bring up a detachment of the 43rd, which chanced to be at no great distance.

Whilst this was doing, the enemy's little column began its retreat, which it conducted with singular steadiness and great order. The 14th Dragoons, seeing this, prepared to launch another squadron against it; and it was already in speed for the purpose, when Colonel Arenschild, of the hussars, observed cavalry advancing both in front and flank, and checked the movement. It was much to be regretted afterwards that he took this step, for the horse which alarmed him proved to be detachments from our own people on their return from pursuing the enemy's dragoons, the whole of whom they had captured. The French infantry lost no time in availing themselves of the indecision of our cavalry. They marched on, and returned to their main body, without having lost a single prisoner, or suffered in killed or wounded.

In his life of his brother Charles, Sir William Napier writes thus concerning this singular combat:

Certainly, both they and their opponents were noble soldiers! And so was William Campbell the Brigade-Major, known then and afterwards throughout the army for every generous quality. He was sententious of speech, quixotic of look, but handsome and strong; and his sentiments of honour were worthy of a Spanish *don*, his courage as high, yet purged of folly; he was indeed a gallant English gentleman in thought, look, word, and deed. In this combat he charged so home that his horse was killed close to the French bayonets; but being himself unhurt, he arose, and though alone, slowly stalked away, disdaining haste as he disdained danger. The gallant French captain, Guache, would not let his men slay the proud soldier. Thus, all was noble on both sides, and William Campbell escaped death.

I wish particularly to direct the attention of my readers to this heroic soldier, William Campbell, because in a later portion of this volume a letter of his on the death of General Craufurd will appear, and also a most interesting letter addressed to him by Craufurd's widow concerning her husband's nature and character about a year after his death. Between William Campbell and Robert Craufurd there existed one of those strong, profound, and tender friendships which are amongst the very best and finest things in human life, but which are hardly ever found except between people endowed with very exceptional gifts of heart and soul. It was from William Campbell that Sir William Napier obtained conclusive evidence that Craufurd and Picton did meet on the day of the combat at the Coa; and that Picton did refuse to come to the assistance of the Light Division in its hour of supreme peril. As Campbell wrote of that memorable meeting:

> Slight was the converse, short the interview; for upon Craufurd's asking inquiringly whether General Picton did not consider it advisable to move out something from Pinhel in demonstration of support, or to cover the Light Division, in terms not bland, the general (Picton) made it understood that 'he should do no such thing.' This, as you may suppose, put an end to the meeting, further than some violent rejoinder on the part of my much-loved friend, and fiery looks returned.

This testimony of William Campbell was given in the year 1835, when Craufurd had been dead for more than twenty-three years. But deep souls never forget what manner of men their greatest friends were, or lose their affection for them.

Craufurd himself was excessively annoyed at the ill success of the attack on the little party of marauding Frenchmen. In a letter written to his wife on July 17, 1810, he says:

> I had a little affair the other day which terminated very unsatisfactorily. I went out in hopes of cutting off some of the enemy's parties, but succeeded only in part; and the failure of the rest was attended with some mortifying circumstances, and occasioned by a series of unlucky accidents.

In accordance with the view here expressed, Craufurd made his report to Lord Wellington, in which he threw no blame on any part of his troops. But many other officers of the English Army were not so just and fair; and they virulently assailed the reputation of the English cavalry engaged in this little affair with the French. In fact, the business evoked more talk and more ignorant censoriousness than many an important battle. But fortunately, Wellington determined to put a stop to this. So, he addressed to Craufurd the following letter, one of the very best that he ever wrote, well suited to give an idea of the great sense of justice, the keen good judgment, and the right feeling which characterised the manly and comprehensive mind of the great commander.

The letter has been printed in Gurwood's edition of Wellington's Despatches, but the original is in my possession. One of my reasons for giving it here is because I think that in many respects it is well calculated to teach a much-needed lesson to some ignorant and slanderous gossips of our own day, who think nothing of staining the splendid reputation of renowned regiments by their gross exaggerations and misrepresentations of those checks and accidents which, from time to time, happen and must happen to all troops engaged in real war. Alas! in these days we have no Wellington, to shut the mouths of venomous critics with direct incisive words of penetrating rebuke.

Alverca, July 23, 1810.

My Dear General,

I received in the night your letter of the 22nd.

I have been much annoyed by the foolish conversations and reports and private letters about the 16th Light Dragoons. General Cotton wrote to me shortly after the affair of the 11th, to request that the conduct of that regiment might be inquired into; to which I replied that you, in your report, had not made any charge against the 16th, and that it would not be just towards that regiment to make their conduct the subject of inquiry for a failure which appeared to me to have been produced by various unfortunate accidents which could not be prevented.

Two or three days afterwards General Cotton came here, and told me that he had traced some of those reports and conversations to General Stewart, the A.G. Upon which I had General Stewart and him before me, after having pointed out to the former the inconvenience and impropriety of a person in his situation circulating any reports about the troops; and I declared my determination, if I heard any more of it, to oblige him to come forward with a charge against the 16th. So, the matter stands here.

In respect to the business itself, it appeared to me from the first that it would and must have succeeded, notwithstanding the gallantry and steadiness of the French infantry, if various accidents had not prevented the execution of the plan as first formed; and I have stated this as my opinion in the report which I have made upon the business. Your own report points out clearly the variations from the original plan, and the different accidents which occurred in the execution; among which certainly must be classed the charge of the first squadron of the 16th to the left of the hussars, and the delay between the first charge and the charge by Talbot, owing to the first and second squadrons of the 16th having gone off after the cavalry.

But even then, the infantry would not have got away, if the squadrons coming out of Barquilla had not been taken for the enemy.

I can only say that I have never seen an attack by our troops in which similar, if not greater, accidents and mistakes had not occurred, and in which orders had not been given, for which no authority had proceeded from the commander, and in which there were not corresponding accidents and failures. This is to be attributed to the inexperience of our officers, and, I must add, to some good qualities in them as well as in the troops.

All this would not much signify, if our staff and other officers would mind their business, instead of write news and keep coffee houses. But as soon as an accident happens, every man who can write, who has a friend who can read, sits down to write his account of what he does not know and his comments on what he does not understand; and these are diligently circulated and exaggerated by the idle and malicious, of whom there are plenty in all armies. The consequence is that officers and whole regiments lose their reputation; a spirit of party, which is the bane of all armies, is engendered and fomented; a want of confidence ensues, and there is no character however meritorious, and no action however glorious, which can have justice done to it.

I have hitherto been so fortunate as to keep down this spirit in this army, and am determined that I will persevere.

In respect to the 16th Light Dragoons, they appear in this affair to have conducted themselves with the spirit and alacrity of soldiers. They failed in the intelligence and coolness and order which can be acquired only by experience; but it would be too hard to impute to them alone the failure of complete success, which may be traced likewise to other accidental circumstances; and it would be equally cruel to allow the reputation of this regiment to be whispered away by ignorance, idleness, and slander.

You and I agree entirely upon the whole matter; and I have gone into this detail, just to explain to you what has passed here, and upon what principle I have acted.

Ever yours most faithfully,

Wellington.

After reading this admirable letter, I cannot help wondering what Wellington or Craufurd would have said to the gross exaggerations which were so diligently circulated concerning the very vexatious repulse of one of the old Light Division regiments (the 43rd) in the New Zealand war in the year 1861. This later repulse was certainly of no more importance than that of the English cavalry in their unfortunate attack above referred to Many of the very same men who lost their heads for a time, in the great confusion of the moment at the gate Pah, when so many of their officers were killed or wounded, not long afterwards triumphantly routed the enemy. If anyone wishes to see a really fair account of the whole business, I would beg to refer him to a very interesting book called *Bush Fighting in New Zealand*, by Sir J. Alexander, this is republished by Leonaur as *Bush Fighting*.

Returning now to the days preceding the combat at the Coa, I must notice the fact that General Picton certainly owned that he was ordered to give support to the Light Division; for he wrote the following letter to Craufurd. The original is in possession of General Craufurd's family.

Pinhel, July 4, 1810.

Sir,

It being important that I should communicate to you, with as much expedition as possible, the events that may take place on these parts of the Coa which I am instructed to observe, I have to request that you will have the goodness to station a dragoon at Valverde, with orders to forward such communications as I may have occasion to make, in the most expeditious manner; and I have also to request as early information as possible of your movements, that I may be enabled to co-operate with them, in obedience to his Excellency the Commander of the Forces' instructions of the 2nd instant.

I have the honour to be,

Your faithful humble servant,

Th. Picton, M.G.,
Commanding 3rd Division.

Ciudad Rodrigo surrendered on July 10; and the Spanish troops, much grieved and irritated, separated from the Light Division and marched in a different direction.

On July 11, Wellington wrote to Craufurd thus:

I have received your letters of this day. The fall of Ciudad Rodrigo was to be expected, and the defence has been greater than we had a right to expect.

I regret poor Talbot; he is a great loss. (Talbot was Colonel of the 14th Light Dragoons, and a first-rate cavalry officer.)

I have looked over my instructions to you, and I see nothing to add excepting the word threaten in the fourth paragraph; that is to say, it will run, in case the enemy should threaten to attack General Craufurd, instead of in case the enemy should attack General Craufurd. In short, I don't wish to risk anything beyond the Coa; and indeed, when Carrera is clearly off, I don't see why you should remain any longer at such a distance in front of Almeida.

It is desirable that the communication with Almeida should be kept open as long as possible, in order that we may throw into that place as much provisions as possible; and therefore, I would not wish you to fall back beyond that place, unless it should be necessary. But it does not appear necessary that you should be so far, and it will be safer that you should be nearer, at least with your infantry.

On July 13 the commander-in-chief says in a letter to the leader of the Light Division:

I shall be obliged to you, if you will direct your posts on the left to report all extraordinaries to Major-General Picton's posts on the Coa; and they might fall back upon them, if necessary.

And on the 14th, Wellington observes:

It is strange that the enemy have made no movement since the fall of Ciudad Rodrigo. I should almost doubt their being in possession of the place, and should be inclined to believe that the cessation from fire has been an agreement for a certain number of days, to see whether they would be relieved; as whatever may be the enemy's ultimate plan of operations, it must be desirable to them at least to see the banks of the Coa. I think you will do well to move your infantry to Junca; but you had better retain all your cavalry till you will withdraw across the Coa.

From these extracts I think it is plain that those of Craufurd's critics are quite wrong who have said that he was ordered to retreat over the Coa a long time before the day on which he was attacked suddenly by the French, July 24. Even so late as July 16, Wellington writes thus to General Craufurd:

It is desirable that we should hold the other side of the Coa a little longer; and I think that our doing so is facilitated by our keeping La Conception. At the same time, I don't want to risk anything in order to remain at the other side of the river, or to retain the fort; and I am anxious that, when you leave it, it should be destroyed.

On July 22 Wellington did seem to think that Craufurd should cross the Coa, but not very decidedly. He writes thus:

I order two battalions to support your flanks; but I am not desirous of engaging in an affair beyond the Coa. Under these circumstances, if you are not covered where you are, would it not be better that you should come to this side, with your infantry at least?

On July 24, the very day of Craufurd's fierce combat on the Coa, Wellington wrote him an interesting letter, though not on that subject. He says:

I believe I omitted to tell you that I had got lately the emplacement of the whole French Army of June 1, which is a very curious document, and gives a tolerable notion of their whole force in Spain, which is not less than 250,000 men. But I don't think they have means of reinforcing it much further. This document, together with the returns which I have of the French corps in our front, gives me a knowledge of the names of all the principal officers, etc., employed with those corps; and any paper which may fall into your hands, such as a requisition upon a village signed by an officer or commissary, would be of use to me, as it would serve to show in some degree their disposition, and would aid other information.

I have observed that the French are singularly accurate in preserving the different *corps d'armée* in the order in which they
are first arranged in the line of battle. The corps of Key, Soult,
Mortier, Victor, and Sebastiani are at this moment in the same
situation in respect to each other that they held before the Battle of Talavera. And Junot's corps has come in, and has been
placed upon the right of the whole. Knowing the names of
the officers, the numbers of the regiments and battalions, and
the names of the commissaries attached to each corps, and the
general order in which they stand in the line, the name of any
person making a requisition in any place must aid me in forming an opinion of the disposition of the army.

2 p.m. I have heard both from Pinhel and Valverde that there
was a firing in your front as late as nine this morning; but I conclude that I should have heard from you if it had been serious.

On the 21st the enemy's cavalry had again advanced, Fort Conception was blown up, and Craufurd, on the 22nd, drew his whole force
back near Almeida, observing with piquets of cavalry the different
roads on the great plain in front.

Napier now writes concerning General Craufurd:

He had kept a weak division for three months within two
hours' march of sixty thousand men, appropriating the resources of the plains entirely to himself; but this exploit, only to be
appreciated by military men, did not satisfy his feverish thirst of
distinction. He had safely affronted a superior power; and, for-
getting that his stay beyond the Coa was a matter of sufferance
and not of real strength, he with headstrong ambition resolved,
in defiance of reason and the reiterated orders of his general, to
fight on the right bank. He had four thousand British infantry, eleven hundred cavalry, and six guns in position, on a line
oblique to the Coa. The right was on some broken ground, the
left, resting on an unfinished tower eight hundred yards from
Almeida, was defended by the guns of that fortress; his cavalry
was on the plain in front; but his back was on the edge of a ravine forming the channel of the Coa; and the bridge, more than
a mile distant, was in the bottom of the chasm.

Sir William Napier was much mistaken in saying that Craufurd
"resolved" to fight under these circumstances. I will give Craufurd's

own letter written to the *Times* on this subject rather further on; and, *concerning his own intentions*, it must be admitted that he was a better judge than Napier. Sir George Napier (in his *Early Military Life*) represents things much more accurately when he says:

> Craufurd, however, let his vanity get the better of his judgment, and delayed so long that at last the enemy made a sudden attack.

That is the real truth about the business. And this was Lord Wellington's view. In a letter to Lord Liverpool, written on July 27, he says:

> Unfortunately, General Craufurd did not begin to retire till the last moment.

The commander-in-chief evidently never thought that Craufurd intended to defy this large French Army, contrary to his orders; but he did think that the pugnacious leader of the Light Division lingered too long before beginning his retreat. No doubt Wellington would have been far more displeased with Craufurd than he was, if he had regarded his error of judgment as accompanied by deliberate disobedience.

Still, the interesting question remains, why did General Craufurd not cross the Coa two or three days earlier? Lord Londonderry tells us that Craufurd thought that:

> The French would respect the fortress of Almeida, that they would not push him very rapidly, and hence that he would be able to make a regular retreat at any moment.

In the *Life of Sir William Napier*, by H. A. Bruce, in some "Notes of Conversations with the Duke of Wellington," we find the following remark by the historian of the Peninsular War:

> Colonel ———, of Almeida, was very negligent in not putting some men into the windmill in front of the works. It would have delayed the investment, and have given time to General Craufurd to withdraw his division in safety.

And in his vivid description of the fight by the Coa, Sir William Napier writes:

> Massena claimed to have taken two pieces of artillery, which was true; for the iron guns intended to arm the unfinished tower near Almeida were lying at the foot of the building, and thus fell into his hands. They belonged, however, to the garrison, not

to the Light Division; and that they were not mounted and the tower garrisoned was a great negligence. Had it been otherwise, the French cavalry could not have charged the left of the position, and the after-investment of Almeida itself would have been retarded.

These remarks of Sir William Napier are peculiarly significant, because he held that the supreme danger to the Light Division in this combat arose from the French cavalry, which he thought might have annihilated it.

It is evident, then, that Craufurd placed too much confidence in the governor and garrison of Almeida. He considered himself bound to prevent the investment of this fortress as long as he possibly could; and so, at last the enemy made a sudden and unexpected attack upon him, so that he could not retire without a fight. His judgment was erroneous, no doubt, to some extent. But he knew well that it was important to Lord Wellington's general plans that the French should be delayed as long as possible before Almeida. This is plain from the disgust and dissatisfaction afterwards caused to the commander by the unfortunate and premature fall of this place. In short, Craufurd's fault was excess of zeal, attempting too much, a not very uncommon fault with natures so fiery and eager as his was. Yet of him Sir George Napier wrote:

When his reason was not obscured by passion, few men possessed more clearness of judgment.

In justice to Craufurd it should also be remembered that, in the case of his other generals of division, Lord Wellington had sometimes to make a different but no less real complaint; he blamed them for timidity and want of confidence and enterprise. Thus, only a few months after Craufurd's death, when Hill was conducting some very critical operations, they were to a considerable extent marred by the timidity of some of the generals concerned, especially of the incompetent Erskine. In his history of the Peninsular War, Napier, with reference to this, says of Wellington:

To the ministers, however, he complained that his generals, stout in action personally as the poorest soldiers, were commonly so overwhelmed with fear of responsibility, when left to themselves, that the slightest movement of the enemy deprived them of their judgment, and they spread unnecessary alarm far and wide.

Certainly, the great commander never had occasion to make a complaint of that sort against General Craufurd. Of him it was justly remarked in a biography of another gallant officer (General Le Marchant):

> Others shunned responsibility; he courted it.

This singular boldness had its advantages. Concerning the four and a half months of supremely difficult outpost work which preceded the fight at the Coa, Sir James Shaw Kennedy, who had ample means of knowing, wrote thus:

> He (Craufurd) almost led the commander-in-chief into it by the enthusiastic zeal with which he entered upon it, and the activity and ability with which he carried it through.

To such a leader something in the way of occasional errors of judgment may surely be forgiven.

Sir William Napier's account of the combat at the Coa is very vivid and graphic; but it is so well known that I think it will be more interesting to give here another account by an officer who was also engaged in that fight.

Colonel Leach, of the 95th Rifles, describes it thus:

> Soon after daybreak the whole of Marshal Ney's corps, consisting of troops of all arms to the amount of about 25,000 men, advanced for the purpose of investing and laying siege to Almeida, and of driving General Craufurd's corps of observation over the Coa, should it be found on the same side of the river.
>
> General Craufurd placed his infantry in line amongst some rocky ground and stone walls, his left being within seven or eight hundred yards of Almeida, and his right thrown back in a convex form towards the Coa. Our cavalry posts in the plain were soon forced back on the infantry, and a brisk cannonade commenced. The advance of the French cavalry were brought to bay by our infantry in the intersected ground; but Marshal Ney, having more than 20,000 infantry at his back, was not long to be delayed in this manner. Although the left of our line was under the protection of the guns of the fortress, the French assailed it with great impetuosity; and the right and centre also soon found itself beset with a swarm of light troops, supported

115

by heavy columns constantly advancing, and aided by their artillery, which cannonaded us warmly.

The baggage, artillery, cavalry, and the two Portuguese light battalions were directed to retire instantly to the bridge over the Coa, and to gain the opposite bank without delay. Those who have seen and know this narrow and difficult defile need not be informed that to keep at bay as many thousand infantry as Marshal Ney might think proper to send forward, whilst the road was choked with troops, baggage, and artillery, which it was absolutely necessary should be covered and protected during a retreat of a mile or more, and until they had crossed the bridge in safety, was no easy matter.

The troops destined to cover the retreat consisted of our own battalion and a considerable part or the whole of the 43rd and 52nd Regiments. No further description of this rocky defile is necessary, than that the road is very narrow, and as bad as the generality of mountain roads in the Peninsula are; and, moreover, that it is overhung by huge rocks in many places, from which, had our pursuers been permitted to possess themselves of them, they might have annihilated the troops underneath, without their being able to retaliate. And thus, the only option left them would have been a walk to Verdun as prisoners of war, or an instantaneous passage across the Styx instead of the Coa. By this time the fight had begun in good earnest; and, in order that my story may not be too long, it will be sufficient to say that, from the commencement of the action at the edge of the plain until we reached the river, every inch of ground admitting of defence was obstinately contested by the rear-guard, which was followed by fresh troops every instant arriving to support their comrades. The French artillery failed not to help us along, whenever they had an opportunity, with a nine-pound shot.

As the rear-guard approached the Coa, we perceived that a part only of our cavalry, infantry, and artillery had yet crossed the bridge; it became therefore indispensably requisite for us to keep possession of a small hill looking down on and perfectly commanding the bridge, until everything had passed over, cost what it might.

I trust I shall be pardoned for saying that the soldiers of the old and gallant 43rd, and that part also of our own battalion whose lot it was to defend this important hill against a vast superiority of numbers, proved themselves worthy of the trust.

In ascending the hill, a musket-shot grazed the left side of my head, and buried itself in the earth close by. Both my subalterns, who were brothers, were severely wounded in the defence of this hill; and we had but barely time to send them, with other wounded officers and men, across the river, ere we were obliged to retire, and to make a push in double-quick time to reach the bridge, the whole time exposed to such a fire from the hill which we had just abandoned, as might have satisfied the most determined fire-eater in existence.

If any are now living of those who defended the little hill above the bridge, they cannot fail to remember the gallantry displayed by Major Macleod of the 43rd, who was the senior officer on the spot. How either he or his horse escaped being blown to atoms, when in the most daring manner he charged on horseback, at the head of a hundred or two skirmishers of the 43rd and of our regiment mixed together, and headed them in making a dash at a wall lined with French infantry which we soon dislodged, I am at a loss to imagine. It was one of those extraordinary escapes tending strongly to implant in the mind some faith in the doctrine of fatality.

The whole of General Craufurd's corps at length gained the opposite bank of the Coa, and was strongly posted near the bridge, behind walls, rocks, and broken ground. The torrents of rain which fell the night before had so swollen the river that all the fords were at that moment impassable; a fortunate circumstance, as the only way by which we could now be attacked was over the narrow bridge, on which we could bring a destructive fire; and we likewise commanded the approach to it from the opposite side with musketry. An incessant fire was kept up across the river by both parties; and, after it had continued some time, the French sent a party of grenadiers to storm the bridge, with the vain hope of driving us from our new position. They advanced most resolutely in double-quick time, and charged along the bridge; but few, if any, went back alive, and most of those who reached our side of it unhurt were killed afterwards. This experiment was repeated, and it is almost needless to add that it met the same fate each time.

The French officer who directed those attacks on the bridge, might have known, before he caused the experiment to be made, that a few hundred French grenadiers, advancing to the tune of '*Vive l'Empereur!*' '*En avant, mes enfans!*' and so forth, were not likely to succeed in scaring away three British and two Portuguese regiments supported by artillery. It was a piece of unpardonable butchery on the part of the man who ordered those brave Grenadiers to be thus wantonly sacrificed, without the most remote prospect of success. They deserved a better fate; for no men could have behaved with more intrepidity.

The total loss of the Light Division was from three to four hundred men. Thus, ended the affair of the Coa, a day which will not easily be forgotten by those who were present. And I may also add that, although an overwhelming French force obliged the Light Division to retreat, and to contend with it under every possible disadvantage, until it had gained the opposite bank of the river, the retreat was so well covered and protected by the excellent disposition of the troops forming the rear-guard, that we may, without being accused either of vanity or bravado, look back upon it as a day of glory and not of defeat.

Here the narrative of Colonel Leach ends. Napier tells us that:

Craufurd retired in the night behind the Pinhel River.

He also says of this fierce and difficult combat:

There was no room for a line, no time for anything but battle. Every captain carried off his company as an independent body; and joining as he could with the riflemen and 52nd, the whole presented a mass of skirmishers, acting in small parties and under no regular command, yet each confident in the courage and discipline of those on his right and left, and all keeping together with surprising vigour.

Napier also says:

It was at first supposed that Lieutenant Dawson and half a company of the 52nd, which had been posted in the unfinished tower, were also captured; but with great intelligence he passed all the enemy's posts in the night, crossed the Coa at a distant ford and rejoined his regiment. Ney lost one thousand men, and the slaughter at the bridge was fearful to behold.

As might have been expected from the nature of the combat and the splendid qualities of the soldiers of the Light Division, occasion was here given for many an exhibition of high courage and unflinching self-sacrifice amongst Craufurd's men. The two following stories are related by Sir William Napier, and may serve to show us what manner of men the privates and non-commissioned officers of the famous 43rd Light Infantry then were. There was a young soldier named Stewart, nicknamed "The Boy," as he was only nineteen years old, and of gigantic stature. He had fought bravely and displayed great intelligence beyond the river, and was one of the last men who came down to the bridge; but he would not pass. Turning round, he regarded the French with a grim look, and spoke aloud as follows:

So, this is the end of our boasting! This is our first battle, and we retreat! The Boy Stewart will not live to hear that said.

Then striding forward in his giant might, he fell furiously on the nearest enemies with the bayonet, refused the quarter they seemed desirous of giving, and died fighting in the midst of them.

"The Boy" was a native of the north of Ireland. Much as one must regret the loss of so gallant a soldier through his rashness, it is certainly not for me, the grandson of his general, to condemn him; for "The Boy" had indeed a double portion of his leader's fiery pride; and both were made of the same stuff as the unyielding warriors at Thermopylae. Peace be with the noble spirit of "The Boy"!

Still more touching and more heroic was the grand and sublime self-sacrifice of another warrior of the gallant 43rd, Sergeant Robert McQuade, During Major Macleod's rush this man, also from the north of Ireland, saw two Frenchmen level their muskets on rests against a high gap in a bank, awaiting the uprise of an enemy. Sir George Brown, then a lad of sixteen, attempted to ascend at the fatal point; but McQuade, himself only twenty-four years of age, pulled him back, saying with a calm, decided tone, "You are too young, sir, to be killed." And then, offering, his own person to the fire, fell dead, pierced with both balls!

★★★★★★

It may interest some of my readers to know that Sir George Brown lived to be Colonel-in-Chief of the Rifle Brigade, and that he was profoundly devoted to the memory of General Craufurd, and always kept a little portrait of him n his own room. Through the kindness of Sir G. Brown's great-nephew, Colonel Leslie of the Cameron Highlanders, this portrait was copied, and a photograph of it now hangs in the officers' mess-room of the 43rd; and it has been used for the frontispiece of this volume.

★★★★★★

Of such grand material were then the non-commissioned officers of the incomparable Light Division. Assuredly young Brown had then and there read to him a better lesson in true self-sacrifice, true heroism, and true religion than ever issued from the lips of a preacher! When one remembers the genuine moral greatness and nobleness so often exhibited, throughout our long history, by what the world calls our "common soldiers;" when one realises, for instance, how splendid were the loyalty and devotion to duty displayed by our ignorant soldiers during the wreck of the Birkenhead, it makes one's blood boil with indignation to think that they are habitually looked down upon and treated with contumely by the respectable and selfish Pharisees of a stupid conventionalism, by men whose very religion is often steeped in meanness, and utterly devoid of that spirit of self-sacrifice which is in truth the very essence of Christianity and the crowning glory of our human nature.

For my part, I own freely that I have lived on terms of friendship and affection with many private soldiers, and that I care far more for their opinion than for that of mere respectability. Soldiers have many besetting faults and sins; but in the vast majority of cases I understand the causes of their sins so well, that their offences in no way alienate my strong hereditary sympathy. To be "numbered with the transgressors" as the ordinary world reckons transgressors often seems to me no unenviable fate; for amongst these reputed outcasts I have often found many fine qualities and many of the warmest hearts that I have known amongst all the sons of men. Quite lately British soldiers were described as "scum" in the columns of a fashionable newspaper. Educated writers ought, I think, to be ashamed to use such unfair and ungenerous language of a large class of men to whom we all owe much.

When I think of the many privations and vexatious annoyances to which the soldier is still often subjected, and which he usually bears with great patience and good temper, it seems to me that he is far more deserving of the gratitude than of the contempt of the people of his country. And I know well, by prolonged personal experience, that if one wishes to detach him from his sins and to elevate his moral nature, this is best effected by intelligent and unrestrained sympathy, and not by harsh and unsparing condemnation.

A great many soldiers have very strong feelings; and it is by appealing to these that one moves them most. I have noticed that in religious services the men very often like best some of our hymns which second-rate religionists are wont to stigmatise as "sentimental." No preacher will ever touch the hearts of English soldiers who expects cold prudential self-regard to work those wondrous moral miracles of regeneration, which love and pity wrought freely in the sin-stained but loyal hearts of simple Galilean peasants in the days of old.

Marshal Massena appears to have been a very boastful and untruthful person, and in his official report of the combat on the Coa he indulged himself with some statements contrary to facts and at the same time discreditable to the conduct of the Light Division. General Craufurd, though he had many faults, always thoroughly identified himself with his men, and was as jealous of their reputation as of his own. Consequently, he published the following long letter in the *Times* of November 21, 1810. This letter is highly characteristic; it also contains Craufurd's defence of his own arrangements, and also shows clearly that he never resolved (as Napier said he did) to fight against any large force of the enemy on the French side of the river. All that he hoped or designed to do was to prevent the investment of Almeida by any small or moderate number of troops.

> Marshal Massena, not content with the gross misrepresentations which were contained in his first official account of the action of the 24th of July, near Almeida, has in a subsequent despatch reverted to it in a tone of boasting wholly unjustified by the circumstances; assuring the War Minister that his whole army is burning with impatience to teach the English Army what they taught the division of Craufurd in the affair of Almeida.
>
> Brigadier-General Craufurd has therefore determined to give this public contradiction to the false assertions contained in Marshal Massena's report of an action which was not only highly honourable to the Light Division, but which positively terminated in its favour, notwithstanding the extraordinary disparity of numbers. A corps of 4000 men remained during the whole day in presence of an army amounting to 24,000. It performed, in the presence of so superior a force, one of the most difficult operations of war, namely, a retreat from a very broken and extensive position over one narrow defile.
>
> It defended, during the whole of the day, the first defensible position that was to be found in the neighbourhood of the place

where the action commenced; and in the course of the affair, this corps of 4000 men inflicted upon this army of 24,000 a loss equal to the double of that which it sustained. Such were the circumstances of the action in which Brigadier-General Craufurd's corps was opposed to the army commanded by Marshals Massena and Ney on July 24; and it is therefore indisputable that they had the best of it

From Marshal Massena's official despatch, containing a statement of the force to which we were opposed, it appears that the cavalry consisted of the 3rd Hussars, 15th Chasseurs, 10th, 15th, and 25th Dragoons, and that the whole of the infantry of Ney's corps was present, except one regiment of the division of Marchand. The infantry of Ney's corps, according to the intercepted official returns, amounted at that time to upwards of 22,000 effectives, and the cavalry regiments were certainly between 600 and 700 each. It therefore appears that the force with which Marshals Massena and Ney advanced to attack the Light Division on the morning of July 24, consisted of 20,000 infantry, and between 3000 and 4000 cavalry; to which were opposed three English battalions (43rd, 52nd, and 95th), two Portuguese battalions (1st and 3rd Chasseurs), and eight squadrons of cavalry, making, in the whole, a force of about 3200 British, and 1100 Portuguese troops.

Almeida is a small fortress situated at the edge of the declivity forming a right bank of the valley of the Coa, which river runs from the south to the north, and the bridge over which is nearly an English mile west of the town. From July 21 to 24 the chain of our cavalry outposts formed a semi-circle in front of Almeida, the right flank being *appuyé* to the Coa, near As-Naves, which is about three miles above the place, and the left flank also *appuyé* to the river near Cinco-Villa, which is about three miles below the fortress. The centre of this line was covered by a small stream; and on the principal roads by which it was expected the enemy would advance, namely, on the right and centre of the position, the cavalry posts were Supported by piquets of infantry.

The only road which our artillery and the body of our cavalry could make use of, to retreat across the Coa, was that which leads from Almeida to the bridge. The nature of the ground made it difficult for the enemy to approach this road on our left, that is to say, on the north side of the town; and the infantry of the division was, therefore, placed in a position to cover it on the right or south side, having its right flank *appuyé* to the Coa above the bridge, its front covered by a deep and rocky ravine, and its left in some enclosures near a windmill, which is on the plain, about eight hundred yards south of the town. The governor had intended to mount a gun upon the windmill; and one was actually in it, but quite useless, as it was not mounted. Another gun, also dismounted, was lying near the mill. These are the guns which Marshal Massena says he took in the action. On the morning of the 24th the centre of our line of piquets was attacked, namely, that which occupied the road leading from Almeida to Val de la Mula, which village is about four English miles east of the fortress. These piquets were supported by the 14th Light Dragoons and two guns; but when the head of a considerable column, with artillery, presented itself, and began to form on the other side of the rivulet, the piquets were withdrawn. The enemy then passed the rivulet, a cannonade took place, and they formed a line of fifteen squadrons of cavalry, at a distance of about a mile from the abovementioned windmill, with artillery in its front, and a Division of about seven thousand infantry on its right. Other troops were seen, though not so distinctly, advancing upon our right.

It being now evident that we were opposed to such a force as to render it impossible for Brigadier-General Craufurd to prevent the investment of the place, he determined to cross the Coa. He ordered the artillery and cavalry to move off by the road leading from the town to the bridge, and the infantry to follow, retiring across the vineyard in the same direction. The infantry were directed to move in echelon from the left, it being necessary to hold the right to the last, in order to prevent the enemy approaching the bridge by a road coming from Junca, and which runs along the bottom of the valley close to the river.

Some companies, which formed the left of our line, were in a vineyard so completely enclosed by a high stone wall, that it was quite impossible for cavalry to get into it; but the preceding night had been excessively severe, and some of the troops stationed in the vineyard had unfortunately pulled down the wall in many places, to make use of the stones to form a shelter against the violent rain. This wall, which Brigadier-General Craufurd had considered as a complete defence, was, therefore, no longer such; and after our artillery and cavalry had moved off, the enemy's horse broke into the enclosure and took several prisoners.

Our total loss in prisoners and missing amounted to about sixty, after all those who were at first returned as such had contrived to rejoin their regiments. The 43rd Regiment, having been on the left of the line, was the first that arrived near the bridge. The brigadier-general ordered some companies of it to occupy a height in front of the bridge, and the remainder to pass on and form on the heights on the other side of the river. Part of the 95th Rifles, and the 3rd battalion of Chasseurs, who arrived next, were formed on the right of those companies of the 43rd Regiment that were in front of the bridge. This position was maintained until everything was over, and until one of the Horse Artillery ammunition waggons, which had been overturned in a very bad situation, was got up and dragged to the other side by the men. During the remainder of the day the bridge was most gallantly defended by the 43rd and part of the 95th Regiments, and after it was dusk, we retreated from the Coa.

To retire in tactical order over such ground, so broken, rocky, and intersected with walls, as that which separated the first position from the second, would have been impossible, even if not under the fire of the enemy; and the ground on the other side of the river was equally unfavourable for reforming the regiments. Whoever knows anything of war, knows that in such an operation, and upon such ground, some derangement of regular order is inevitable; but the. retreat was made in a military, soldier-like manner, and without the slightest precipitation. In the course of it the enemy, when he pressed, was attacked in different places by the 43rd, 52nd, and 95th Regiments, and driven before them.

With respect to the enemy's loss, it is, of course, difficult to say what it was, because we know that, from the commencement of the revolutionary war, no French official report has ever contained true statements on this point. Upon this occasion Marshal Massena says, 'We have taken one stand of colours, four hundred men, and two pieces of cannon; our own loss amounted to nearly three hundred killed and wounded.' He took no colours; the cannon were the two dismounted guns belonging to the fortress, which were lying in and near the windmill; and instead of four hundred prisoners, he took only about sixty, supposing every one of those we returned as missing, to have fallen alive into the enemy's hands. Now, if in the same paragraph in which he states his own loss at three hundred, he calls sixty prisoners four hundred, we may fairly infer that he is not more accurate in the one statement than in the other; and this circumstance, as well as the usual practice of their service, and the probability of the thing from what we could observe, fully justify us in assuming it to have been from six to seven hundred. Ours amounted in killed, wounded, and prisoners, to three hundred and thirty.

Such is the true account of this affair, upon which the marshal prides himself so much, but in which it is certain that the advantage was on our side. We could not pretend to prevent the investment of the place; but in our retreat we did not lose a gun, a trophy, or a single article of field equipage; and we inflicted on the enemy a loss certainly double that we sustained.

The account, contained in the commencement of the marshal's despatch, of what had passed on July 21, is equally contrary to the truth. He talks of having forced the passage of the little rivulet that runs between Almeida and Val de la Mula on the 21st; whereas our piquets remained there, and not a single Frenchman passed it until the morning of the 24th. He says that many of our sharp-shooters fell into their hands on the 21st; the truth is that they did not take a single man. The retreat of the 14th Dragoons from Val de la Mula was conducted in the most slow and regular manner, and all our intentions with respect to Fort Conception were completely fulfilled.

(Signed)

Robert Craufurd,
Brigadier-General.

Charles Napier was present at the combat on the Coa. He drew up a long list of the errors committed by General Craufurd on this occasion, and this list has been published in his life by his brother, Sir William. Charles Napier said that he made the list for his own instruction; but men are very often not conscious of their really determining motives; and the strong language used by Charles Napier on this occasion makes it plain that detestation of his general was his chief incentive. Substantially, I imagine that most of his criticisms were correct; but the edge of them is considerably blunted when one remembers that General Craufurd had *not* "resolved" to withstand the whole army of Massena, but was attacked suddenly. Sir William Napier, who really believed that his general had "resolved" to fight, agrees with the censure passed on Craufurd by Charles Napier; but his judgment was much fairer than that of his brother. Remembering what the Light Division owed to Craufurd, or at all events remembering some part of it, William Napier adds:

> Still, he was a great officer.

Mr. Bruce, in his more recent life of Sir Charles Napier, omits this last remark of Sir William, and so conveys to his readers a rather misleading idea of the great historian's deliberate opinion of his famous leader.

But even William Napier's judgment of this matter was inevitably biased to a considerable extent by his fervent adoration of the great Sir John Moore. He said:

> Only Moore's regiments could, with so little experience, have extricated themselves from the danger into which they were so recklessly cast. Their matchless discipline was their protection; a phantom hero from Corunna saved them.

This seems hardly accurate or fair. The Light Division had been under Craufurd for more than a year in the Peninsular War when the fight at the Coa occurred; and some of its men had been with him at Buenos Ayres, and in the harassing retreat to Vigo. Captain Kincaid, of the 95th Rifles, speaks, I believe, with far greater accuracy and discriminating justice when he says:

> He (that is, Craufurd) received the three British regiments under his command finished by the hands of a master in the art, Sir John Moore, and as regiments they were faultless; but to Craufurd belonged the chief merit of making them the war Brigade which they became, alike the admiration of their friends and foes.

And again, this same writer says of Craufurd:

> He had introduced a system of discipline into the Light Division which made them unrivalled. . . . It was not until a short time before he was lost to us for ever, that we were capable of appreciating his merits, and fully sensible of the incalculable

advantages we derived from the perfection of his system.

And so, I think that Sir William Napier's picturesque language about the "phantom hero from Corunna" requires modification to a certain extent. According to Sir James Shaw Kennedy, whose ability Napier thoroughly admits or rather asserts, the four or five months of remarkable outpost work which preceded the fight at the Coa, must in the nature of things have been a most effective education for Craufurd's troops, and must have trained them in vigilance and in rapidity of movement to a far greater extent than any teaching by Sir John Moore ever did. I suppose that the. soldiers of the British army have never performed any other exploits in the way of outpost work equal to that carried on between the Rivers Coa and Agueda; and Craufurd's men were fresh from that supremely difficult work when they encountered Marshal Massena and his numerous forces.

Napier was evidently correct in saying that Craufurd and Picton met on the day of this combat on the Coa, and that the latter refused to move to the assistance of the Light Division; but why Picton thus refused no one has ever been able to find out.

In his *Narrative of the Peninsular War*, Lord Londonderry, who knew Craufurd most intimately, evidently thinks that he ought not to have fought on the French side of the Coa; but still he writes:

Yet was Craufurd an officer of singular ability and bravery, and certainly one of the best in the army, as all his proceedings on other occasions showed; and even here he did as much, or perhaps more, than most men in a similar situation could have performed.

It ought also to be borne in mind that though the leader of the Light Division erred gravely in judgment on this occasion, yet his error was no worse than many committed by French marshals whose general reputations yet stand deservedly very high on the whole.

Lord Wellington was on this occasion much vexed and annoyed with General Craufurd; yet he passed no direct censure on him, and never deprived him of his command for a single day; he only omitted to *thank* Craufurd, while greatly praising the conduct of the officers and men of his division.

It is much to be wished that those who compile military histories would study to be accurate so far as is possible. Sir R. Levinge, in his *Historical Records of the 43rd Regiment*, inserts, with apparent approval and sanction, a letter from a young subaltern named Booth, in which

127

it is declared that Lord Wellington had deprived General Craufurd of the command of the Light Division, and given it to Sir Brent Spencer. This is totally untrue; and Sir R. Levinge might easily have discovered its untruth, by looking into Gurwood's edition of Wellington's Despatches, wherein he would have made the discovery that, directly after the fight at the Coa, Wellington writes to Craufurd as still in possession of his old command, that he continues to do so, and that whilst Craufurd lived, his division was never intrusted to other hands except for a few months much later on in the war, when General Craufurd went home on his own private affairs, greatly contrary to Lord Wellington's expressed wishes. This can easily be proved by a reference to the despatches which I have mentioned; and it seems rather strange that the *Historical Records of the 43rd Regiment* should contain such a grave and gratuitous error.

Craufurd himself felt keenly Wellington's disapprobation and implied censure. And he was also very anxious to know what was said on the subject at home in England. Accordingly, he wrote to make inquiries through his wife and his brother, General Charles Craufurd. And they tell him that very little has appeared on this business in the newspapers, excepting a rumour that the Light Division had been taken away from him and given to "General William Stewart, a brother of Lord Galloway." But General Charles Craufurd says, in a letter to his brother Robert, that he put down this rumour to political spite, as the intimate friendship of the leader of the Light Division with Mr. Windham caused him to be much disliked by certain people belonging to a different political set.

I have in my possession a letter written by Wellington to Craufurd the day after the battle, namely July 25, at 6 p.m., in which nothing much is said about the affair, and directions are given quite in the usual way; and the tone and style are the same as ever. And on the following day, July 26, the commander-in-chief again writes to his subordinate general in his customary manner. In fact, notwithstanding Craufurd's dangerous error of judgment, Wellington seems never to have contemplated removing him from his command, or to have revoked the remarkable words which he had addressed to him only a few months ago—on April 9, 1810:—

Since you have joined the army, I have always wished that you should command our outposts, for many reasons into which it is unnecessary to enter.

Before many months had passed, "the masterly dispositions"—as Napier calls them—of his troops at Busaco by the leader of the Light Division were destined to prove conclusively that Lord Wellington was right, and that General Craufurd was a far abler man than some of his indignant regimental officers were willing to confess him to be, when they heaped abuse on him and yearned for his removal on account of his memorable fight against the enemy beside the River Coa.

CHAPTER 6

Services under Wellington Concluded

On July 28, the Light Division arrived at Celorico, and made huts for themselves there. And about this time Lord Wellington directed that the Division should be divided into two brigades, and be commanded as follows: the first Brigade by Lieutenant-Colonel Beckwith, consisting of one half of his own battalion the 95th Rifles, the 43rd Regiment, and the 3rd Portuguese Caçadores; the second Brigade by Lieutenant-Colonel Barclay of the 52nd, consisting of his own regiment, the other part of the 95th Rifles, and the 1st Portuguese Caçadores.

Immediately after Craufurd's retreat across the Coa, on July 24, Massena commenced the siege of Almeida, though in a rather dilatory manner. The Governor of Almeida was Colonel Cox, an English officer in the Portuguese service; and Wellington expected the place to hold out for a considerable time, and thus delay the advance of the French.

Writing to General Craufurd, on July 27, to explain his arrangements to him, Wellington remarks:

> Whatever may be the enemy's intentions (which I think are to dash at us as soon as they will be prepared, and make our retreat as difficult as possible), we shall be in such a situation as to be able to effect it without being much pressed, or to move forward again if a blow can be struck with advantage.

In this letter the commander says that:

> These circumstances and the general view of our situation have determined me to make a move to the rear with our infantry, with the exception of the fourth division, which I will leave in observation on Guarda.

Sir William Napier, writing concerning this period of the war, says:

In these positions, expecting a vigorous defence from Almeida, he (Wellington) hoped to delay the enemy for two months, when the rainy season would give him further advantages in defence of the country. His original intention had been to keep the Light Division always on the Cabeça Negro, a rugged hill overhanging the bridge of the Coa, expecting thus to keep open his communication with the fortress, or to make the French invest the place with their whole army. Craufurd's rashness marred this plan; and his despondency after the action on the 24th rendered it imprudent to renew the project.

General Craufurd's apparent "despondency" was certainly not caused by any apprehension of the French forces, as is sufficiently evident from his almost bringing on a premature action with them a few weeks later, just before the Battle of Benaco. The occupation of this rugged hill overlooking the Coa would have suited him remarkably well; and one cannot help regretting that Lord Wellington did not mention to Craufurd his plans a little earlier, and then the unnecessary fight on the Coa would almost certainly have never taken place.

From an inspection of Craufurd's correspondence with his brother, I am enabled to confirm Sir William Napier's statement that he was then suffering from "despondency;" but the cause of this dejection was not what Napier, and perhaps Wellington, took it to be. It was the great Commander's own displeasure which was depressing the spirits of the fiery leader of the Light Division. Until after the Battle of Busaco where Craufurd earned the very warmest eulogy from his much-respected chief the two men were not any longer on comfortable terms; and this Craufurd felt keenly, as he always entertained the very highest opinion of his commander's abilities and soundness of judgment. The writer of General Craufurd's life, in Mr. Leslie Stephen's valuable *Dictionary of National Biography*, is very much mistaken in his assertion that "Craufurd cared little for Wellington's censure." On the contrary, he cared a great deal for it; and his correspondence affords ample evidence of this.

Mr. Hooper, in his *Life of Wellington*, justly enough describes the leader of the Light Division as "always burning to fight"; but, like many men of passionate temperament, he was extremely sensitive. Lord Wellington was well aware of this fact, but its full significance may at times have escaped his observation. The simple circumstance that his chief had not praised him for his services at the action on the

Coa, disquieted the mind of the eager and impetuous subordinate. Actual censure Craufurd could never have borne; he would have given up his command at once.

About August 26, the French batteries opened on the fortress of Almeida; and a few hours after the bombardment commenced, most unfortunately a shell exploded in the great magazine, blew half the town about the ears of the garrison, and so injured the works that the Governor was obliged to capitulate. This was most disadvantageous to Wellington, as Marshal Massena was now able to prosecute his march on Lisbon some weeks earlier than had been expected.

Early in September the army began to retreat to Coimbra, and many people thought that it would soon embark at Lisbon for England. But about the 20th of this month the Light Division crossed the River Mondego by a ford, and found themselves on the main road leading from Vizeu to Coimbra. As they were approaching the Sierra de Busaco, Craufurd's eagerness to fight nearly brought on a premature engagement; but Lord Wellington arrived at the post in time, and ordered him to retire to Busaco. There on the heights, on a spur of the mountain jutting out very considerably, the Light Division took up its position.

Sir William Napier gives September 29 as the date of the Battle of Busaco; but I suppose this must be a misprint, as all the other authorities give the 27th.

In this battle the Light Division and its leader earned undying distinction. Ney's attack upon Craufurd was repulsed in the most brilliant and effective manner. Napier remarks:

Ney's attack had as little success. From the abutment of the mountain upon which the Light Division was stationed, the lowest parts of the valley could be discerned; the ascent was steeper than where Reynier had attacked; and Craufurd, in a happy mood of command, made masterly dispositions. The table-land between him and the convent was sufficiently scooped to conceal the 43rd and 52nd Regiments drawn up in line; and a quarter of a mile behind them, on higher ground, and close to the convent, the German infantry appeared to be the only solid line of resistance on this part of the position. In front of the British regiments, some rocks, overhanging the descent, furnished natural embrasures in which Ross's guns were placed; and beyond them the Riflemen and *Caçadores* were planted as skirmishers, covering the slope of the mountain.

While it was still dark, a straggling musketry was heard in the deep valley; and when the light broke, three heavy masses, detached from the sixth corps, were seen to enter the woods below and throw forward a profusion of skirmishers. One of these, under General Marchand, emerging from the dark chasm and following the main road, seemed intent to turn the right of the Light Division; a second under Loison made straight up the face of the mountain against the front; the third remained in reserve. Simon's Brigade, leading Loison's attack, ascended with a wonderful alacrity; and though the light troops plied it unceasingly with musketry, and the artillery bullets swept through it from the first to the last section, its order was never disturbed, nor its speed in the least abated. Ross's guns were worked with incredible quickness, yet their range was palpably contracted every round; the enemy's shot came singing up in a sharper key; the English skirmishers, breathless and begrimed with powder, rushed over the edge of the ascent; the artillery drew back, and the victorious cries of the French were heard within a few yards of the summit.

Craufurd, standing alone on one of the rocks, had been intently watching the progress of this attack, and now with a shrill tone ordered the two regiments in reserve to charge; the next moment a horrid shout startled the French column, and eighteen hundred British bayonets went sparkling over the brow of the hill. Yet so brave, so hardy were the leading French that each man of the first section raised his musket, and two officers and ten soldiers fell before them. Not a Frenchman had missed his mark. They could do no more. The head of their column was violently thrown back upon the rear; both flanks were overlapped at the same moment by the English wings; three terrible discharges at five yards' distance shattered the wavering mass, and a long trail of broken arms and bleeding carcases marked the line of flight.

Sir George Napier, in his book, gives one or two interesting details not mentioned by his brother. He says:

General Craufurd himself stood on the brow of the hill watching every movement of the attacking column; and when all our skirmishers had passed by and joined their respective corps, and the head of the enemy's column was within a very few yards of him, he turned round, came up to the 52nd, and called out, 'Now, 52nd, revenge the death of Sir John Moore! Charge! Charge! Huzza!'; and waving his hat in the air, he was answered by a shout that appalled the enemy, and in one instant the brow of the hill bristled with two thousand British bayonets wielded by steady English hands, which soon buried them in the bodies of the fiery Gaul! . . .

Poor Colonel Barclay received a severe wound, of which he afterwards died in England. . .

We kept firing and bayonetting till we reached the bottom, and the enemy passed the brook and fell back upon their main body, which moved down to support them and cover their retreat. All this was done in a very short time, that is, it was not above twenty minutes from the charge till the French were driven from the top to the bottom of the mountain like a parcel of sheep. I really did not think it possible for such a column to be so completely destroyed in a few minutes as that was, particularly after witnessing how gallantly they moved up under a destructive fire from the artillery and a constant galling one from our sharpshooters.

Colonel Leach, of the 95th Rifles, also wrote thus concerning the hopeless repulse of the French on this occasion:

The instant the attacking columns were turned back, they were exposed to the fire of our whole division; whilst our battalion and some *Caçadores* were ordered to pursue and to give them a flanking fire; and the horse artillery continued to pour on them a murderous fire of grape, as they were struggling through the narrow streets of Sula, and trampling each other to death in their great haste to escape. Men, muskets, knapsacks, and bayonets rolled down the side of the mountain in such a confused mass as it is impossible to convey a just idea of.

Lord Londonderry also declared:

Never was rout more complete than that which followed the movement. The enemy, unable to retreat and afraid to resist, were rolled down the steep, like a torrent of hailstones driven before a powerful wind.

Sir William Napier writes concerning the remainder of that memorable day:

> Loison did not renew the action; but Marchand, having formed several small bodies, gained a pine-wood halfway up the mountain on the right of the Light Division, and sent a cloud of skirmishers against the highest part. On that steep ascent, however, Pack's men sufficed to hold them in check, and half a mile higher up Spencer showed a line of the Foot Guards which forbade any hope of success. Craufurd's artillery also smote Marchand's people in the pine-wood; and Ney, who was there in person, after sustaining this murderous cannonade for an hour, relinquished that attack also. The desultory fighting of the light troops then ceased, and at two o'clock parties from both armies were, under a momentary truce, mixed together, carrying off wounded men.

Thus, ended the glorious Battle of Busaco so far as the Light Division was concerned. To general, and officers and men, this victory must have been peculiarly gratifying; for it was a crushing and effective reply to the mendacious boasting of Marshal Massena concerning the combat on the Coa. The French Marshal had assured the War Minister that:

> His whole army was burning with impatience to teach the English Army what they taught the division of Craufurd in the affair of Almeida.

Well, on the mountain side of Busaco they once more encountered "the Division of Craufurd," and the results were so overwhelmingly disastrous that the arrogant and vainglorious Massena appears *this time* to have been so genuinely impressed with the prowess of the Light Division and its leader that he actually forgot to brag and, in order to account for his own failure, even exaggerated the vehement and irresistible attack made by the 43rd and 52nd Regiments when they emerged from the hollow in which they had been so skilfully hidden by their leader. In a letter to Craufurd, written on November 12 following, Lord Wellington said:

> If you could come over here someday, I would show you Massena's despatch on Busaco, which I have got, from which it appears that you attacked Loison '*en deux colonnes serrées en masse!*'

Captain Kincaid relates the following amusing story as one of the results of this famous battle:

On the day of the battle, the 27th, the French general, Simon, who led the attack upon our division, was wounded and taken prisoner; and as they were bringing him in, he raved furiously for General Craufurd, daring him to single combat; but as he was already a prisoner, there would have been but little wit in indulging him in his humour.

General Craufurd and his division were warmly praised by Lord Wellington for their brilliant services on this momentous occasion; and a complete reconciliation was now effected between the great commander-in-chief and his well-trusted subordinate general.

The splendid victory much delighted our people at home, as is made manifest by the following letter addressed to the leader of the Light Division by his brother, General Charles Craufurd, who had himself seen so much service with the Austrian Army in earlier days.

Drakelow, October 19, 1810.

My Dearest Brother

Most sincerely do I congratulate you on having again distinguished yourself in so brilliant a manner. The victory of Busaco was indeed a glorious one! Thank God for it, for the part you bore in it, and for your safety! As the Portuguese troops conduct themselves so well, and as the French have felt their equality at least and our decided superiority both at Busaco and on the Coa, I think one may be justified in being sanguine as to the result of the campaign.

Really this behaviour of the Portuguese, combined with these victories and the other which probably has by this time taken place, must electrify the Spaniards as well as Portuguese in such a manner as to render them very formidable to their enemy. The cause seems to revive.

Lord Wellington has conducted his operations capitally, and I have no doubt of his bringing them to a happy termination, and adding fresh laurels to the many he has already gained. You, too, have an ample portion, I assure you. You always had a great opinion of Lord Wellington's abilities, and you are now proved to be right.

The duke told me, when here a few days ago, that he read lately in one of the papers an account of Whitelocke's affair at Buenos Ayres, by the second in command to Liniers, in which it was asserted that, if you had been allowed to advance into the town that same evening after defeating Liniers, as you proposed to do, you would certainly have taken the place.

The duchess desires her kindest remembrances and begs you to be convinced that she most heartily rejoices in the great honour you are incessantly acquiring. I suppose you will soon have a regiment of course.

> Believe me always,
> My dearest Robert,
> Your most truly affectionate brother,
> C. Craufurd.

★★★★★★

General Charles Craufurd, afterwards General Sir Charles Craufurd, G.C.B., had married the Duchess of Newcastle, widow of Thomas, third duke. She was a daughter of the Earl of Harrington.

★★★★★★

It will be seen from this letter that Robert Craufurd and his brother Charles were singularly devoted to each other. My grandfather always greatly admired and revered the serene temperament and unruffled magnanimity of his elder brother, which were such a contrast to his own internal storm and strife. When writing to his wife, Robert Craufurd's habitual expression on this subject was, "Charles is the very best of men."

After the Battle of Busaco the army began moving off to the famous lines of Torres Vedras, but without any precipitation. The Light Division retired to Coimbra, then to Pombal, then to Battalha, and then to Alemquer, and finally to Aruda, On October 11, Lord Wellington wrote a long letter to Craufurd from a place near Sobral. He says:

> I hope your men are well put up in Aruda in this terrible weather. I don't think the enemy's plan is quite decided yet. He has still some troops at Alemquer, and there is a body of cavalry and infantry (I saw of the latter about 300 men) on this side of Alemquer. I mean however, to hold the town of Sobral as long as I can.
>
> The peasants say that they were marching this morning upon

137

Villa Franca; which is to attack our right, where Hill is. They can make no impression upon the right by the high road positively; and they must therefore endeavour to turn Hill's position upon the Sierra of Alhandra, by its left. This is a tough job also, defended as the entrances of the valleys are by redoubts, and the villages by abattis, etc. However, that is what they must try. . . . From this statement, however, you will see how important the situation of Aruda and the possession of the Pass of Matos (which by-the-bye itself turns Hill's position) are to our operations.

Aruda itself I don't think could be held for any great length of time against a superior force; but the Pass of Matos can, defended as it is by the two redoubts. I understand from Fletcher also that the redoubts command the road going out of Aruda towards Alhandra; so that, if you should find it most advantageous to give up Aruda, the enemy could not make much use of that road, at least by daylight.

I need say nothing to you about the defence of the Pass of Matos. I think it would be desirable, however, that you should occupy with the 52nd or 43rd the high ground which continues from the right of the right hand redoubt, looking from Matos towards Aruda.

Craufurd thoroughly entered into his commander's designs at this period, and co-operated in the most intelligent manner, so that Sir William Napier wrote thus:

Massena, surprised at the extent and strength of works (the famous lines of Torres Vedras generally) which he had only heard of five days before he came upon them, employed several days to examine their nature. The heights of Alhandra were inexpugnable; but the valleys of Calandrix and Aruda attracted his attention. By the former he could turn Alhandra and reach the weakest part of the second line; but the abattis and redoubts, hourly strengthening, gave little encouragement to attack there. The ground about Aruda did not give him a view of the troops, although he frequently skirmished to make Craufurd show his force; but that general, by occupying Aruda as an advanced post, had rendered it impossible to discover his true situation without out a serious affair, and in an incredibly short space of time he secured his position in a manner worthy of admiration.

Across the ravine on the left, a loose stone wall, sixteen feet thick and forty feet high, was raised; across the great valley of Aruda a double line of abattis was drawn, not, as usual, of the limbs of trees, but of full-grown oaks and chesnuts digged up with all their roots and branches, dragged by main force for several hundred yards, and then reset and crossed so that no human strength could break through. Breastworks, at convenient distances to defend this line of trees, were also cast up; and along the summits of the mountain, for a space of nearly three miles, including the salient points, other stone walls six feet high by four in thickness, with banquettes, were piled up! Romans never raised greater works in the time!

Thus, General Craufurd *again* baffled his boastful enemy, Marshal Massena.

As this volume is merely a memoir, and makes no pretence to be anything like a history, I need not attempt to describe the famous lines of Torres Vedras, which the far-seeing sagacity of Wellington had prepared as a barrier against the French around Lisbon. A few brief extracts from Sir William Napier will suffice. The lines consisted of three distinct ranges of defence, of which the third was intended to cover a forced embarkation, if necessary.

Of these stupendous lines the second, whether for strength or importance, was the principal; the others were appendages, the third a mere place of refuge. The first line was originally designed as an advanced work, to stem the primary violence of the enemy and enable the army to take up its ground on the second line without hurry or pressure. But while Massena remained inactive on the frontier, it acquired strength, which was now so much augmented by the rain that Wellington resolved to abide the attack there permanently.

These celebrated lines were great in conception and execution, more in keeping with ancient than modern military labours; and it is clear that the defence was not dependent, as some French writers suppose, upon the first line. If that had been stormed, the standard of Portuguese independence would still have floated securely amidst the rocks of the second line. But to occupy fifty miles of fortification, to man one hundred and fifty forts, and work six hundred guns required many men; and numbers were not wanting. A great fleet in the Tagus, a superb body of marines sent out from England, the civic guards of

Lisbon, the Portuguese heavy artillery corps, the militia and *ordenança* of Estremadura, furnished a powerful reserve to the regular army. The native gunners and the militia supplied all the garrisons of the forts on the second and most of those on the first line; the British marines occupied the third line; the navy manned the gun-boats on the river, and aided in various ways the operations in the field. The recruits from the depots and the calling in of all the men on furlough rendered the Portuguese Army stronger than it had yet been, while the British troops, reinforced from Cadiz and England, and remarkably healthy, presented such a front as a general would desire to see in a dangerous crisis.

Another writer tells us that:

The Peninsula on which Lisbon stands, is traversed by two lofty heights which stretch from the River Tagus to the ocean, varying in altitude and abruptness, and running in a parallel direction, at a distance of from six to nine miles. Through the passes in these mountains run the four great roads that communicate between Lisbon and the interior.

Colonel Leith Hay explains the mode in which these formidable lines would have been defended:

No British soldiers, with the exception of artillery, would have acted within the walls. Some Portuguese infantry, with the militia and *ordenança*, were destined to compose the garrisons; while the whole allied army, numerous, brilliant in equipment, high in spirit, confident in its great commander, was prepared to move in every direction, to cover the summits of mountains, to descend into valleys, or to pour in torrents on any luckless column that, with diminished numbers, might have forced their way past the almost impenetrable obstacles of this grand position.

Napier tells us that:

More than one hundred and twenty thousand fighting men were rationed within the lines, seventy thousand being regular troops.

The position of the French was far from being well-secured or comfortable; for whereas the allies had abundant supplies, which could always be brought by sea, the French had behind them an exhausted district, and a very unfriendly population, and a host of irregular troops waiting only an opportunity to become actively aggressive.

Marshal Massena found it impossible to attack the famous lines; and about the middle of November he withdrew to Santarem. There the French strengthened their position, and determined to remain. But Napier tells us that:

> Craufurd, however, still thought a rear-guard only was at Santarem; his spirit was chafed; he seized a musket and, followed by a sergeant, advanced in the night along the causeway, to commence a personal skirmish with the French piquet; he escaped from its fife miraculously and came back convinced that Massena was not in flight.

The two armies remained here in a state of comparative inactivity for about three months. Colonel Leach, of the 95th Rifles, speaks thus of a certain addition now made for a time to the Light Division:

> When we arrived here from the lines of Torres Vedras, the Duke of Brunswick's Oels' corps of infantry, which had recently reached Portugal, was sent to join the Light Division. They deserted to the French in such numbers that we had a *lease* of them but for a few weeks. Lord Wellington caused several of them, who had been taken in the attempt to desert to the enemy, to be tried and shot; and immediately afterwards he directed that the corps should be sent away from the Light Division.

This decision of the commander-in-chief was probably in great measure the result of Craufurd's report of these troops, which was most unfavourable; in fact, he detested to have them mingled with his own staunch and admirably trained men.

General Craufurd went home to England on leave at the beginning of February in the year 1811, thinking that no great operations were likely to be undertaken during the winter. In a letter written on December 9, 1810, Wellington said to Craufurd, "Adverting to the number of general officers senior to you in the army, it has not been an easy task to keep you in your command;" and he goes on to say that if the leader of the Light Division went home, it might not be possible to give him back his command on his return to the army. And in another letter on the same subject, written on January 28, 1811, Wellington says that he *assents* to Craufurd going home, but that he cannot *approve*.

During the absence of its old leader the command of the Light Division was temporarily given to Sir W. Erskine, who proved himself to be by no means a brilliant general.

Whilst General Craufurd was away in England, his division was earning much additional distinction, especially at Redinha and in the combat of Sabugal, of which latter action Wellington declared:

> This was one of the most glorious actions British troops were ever engaged in.

Sir W. Erskine arranged things very badly on this occasion, so that Beckwith, who commanded his first Brigade, having with him only one bayonet battalion and four companies of Riflemen, found himself assailing twelve thousand infantry, supported by cavalry and artillery.

Colonel Leach, of the 95th Rifles, gives us the following account of the combat at Sabugal:

> The outline of the plan was that the Light Division and some cavalry should pass the River Coa by a ford at some distance above Sabugal, whilst other divisions assailed the position by fords and the bridge near the town. The operations of the day commenced by the Light Division passing the Coa at a ford of considerable depth, under fire of Reynier's advanced posts, who were driven back on their supports by Colonel Beckwith's Brigade, which first crossed the river.
>
> In this, as in all other mountainous regions, thick fogs appear and disappear very suddenly; and such was the case on the present occasion. Its temporary dispersion discovered Colonel Beckwith's little Brigade almost in contact with the whole of Reynier's corps, which, after a sharp fire, forced back with overwhelming numbers the four companies of the 95th (that composed Colonel Beckwith's advance) on the 43rd regiment; and aware that the number of his opponents was trifling, the French general made an impetuous attack with infantry cavalry, and artillery, to crush and annihilate them before support should arrive. But the 43rd, on which the Riflemen were driven back for support, was a corps not to be meddled with free of expense, as they very soon proved to their antagonists by driving them back, in most gallant style, with the bayonet.
>
> Fearful as were the odds, Colonel Beckwith's Brigade pursued the French into their own position, and inflicted on them a

severe loss; but, being reinforced, they again drove back this handful of men. Our men, however, possessed themselves of some stone walls and broken ground, by which they contrived to hold on until they once more obliged their enemy to retreat; and entering their position with them, our men charged and captured a howitzer.

For the recapture of this, the French were making another grand effort, when the second brigade of the Light Division, with troops also of the 3rd and other divisions, arrived near the scene of action, which obliged Reynier to make a rapid retreat. In less than forty-eight hours afterwards the whole French army was over the Portuguese frontier, and sought shelter under the guns of Ciudad Rodrigo.

Thus, did Massena's invasion of Portugal terminate, and in this manner was his threat fulfilled of '*driving the English into the sea.*'

This combat by the Coa must have been peculiarly gratifying to the Light Division, considering the way in which Marshal Massena had boasted of his former encounter with it beside the same river only eight or nine months before.

Wellington had now saved Portugal. Napier tells us that:

Massena entered Portugal with sixty-five thousand men, and his reinforcements while at Santarem were about ten thousand; he repassed the frontier with forty-five thousand; the invasion, therefore, cost him thirty thousand men.

Wellington now invested Almeida, which was in possession of the French, Colonel Leach informs us that:

The Light Division, with its old friends, the 1st German Hussars, soon took up the same line of outposts on the Azava, which they held last summer, during the period that Massena was laying siege to Ciudad Rodrigo. One brigade was at Gallegos, the other at Espeja, having hussar piquets across the Azava at Carpio and Marialva, and on the Agueda at Moulina dos Flores.

In April, 1811, General Craufurd was on his way back to take the command of his own favourite division, His leading had been much missed during his absence, as Sir W. Cope has remarked; and the following letter from the commander-in-chief will show that he was glad to welcome back his active, vigilant, and enterprising subordinate.

Villa Formosa, April 14, 1811.

My Dear General,

I received this morning your letter of the 9th. You will find your division in your old quarters at Gallegos, and the sooner you can come up to them the better.

We are blockading Almeida, in which there may be about a month's provisions. The greater part of the French Army are gone to the Douro.

Ever yours most faithfully,

Wellington.

General Craufurd.

I notice that in this letter Wellington no longer calls Craufurd a *Brigadier*-General; but I believe he was not actually gazetted as a Major-General till June 4, 1811.

In a letter written about this time to his wife, Craufurd says that he finds that his division has been earning great additional distinction during his absence, and that he "cannot pretend" not to feel much grieved at not having participated in it. The combat of Sabugal was in fact one after Robert Craufurd's own heart; the almost incredible audacity of his Riflemen, his 43rd, and his 52nd was eminently calculated to make him prouder than ever of that unequalled division which he always loved so well, and to which he devoted himself so freely. His strong natural affections caused him to feel keenly the long separation from his wife and children, and in consequence he was always talking of retiring from the army; but it is plain enough that he never could have left it for any great length of time whilst the war lasted. His nature was made for activity, and as one of his own soldiers (Rifleman Harris) said of him, "war was his very element."

Craufurd rejoined his division just before the Battle of Fuentes d'Onoro, which took place on May 5, 1811. He was received with ringing cheers by his men, and these cheers seem to have astonished the French. Costello (a non-commissioned officer of the 95th Rifles) tells us that "while things were in this state, General Craufurd made his reappearance amongst us from England, and was welcomed with much enthusiasm by the division. Although a strict disciplinarian, the men knew his value in the field too well not to testify their satisfaction at his return. The *Caçadores*, particularly, caused much laughter among us by shouting out in Portuguese, the moment they caught sight of him, 'Long live General Craufurd who takes care of our bellies!'; meaning by this exclamation they got their rations regularly while under his command. The general seemed highly pleased, and bowed repeatedly with his hat off, as he rode down their ranks."

Napier informs us that Wellington at this period had only thirty-two thousand infantry, twelve hundred cavalry in bad condition, and forty-two guns, whereas on the side of the enemy, "forty thousand French infantry, and five thousand horse, with thirty-six pieces of artillery were under arms." Thus, the enemy were enormously superior in cavalry, especially as, according to Napier, not more than a thousand English troopers were actually in the field.

> The French, therefore, drove in all the cavalry out-guards at the first shock, cut off Ramsay's battery of horse artillery, and came sweeping in upon the reserves of cavalry and upon the 7th Division. Their leading squadrons, approaching in a disorderly manner, were partially checked by fire; but a great commotion was observed in their main body; men and horses were seen to close with confusion and tumult towards one point, where a thick dust and loud cries, and the sparkling of blades and flashing of pistols indicated some extraordinary occurrence.
> Suddenly the multitude became violently agitated, an English shout pealed high and clear, the mass was rent asunder, and Norman Ramsay burst forth, sword in hand, at the head of his battery, his horses breathing fire, stretched like greyhounds along the plain; the guns bounded behind them like things of no weight, and the mounted gunners followed close, with heads bent low and pointed weapons, in desperate career. Captain Brotherton of the 14th Dragoons, seeing this, instantly rode forth and with his squadron shocked the head of the pursuing troops, and General Charles Stewart, joining in the charge, took the French Colonel Lamotte, fighting hand to hand; but then the main body of the French came on strongly, and the British cavalry retired behind the Light Division which was immediately thrown into squares.

Owing to the progress of the French in another part, it became absolutely necessary that the original concentrated position above Fuentes d'Onoro should be quickly regained by the English troops. Accordingly, Napier says:

> The 7th Division were therefore ordered to cross the Turones and move down the left bank to Frenada, while the Light Divi-

sion retired over the plain; the cavalry covered this movement, and the 1st and 3rd Divisions and the Portuguese were at the same time placed on the *steppe* of land before described, perpendicular to the ravine of Fuentes d'Onoro. General Craufurd, who had resumed the command of the Light Division, covered Houstoun's passage across the Turones, and then retired slowly over the plain in squares, followed by the French horsemen, who continually outflanked, but never dared to assail him. . . . Many times, Montbrun feigned to charge Craufurd's squares, but always he found them too dangerous to meddle with, and this crisis passed without a disaster; yet there was not, during the whole war, a more perilous hour.

An officer of the Light Division, Colonel Leach, speaks with justifiable pride of the conduct of that famous band of men on this occasion.

The British right being turned at Navis d'Avair, the mass of French cavalry, with artillery, continued to advance along the plain, threatening to cut off the Light Division from the position on the heights. We were therefore directed to retire from the wood, to form squares of battalions, and to fall back over the plain on the 1st Division. The steadiness and regularity with which the troops performed this movement, the whole time exposed to, a cannonade and followed across a plain by a numerous cavalry ready to pounce on the squares, if the least disorder should be detected, has been acknowledged by hundreds of unprejudiced persons (unconnected with the Light Division) who witnessed it from the heights, to have been a masterpiece of military evolutions.

After much desperate fighting, in which "the 71st, 79th, the 2nd battalion of the 24th, and all the regiments employed in the defence of the village, rivalled each other in gallantry and good conduct," Lord Wellington was victorious; and as Colonel Leach remarks:

Thus, did Massena utterly fail in every attempt, and left the village and the ground near it covered with killed and wounded.

The marvellous coolness and steadiness of the Light Division on this occasion have called forth many expressions of admiration from those well qualified to judge. But General Picton, always jealous of Craufurd, thought proper to speak disparagingly of his brother general and the troops under his command; and Sir William Napier has given the flattest contradiction to Picton's assertions. This is contained in an appendix in the last volume of the *History of the War in the Peninsula*, wherein Napier writes thus:—

> Again, General Picton, writing of the Battle of Fuentes d'Onoro says, 'The Light Division, under General Craufurd, was rather roughly handled by the enemy's cavalry, and had that arm of the French army been as daring and active upon this occasion as they were when following us to the lines of Torres Vedras, they would doubtless have cut off the Light Division to a man.' Nevertheless, as an eye-witness, and being then a field-officer on the staff, I was by Mr. Robinson's rule entitled to see, I declare most solemnly that the French cavalry, though they often menaced to charge, never came within sure shot distance of the Light Division. The latter, with the exception of the 95th Rifles, who were skirmishing in the wood of Pozo Velho, was formed by regiments in three squares, flanking and protecting each other; they retired over the plain leisurely without the loss of a man, without a sabre-wound being received, without giving or receiving fire; they moved in the most majestic manner, secure in their discipline and strength, which were such as would have defied all the cavalry that ever charged under Tamerlane or Genghis.

About May the 10th the Light Division found itself once more in its old quarters at Gallegos and Espeja. On the night of May, the 10th, the French garrison in Almeida contrived to effect its escape, very much to the annoyance of Lord Wellington. Besides carrying off successfully the greater part of his men, the French general, Brennier, also rendered the fortress useless to the allies by mining the principal bastions and destroying the guns.

The English generals whom Napier blames for their negligence on this occasion were General Campbell and Sir W. Erskine. A recent compiler of military history throws the blame on Craufurd, who had absolutely nothing to do with the affair. Napier's account of the vexatious affair is perfectly clear, and it is much to be wished that compilers would not gratuitously circulate erroneous statements about renowned leaders.

Concerning this escape of the garrison of Almeida Lord Londonderry wrote:

It seemed as if, by this untoward event, all the advantages obtained by the battle of Fuentes d'Onoro were thrown away.

He also says that General Campbell was the person to, blame for this.

Lord Wellington issued a severe and caustic rebuke to the officers of his army in consequence of this business; and it is said that in a private letter he declared that he:

> . . . .began to be of opinion that there is nothing on earth so stupid as a gallant officer.

About this time Marshal Marmont arrived from France to take command and to supersede Massena, the old enemy of the Light Division.

About May the 22nd intelligence reached the army of the sanguinary battle fought at Albuera, between the French under Marshal Soult and the little army under Marshal Beresford.

Towards the end of the month of May the Light Division received orders to move towards Marshal Beresford on the Guadiana, as Marmont was now endeavouring to form a junction with Soult in order to raise the siege of Badajoz, which Beresford had now again commenced. On June 23:

> Craufurd's troops bivouacked on the hottest and most parched piece of ground in the Peninsula, lying between Aronches and Campo Mayor, and on the left bank of the Caya. In this neighbourhood Lord Wellington had concentrated his whole army.

Marshals Soult and Marmont having united their forces, amounting according to Colonel Leach to about eighty thousand men, Wellington was obliged to raise the siege of Badajoz. The British Army remained in position on the Caya for about a month. Then the two French Marshals, not liking to attack, broke up from the Guadiana, after having garrisoned and provisioned Badajoz.

On July 20 the army marched in a northern direction, retracing its steps. Only General Hill's Division, with some cavalry, remained in Alemtejo

About August the 10th the Light Division and its old companions, the German hussars, were once more advanced across the Agueda. Napier says that:

> Wellington reached the Coa on August 8, intending first a close

blockade of Ciudad Rodrigo, and finally a siege. He was too late; the place had been revictualled for two months on the 6th by Bessières' convoy, and the blockade being necessarily relinquished, the troops were quartered near the sources of the Coa and Agueda.

Early in September, however, Wellington had formed his blockade, and fixed his own headquarters at Guinaldo.

The following letter from the commander-in-chief to General Craufurd, written at this time, will show that his confidence in the ability of the leader of the Light Division remained as great as ever. As usual, the post requiring the greatest vigilance and daring was assigned to Craufurd's troops.

Guinaldo, August 18, 1811.

My Dear General,

I heard of the misfortune which occurred to one of your brigades of mules, but I hope it is not so extensive as you imagine. The commissary-general will remedy it. I don't know how they came to pass by St. Martin; and it is still more difficult to account for the surprise of our piquet there. But I understand that the whole party, Germans, English, Spaniards, and muleteers were looking at a procession when the French entered the town.

It is very unfortunate that the cavalry, who I had ordered to Gata, were not sent to that place. If they had been, this misfortune would not have occurred, and I should have known of the enemy's being at Gata sufficiently early to attempt something upon them.

I heard last night (but not from good authority) of a party being collected at Granadilla—probably for another reconnoissance. I am going over to Cesmiro this morning, in order to look at the country on the other side of Ciudad Rodrigo, and I shall not be back till tomorrow; but if anything comes near enough to you to enable you to strike a blow without incurring much risk, I wish you would do it. You see by Grant's account of the 16th how the last reconnoissance got off. I think the next would be directed more towards Escarigo.

It is not impossible that they might wish to open a communication with Ciudad Rodrigo, in which case I mean to assemble the army about Pedro de Toro; and you might collect your divi-

149

sion at once at Zamorra, and be in readiness to fall upon anything, not too large for you, which should attempt to cross the
plain. I consider Monsagro to be a point at which you ought
to have an intelligent officer, who would be able to give you
information of all that passes in the *Sierra* on that side.

Ever yours most sincerely,

Wellington.

About this time many officers and men of the Light Division died,
having brought malignant fever with them from the unhealthy camp
on the Caya in Alemtejo. The division was now reinforced by five
companies of the 3rd battalion of the 95th Rifles, under Lieutenant-
Colonel Barnard. They arrived at Lisbon from Cadiz, and had been
present at the memorable battle of Barossa. Two companies also of the
2nd battalion of the same regiment had been sent from England to
join the Light Division within the last six or eight months, these being
the most effective men that could be collected from a battalion which
went to Walcheren, in 1809, upwards of a thousand strong. Probably
some of these men belonging to the 2nd battalion had been with
Craufurd in his retreat to Vigo, but the faithful "Rifleman Harris" was
not one of them.

Marshal Marmont had assembled his whole army, and was intend-
ing to raise the blockade of Ciudad Rodrigo and to throw into it
a large convoy of provisions. His advanced guard was on the River
Agueda, and some of his cavalry watched the Light Division, which
occupied a very extended line of country behind the Vadillo, a river
flowing into the Agueda, which latter stream separated Craufurd's
troops from the rest of the army, and rendered their position a very
dangerous one. On September 25, some of Wellington's troops were
fiercely engaged in the combat at El Bodon;

> But the Light Division, being at the time on the Vadillo, some
> leagues off, could only hear the distant cannonade, and were
> kept many hours in a state of uncertainty and anxiety, knowing
> that, unless the troops on the left bank of the Agueda were able
> to keep the French in check, they must necessarily be cut off
> from the main body of the army and scramble into the moun-
> tains, at whose base they were in position.

Colonel Leach further says that:

> The same night the Light Division marched from the Vadillo,

and on the 26th, crossing the Agueda by a ford near the mountains, joined the 3rd and 4th Divisions in the position at Guinaldo.

Napier says:

> The Light Division should have marched by Robledo to Guinaldo, and Craufurd received the order at three o'clock, heard the cannonade, and might have reached Guinaldo before midnight; but, fearing a night march, he only moved to Cespedosa, one league from the Vadillo, which river was immediately passed by fifteen hundred French.

Napier adds that the English position at Guinaldo was occupied by only 14,000 men, of which about 2600 were cavalry. General Graham was ten miles distant; the Light Division being at Cespedosa and debarred from the direct route by the ford of Garros, was sixteen miles distant; the 5th Division, posted at Payo in the mountains, was twelve miles distant. Meanwhile Marmont united 60,000 men in front of Guinaldo. Wellington was then dangerously menaced, but he would not abandon the Light Division, which, being intercepted by the French cavalry at Robledo, and compelled to make a circuit, did not arrive until after three o'clock in the evening. Then the danger was over; as Napier remarks:

> Marmont's fortune was fixed in that hour!

Lord Wellington was much annoyed with General Craufurd on this occasion, and to this affair really refer the following remarks in the *Private Journal of F. S. Larpent, Judge-Advocate-General of the British Forces in the Peninsula*:

> On one occasion, near Guinaldo, he (Craufurd) remained across a river by himself, that is, only with his own division, nearly a whole day after he was called in by Lord Wellington. He said he knew he could defend his position. Lord Wellington, when he came back, only said, 'I am glad to see you safe, Craufurd.' The latter said, 'Oh, I was in no danger, I assure you.' 'But I was from your conduct,' said Lord Wellington. Upon which Craufurd observed, 'He is d——d crusty today.'

Mr. George Hooper, in his *Life of Wellington*, and also one or two other writers, have rather absurdly referred this anecdote of Larpent's to the meeting between Wellington and Craufurd after the combat

151

on the Coa. They are manifestly wrong; for, in the first place, Larpent distinctly says that the affair took place near Guinaldo; in the next place, Craufurd knew well that he was in great danger in the battle on the Coa, and was not likely to deny it; and lastly, Wellington himself was personally in *no danger* from Craufurd's fight at the Coa, whereas he was, according to Napier, in the very greatest peril at Guinaldo. If this anecdote is related at all, it might as well be told correctly, and not in such a way as to make both Wellington and Craufurd speak very inappropriately.

From Guinaldo Wellington withdrew his army to Aldea Ponte, except the Light Division and some of the 1st German Hussars, which were left as a rear-guard, and followed the main body of the forces gradually. From Aldea Ponte the army moved to Soita, and there, Wellington gathered together all his troops except the division of General Hill. It was now expected that a great battle would take place; but Marmont, in a few days, withdrew his whole army across the Agueda, and from thence to Salamanca and Placentia. He had been obliged to collect, at great inconvenience, a force vastly superior to that of the allies, particularly in cavalry, and to march a long distance for the purpose of introducing a large convoy of provisions into Ciudad Rodrigo; and by draining Placentia, Salamanca, and other districts of French troops, he afforded an opportunity to the Spaniards of operating on his flanks and rear.

The Light Division, reinforced by some cavalry, now resumed the nominal blockade of Ciudad Rodrigo in concert with Julian Sanchez; and the rest of the army was cantoned on both sides of the Coa, headquarters being fixed at Frenada.

Wellington soon made secret preparations for attacking Ciudad Rodrigo. Napier says:

Almeida was now repaired so far as to resist a sudden attack; and while the recent movement across the Agueda occupied the enemy's attention, the battering-train and siege stores were introduced without notice as an armament for the new works. A trestle-bridge to throw over the Agueda was also secretly prepared in the arsenal of Almeida by Major Sturgeon of the Staff Corps an officer whose brilliant talents, scientific resources, and unmitigated activity continually attracted the attention of the whole army. Thus, the preparations for the attack of Ciudad Rodrigo advanced, while the English general seemed to be only intent upon defending his own positions.

At the beginning of January, 1812, the favourable moment for action, so long watched for by Wellington, came at last. An imperial decree had again remodelled the French armies, which were much reduced in numbers in the Peninsula. The Imperial Guards, 17,000 strong, marched to France in December 1811, being required for the Russian war. Altogether, not less than 40,000 of the best soldiers were withdrawn, and the maimed and worn-out men being sent to France at the same time, the force in the Peninsula was diminished by 60,000 men.

On January 1, 1812) General Craufurd wrote to his wife one of the last letters that he was destined to write; for he received his mortal wound on the 19th of the same month. At this period, he seems to have been troubled by some pecuniary difficulty, and also to have been much longing for reunion with his wife and children. He writes thus:

> There is such a sameness in our life here, and such a uniformity in my feelings and state of mind, and such a settled desire of getting out of this horrid scrape that I am entangled in, that at the end of each week I have only to repeat what I told you at the beginning of it.

He also says:

> I cannot say that Lord Wellington and I are quite so cordial as we used to be. He was nettled at a report which I made of the wants of the division.

General Craufurd also says that he hopes to be reunited to his wife by the end of the year. Perhaps she might have again gone out to him in the Peninsula; or he might have gone home again on leave; but I think it is quite certain that he never could have left the army for any great length of time whilst the war lasted. Even if he had retired from the army altogether, he would inevitably have returned to it before very long; and Lord Wellington knew his merits too well to feel the least hesitation as to giving him a warm welcome again. However, after the fall of Ciudad Rodrigo, the war became so exciting that Craufurd would have been very unlikely to retire.

For the enterprise against Ciudad Rodrigo Wellington had altogether 35,000 men, including cavalry. Napier tells us that:

> Seventy pieces of ordnance had been collected, but from the scarcity of transports only thirty-eight guns could be brought

153

to the trenches; and these would have wanted their due supply of ammunition, if eight thousand shot had not been found amidst the ruins of Almeida.

A pontoon bridge had been thrown across the river some distance below the town. The divisions were to relieve each other in the trenches every twenty-four hours, the frost being very severe. On January 8th, the Light Division marched before break of day and forded the River Agueda. On some rising ground stood the redoubt of San Francisco, which it was necessary to take before operations could be commenced against the town. At nine o'clock at night 300 men belonging to the 43rd, 52nd, 95th, and the 3rd Portuguese Caçadores, under the command of Colonel Colborne, of the 52nd, stormed and carried it. Colonel Leach also tells us that:

All the French troops in the fort, amounting to about seventy men and three officers, were either made prisoners or bayonetted in the assault. Strong working parties immediately commenced the first parallel on the heights where the redoubt stood; and as the garrison kept up an extremely heavy fire, both of shot and shells, without intermission throughout the night, our men worked like rabbits, and before daybreak we were tolerably well covered in the trenches.

Sir William Napier says that:

The siege was advanced several days by this well managed assault.

Colonel Leach further informs us that:

The 1st Division relieved the Light Division on the 9th; and the French being able to overlook us from the top of the cathedral tower, and to see the troops as they arrived to relieve each other, always took that opportunity, when the trenches were crowded with double numbers, to open every gun and mortar which could possibly be brought to bear, and kept up as dreadful a fire of shot and shells as men were ever exposed to. General Craufurd's horse was killed under him by a round shot. Having been relieved by the 1st Division, we went through the freezing operation of fording the Agueda, and returned to our villages late at night, the being some leagues distant from the fortress.

154

Concerning further operations, Napier writes:

> On the 12th the Light Division resumed work; the Riflemen,
> profiting from a thick fog, covered themselves in pits which
> they digged in front of the trenches, and from thence picked
> off the enemy's gunners; yet the weather was so cold, and the
> besieged shot so briskly that little progress was made. On the
> 13th the same causes impeded the labourers of the 1st Division.
> Scarcity of transport also balked the operations. One third only
> of the native carts had arrived, and the drivers of those present
> were very indolent; much of the twenty-four pound ammu-
> nition was still at Villa de Ponte, and intelligence arrived that
> Marmont was collecting his forces to succour the place.
>
> In this difficulty it was resolved to hasten the siege by opening
> a breach with the counter-batteries, which were not quite six
> hundred yards from the curtain, and then to storm the place
> without blowing in the counterscarp; in other words, to over-
> step the rules of science, and sacrifice life rather than time; for
> the capricious Agueda might in one night flood, and enable a
> small French force to relieve the place. The whole army was
> therefore brought up from the distant quarters and posted in the
> villages on the Coa, ready to cross the Agueda and give battle.

On the night of the 13th a convent in the suburbs, in which the
French had three pieces of artillery which enfiladed the trenches, was
stormed and carried with great bravery by some troops of the German Legion belonging to the 1st Division. On the following day the
40th Regiment assailed most gallantly another convent in the suburbs;
and at four o'clock the same afternoon our batteries opened on the
town for the first time. The 3rd Division was in the trenches on the
15th, and the firing from both parties was kept up with great fury.

The Light Division took their turn in the trenches on the 15th,
and Napier tells us that:

> The ramparts were again battered and fell so fast that it was
> judged expedient to commence the small breach at the turret;
> therefore, in the night five more guns were mounted. At day-
> light the besiegers' batteries recommenced, but at eight o'clock
> a thick fog compelled them to desist; nevertheless, the small
> breach had been opened, and the place was summoned, but
> without effect. At night the parallel on the lower Teson was ex-
> tended, and a sharp musketry was directed from thence against

the great breach; the breaching-battery as originally projected was also commenced, and the Riflemen of the Light Division continued from their pits to pick off the enemy's gunners.

On the 17th, the fire on both sides was very heavy, and on the 18th two breaches in the walls having been reported practicable, the 3rd and Light Divisions were ordered to arrive on the ground on the 19th, and to storm the town that night.

The general plan of the attack was as follows: the 3rd Division was to storm the large breach, and the Light Division the smaller one, whilst General Pack's Portuguese Brigade was to make a false attack at a different point. Wellington ended his order for the assault with this sentence, "Ciudad Rodrigo *must* be stormed this evening," and his troops responded nobly to the demand made upon them. The Light Division, as usual, displayed surpassing heroism; and its trusted leader sacrificed his life from his ardent desire to see that the designs of his commander-in-chief were thoroughly carried out.

The storming party of the Light Division was commanded by Major George Napier, an officer of whom General Craufurd always held a very high opinion. In his *Early Military Life*, Sir George Napier writes as follows concerning the storming of Ciudad Rodrigo:

> The next day, as I thought from all I saw and heard from the Engineers that ere long the breaches would be practicable, I went to General Craufurd, and asked him as a favour that he would allow me to command the storming party of the Light Division, whenever the commander-in-chief determined on making the assault. This he promised; and on January 19, 1812, we received orders to move from our cantonments and march to the trenches.
>
> About a mile from the town we halted, and General Craufurd desired me to get one hundred volunteers from each British regiment in the division, with proportionate officers and non-commissioned officers, to form them up in front of the division, and take the command of them in order to lead the assault. I went to the three regiments, *viz.* the 43rd, 52nd, and Rifle Corps, and said, 'Soldiers, I have the honour to be appointed to the command of the storming party which is to lead the Light Division to the assault of the small breach. I want one hundred volunteers from each regiment; those who will go with me come forward.' Instantly there rushed out nearly half the divi-

sion, and we were obliged to take them at chance.

I may add that Sir George Napier lost an arm on this occasion, that he did his work most admirably, and amply justified his general's selection of him for the important position assigned to him. Probably no family in the whole world ever gave to any division at the same time three such splendid soldiers as the brothers, Charles, William, and George Napier.

Edward Costello, a non-commissioned officer of the 95th Rifles, writes thus in his *Adventures of a Soldier*, concerning the party forming the Forlorn Hope:

> General Craufurd, who led us in person, while we stood formed under the wall, addressed us upon the nature of the duty assigned us. It was the last enterprise his gallant spirit was ever destined to direct. On this memorable occasion his voice was more than ordinarily clear and distinct.
>
> ★★★★★★
>
> Note:—I have heard through several old soldiers of this war one having been in a different division that Craufurd's voice was singularly clear, and that it could be heard distinctly even amidst the din of battle.
>
> ★★★★★★
>
> His words sank deep in my memory; and although the shock of many a battle has rolled over my grey locks since that period, I remember some of his language as follows: 'Soldiers, the eyes of your country are upon you. Be steady, be cool, be firm in the assault. The town must be yours this night. Once masters of the wall, let your first duty be to clear the ramparts, and in doing this keep together.

Costello also adds:

> General Craufurd calling out, 'Now, lads, for the breach,' led the way.

This same writer informs us that Craufurd was "beloved by the men." *They* at all events believed in him, though many of his officers disliked him. The soldiers of the Light Division were always ready to follow their trusted leader; so that a military historian wrote of them on this occasion:

> The men, true to Craufurd's orders, cleared the ramparts.

The time taken in the storming of Ciudad Rodrigo seems marvellously short. Colonel Leach says:

> At eight o'clock at night the assault was given, and in less than half an hour both the breaches were carried, after a severe struggle, during which the assailants were exposed to a most destructive fire of musketry and grape, hand-grenades, etc.

Sir William Napier thus describes the part performed by the Light Division on this momentous occasion:

> On the left the stormers of the Light Division, who had three hundred yards of ground to clear, would not wait for the hay-bags, but with extraordinary swiftness, running to the crest of the glacis, jumped down the scarp, a depth of eleven feet, and rushed up the *fausse braie* under a smashing discharge of grape and musketry. The ditch was dark and intricate; the forlorn hope inclined towards the left; the stormers went straight to the breach, which was so narrow at the top that a gun placed across nearly barred the opening.
>
> There they were joined by the forlorn hope, and the whole body rushed up; but the head of the mass, crushed together as the ascent narrowed, staggered under the fire, and, with the instinct of self-preservation, snapped their own muskets, though they had not been allowed to load. Major Napier, struck by a grape-shot, fell at this moment with a shattered arm, but he called aloud on his men to use their bayonets, and all the unwounded officers simultaneously sprang to the front; thus, the required impulse was given, and with a furious shout the breach was carried. Then the supporting regiments, coming up in sections abreast, gained the rampart; the 52nd wheeled to the left, the 43rd to the right, and the place was won.

Napier adds:

> During this contest, which lasted only a few minutes on the breach, the righting at the great breach had continued with unabated violence; but when the stormers and the 43rd came pouring along the rampart towards that quarter, the French wavered; three of their expense magazines exploded at the same moment; and then the 3rd Division, with a mighty effort, broke through the retrenchments. The garrison fought indeed for a moment in the streets, yet finally fled to the castle where Lieu-

tenant Gurwood, who, though severely wounded in the head, had entered amongst the foremost at the lesser breach, received the governor's sword.

Three hundred French had fallen, fifteen hundred were made prisoners, and the immense stores of ammunition, with one hundred and fifty pieces of artillery, including the battering-train of Marmont's army, were captured. The allies lost twelve hundred men and ninety officers in the siege, of which six hundred and fifty men and sixty officers were slain or hurt at the breaches. Generals Craufurd and Mackinnon, the former a person of great ability, were killed, and with them died many gallant men.

Napier's account of Craufurd's services on this occasion is singularly meagre, being nothing more than the passage last quoted. But fortunately, I am able to give much ampler details furnished by the one person in the world most able to give them; I mean the late General Sir James Shaw Kennedy, who was then acting as *aide-de-camp* to the leader of the Light Division.

In the year 1861 General Sir James Shaw Kennedy sent a long letter about General Craufurd's death to the present Sir William Augustus Fraser, who, though not descended from the leader of the Light Division, is a great-nephew of his by maternal descent. Sir William Fraser has published a great portion of this interesting letter in a volume of verses called *Coila's Whispers*; but as this work is very little known to the world in general, I will here give a few extracts, referring my readers to the book itself for fuller information. I may as well state that a copy of Sir James Shaw Kennedy's letter was sent, by the wish of the writer, to my uncle, the late Mr. Robert Craufurd (second son of the general), and so I had the advantage of reading the whole letter before it appeared in *Coila's Whispers*; and my uncle's representative was desirous that the whole letter should appear in this memoir.

After describing the general arrangements for the assault of Ciudad Rodrigo, the letter goes on to say:

While the columns, as above described, advanced to the assault, General Craufurd, keeping to the left of the columns, proceeded directly to the crest of the glacis, about sixty yards to the left of where the columns entered the ditch; and from this spot, at the highest pitch of his voice, continued giving instructions to the column. This brought upon him an intense fire of musketry from the opposite parapets of the *fausse braie* and ramparts, and at a very short distance; for the ditch of the *fausse braie* was very narrow, and even the main ditch was very narrow, and the place had no covered way.

He was thus exposed to a double fire of infantry at a very short distance; the superior slope of the parapet of the *fausse braie* being in the same line as the slope of the glacis, he could not remain many minutes where he was without being hit. Accordingly, he was struck by a musket ball, which passed through his arm, broke through the ribs, passed through part of the lungs, and lodged in or at the spine; and he not only fell, but the shock was so great that, on falling, he rolled over down the glacis.

His *aide-de-camp* then further tells us that there was no one even near them, and that he:

. . . . half dragged and half carried him to where there was an inequality of ground in which he was out of the direct fire from the place.

General Craufurd then thought that he was actually dying, and he begged Shaw Kennedy to say to his wife that he was "quite sure that they would meet in heaven."

The *aide-de-camp* also says:

By accident I met Lord Wellington at the Salamanca gate on the morning of the 20th, and he asked most anxiously for Craufurd. I gave him an unfavourable report of his state. His Lordship called afterwards and saw Craufurd, and they conversed together for some time. Craufurd congratulated Lord Wellington on the great advantage he had gained by taking Ciudad Rodrigo; to which his Lordship replied something in these words, 'Yes, a great blow, a great blow indeed.'

★★★★★★

Note:—I imagine that Wellington was really thinking at this time of Craufurd's imminent death, which the commander-in-chief regarded as "a great blow," whatever others may have considered it. A short extract from one of Craufurd's own letters disproves the assertion that he and Wellington were *never* very cordial or friendly with each other.

★★★★★★

After having written the long letter concerning the death of his old leader in answer to Sir William Fraser, Sir James Shaw Kennedy wrote a shorter letter to my uncle, Mr. Robert Craufurd, in which he says:

> The part of my (former) letter describing the circumstances of your father's death which will probably attract your special attention, are the expressions which he used in regard to your mother immediately after he was wounded, and when he thought himself just dying. Those expressions were the genuine impulses of his mind when under the impression that he was almost instantly to quit this life, and proved to me his deep feeling of affection for your mother; they also proved a truly deep-seated religious conviction. He lived for upwards of four days afterwards; but during the whole of that time had hopes of surviving his wounds, so that what he said was not so striking to my mind. What communications were made to his family I know not, as all that was arranged by Sir Charles Stewart, (Adjutant-General to Lord Wellington's army, and afterwards Marquis of Londonderry), with whom your father was so intimate that they always addressed each other as Robert and Charles.

Even amidst the great sufferings of his last hours Craufurd still felt the keenest sympathy with the officers and men of his beloved division. Major George Napier, being wounded, was in the same house, in a room below that occupied by his dying leader; and he tells us that General Craufurd sent almost hourly messages down to him, to know how he was, and to express his approval of his conduct and his regret that he should never see him again.

The storming of Ciudad Rodrigo, so glorious to the British troops, unfortunately terminated in frightful lawlessness and excesses. Sir William Napier says:

> The town was fired in three or four places; the soldiers menaced their officers and shot each other; many were killed in the market-place; intoxication soon increased the tumult, and at last, the fury rising to absolute madness, a fire was wilfully lighted in the middle of the great magazine, by which the town would have been blown to atoms but for the energetic courage of some officers and a few soldiers who still preserved their senses.

Napier adds that the excuse that:

> The soldiers were not to be controlled will not suffice.

Colonel Macleod, of the 43rd, a young man of a most energetic spirit, placed guards at the breach, and constrained his regiment to keep its ranks for a long time after the disorders commenced; but as no previous general measures had been taken, and no organised efforts made by higher authorities, the men were finally carried away in the increasing tumult.

As regards the men of the Light Division, Craufurd had probably reckoned on being with them personally to keep them in order. The extreme severity with which he punished stealing amongst his men shows plainly that he would have taken the very strongest measures to repress the much worse offences committed on this occasion. Some have endeavoured to make excuses for the odious crimes committed by our soldiers at Ciudad Rodrigo and afterwards at Badajoz. But great officers, such as William Napier or Robert Craufurd, never did this. They well knew that the most sincere regard and affection for the men are quite consistent with the very firmest determination to prevent them from behaving cruelly and vilely.

Those who love English soldiers the best are naturally the most unwilling to pay them the very bad compliment of declaring or insinuating that their natures are so debased and brutal that they cannot help acting like wild beasts, when once their passions are roused. When properly taught and managed, I believe that the British soldier is genuinely capable of displaying every form of magnanimity, not only that comparatively lower form of it involved in "taking a city," but also that more difficult form involved in "ruling his spirit" in hours of sorest trial and supreme temptation.

That the soldier often has in him the elements of moral and spiritual as well as of military glory and greatness is, I think, made clearly manifest by our long annals of heroic self-sacrifice amongst the men of our armies. The marvellous discipline and sublime self-abnegation of the soldiers on the ill-fated ship *Birkenhead* show plainly enough that it is not in vain to appeal to the very noblest and most profoundly human feelings as existing in the breast of the ignorant common soldier.

CHAPTER 7

Craufurd's Funeral

Sir William Fraser, in his *Words on Wellington*, gives us the following interesting information:

One of the most striking pictures I have ever seen was shown many years ago at the Gallery of Illustration. Among a series of dissolving views was one of Wellington standing alone before the High Altar in the cathedral of Ciudad Rodrigo, looking at the coffin of General Craufurd, which was placed on a bier immediately in front of it.

The same writer also says:

General Craufurd was buried in the breach which he had taken, and the bastion bears the name of 'Craufurd's bastion.'

A former well-known chaplain-general to the army, the Rev. G. R. Gleig (author of *The Subaltern*, republished by Leonaur), wrote a very interesting account of Craufurd's funeral in a magazine called the *Gem* in the year 1829. This narrative has been reprinted for private circulation only, and is scarcely at all known by the public. I will therefore print it in this volume, as it gives a perfectly impartial account of the feelings evoked amongst the army in general by Craufurd's premature death. Of course, Mr. Gleig was a very young man when he went out to the Light Division; but he was an acute observer, and his impressions are of some permanent value to any who wish to form a true estimate of a famous leader concerning whom the most opposite opinions have been held by those who knew him.

Mr. Gleig's narrative a somewhat long one is as follows:

It was on a cold rainy afternoon, towards the end of January,

1812, that the little party, of which I was at the head, arrived at the seat of war, and took up its abode in one of the detached cottages which at that time gave shelter to the Light Division. We had landed at Lisbon early in the month, where, upon one pretence or another, we were detained for nearly a fortnight; and we had traversed the country between the capital and the frontier by forced marches; but all our diligence failed in enabling us to reach headquarters in sufficient time to take part in the toils and dangers to which our comrades were immediately exposed. The fortress of Ciudad Rodrigo, of the investment of which we had been aware, was already reduced; and the army was preparing, as men generally believed, to take up once more its line on the Coa. This was abundantly mortifying to an individual like myself, who had not yet seen a shot fired in earnest, and who, at the commencement of his career, experienced an extreme desire to signalise his valour; but the accidents which stood in the way of this laudable inclination were, as I well knew, unavoidable; and I found comfort in the reflection that, in all human probability, the period was not very remote when other and no less favourable opportunities of winning a mural crown would be presented.

I reached the hamlet in which our division was cantoned just four days after the place had been carried by storm, and the scene which met me there was of no ordinary character. Crowded into a few scattered cottages, the soldiers, though destitute of all that the world calls comfort, appeared to enjoy admirable health and the highest spirits. As might be expected, the events of the late siege, and, above air, of its perilous conclusion, formed in every circle the sole topic of conversation, whilst articles of plunder were everywhere offered for sale, and bargains the most absurd, and purchases the most grotesque, were everywhere in progress.

Mingled with this general appearance of hilarity, however, might be discerned here and there signs of the deepest grief, where individuals had lost a friend, and messes a favourite member; and, above all, the name of Craufurd was heard, coupled, as often as it was pronounced, with expressions of the most profound reverence and poignant sorrow. It is needless for me to remind you that the gallant officer in question had long commanded the division, by whom he was regarded, in

164

point of intelligence and military skill, as second only to Lord Wellington, or that his unremitting attention to the wants of the troops secured for him to the full as much of their love as of their respect.

I will not waste time by describing to you the manner in which I was received by my companions in arms, or by giving any outline of the conversation which drew us on from hour to hour in continuation of our vigils. You can easily guess that that was not the least agreeable night of my military life, and that the necessity of causing our mattresses to be spread was not alluded to till the last cup of wine left in the *boraccio* had been drained. But the wine was at length expended; hints were dropped of an early parade on the morrow; and we finally separated with a firm determination of bringing to a close, in the evening after, a conference thus prematurely interrupted.

Whether the fatigues of yesterday's march told heavily upon me, or the wine which I had swallowed overnight acted as a narcotic, I cannot tell; but when I awoke next morning, I found myself alone in the chamber. My comrades had both risen, and were gone abroad; and though I felt that they acted kindly in not disturbing my slumbers, I was nevertheless chagrined at the idea that, on the very first morning of my arrival at headquarters, I should appear slothful. I accordingly arose in all haste, and went to the window.

The sky was clear and bright, and the rain of the preceding day having been succeeded by a bracing frost, everything around wore an aspect widely different from that which it presented when, weary and half famished, and shivering in my saturated garments, I first arrived at my present habitation. The roads, which then wore the appearance of mere tracks across a marsh, were now hard and firm; and the face of the country, though in general bleak and desolate enough, was at least less bleak and desolate than it seemed to be when examined through the veil of a heavy and unintermitting shower.

I saw, too, for the first time, that the brigade to which I was attached inhabited about half-a-dozen hovels scattered at some distance the one from the other, on the north side of the Agueda; and I beheld that romantic stream rolling in all the majesty of a swollen torrent, and chafing against the rough and precipitous rocks which formed its banks. Directly opposite to me stood the town of Ciudad Rodrigo, placed upon one of the three hills which alone break in upon the sameness of the plain, standing even in its ruins with an air of singular majesty above the widely-extended flat which on all sides begirt it. But the object which most forcibly attracted my attention was the parade of the several corps of the division, which were already beginning to assemble. I knew not for what purpose this muster was going on; my fertile imagination readily conjured up a picture of advancing columns of the enemy, and a threatened engagement; so, I made all haste possible in completing my toilet, and hurried forth to take my station.

On reaching the parade ground, I heard that this was the day appointed for the funeral of General Craufurd, and that the whole of his division had been commanded to pay the last tribute of respect to his much-honoured remains. The individual who communicated to me this fact had been his *aide-de-camp*, and as he happened to be an old acquaintance of my own, he very readily complied with my entreaty to be made acquainted with all the circumstances which attended the death of his lamented chief. It appeared that General Craufurd's Division having been appointed to storm the smaller breach, formed by the fall of a round tower, opposite to the convent of San Francisco, advanced at the appointed hour under its gallant leader, and made good with, comparatively speaking, little loss, a lodgement on the summit of the rampart.

Among the number of those, however, whose career of glory was then cut short, poor Craufurd himself happened to be included. He was at the head of the column, (considerably in advance of it, standing on the crest of the glacis, with his *aide-de-camp* only), at once directing and animating his people, when a musket ball took his left arm, and, penetrating into the side, lodged in his lungs. For a moment he struggled, as it were, with the weakness of humanity, and strove to head his brave followers as he had hitherto done, but the effort was fruitless. He failed, and fell back into the arms of one of the soldiers. He was instantly carried to the rear, where the medical attendants bled him twice, and he appeared to derive benefit from the operation.

In the meanwhile, the contest was going on with great obstinacy, and my informant could not, of course, abandon it; but as soon as the town was carried, and everything like fighting ceased, he hurried off to attend the general. The latter was then in a heavy, death-like slumber, into which, soon after the bleeding, he had fallen, and from which he did not awake till long after dawn on the 20th. But he awoke with no favourable symptoms about him; and it soon became evident, as well to the surgeons as to his friends who watched beside his pallet, that all hope of recovery was futile.

I have reason to believe that General Craufurd himself, from the instant of receiving his wound, never entertained an idea of recovery. On the contrary, when General Stewart, (adjutant-general of the army, and afterwards Marquis of Londonderry), who remained with him like a brother, and his other attendants would have flattered him by talking of future operations, he only shook his head and replied in a feeble voice that his futurity, at least upon earth, would be of short duration; and so, it proved to be. Little change took place during the 21st and 22nd; he suffered both then and previously internal agony; but on the 23rd the pain abated, and his anxious friends fondly persuaded themselves that this was a symptom of the recovery for which they wished rather than hoped.

The case was widely different; he spoke, indeed, from that moment with greater composure and apparent ease; but his conversation was now, what it had ever been, even during the paroxysms of his sufferings, of his wife and children. He repeatedly entreated his *aide-de-camp* to inform his wife that he was sure they would meet in heaven,' and that there was a Providence over all, which never yet forsook and never would forsake the soldier's widow and orphans. Thus, passed the moments till about two o'clock in the morning of the 24th, when, for the first time since the night of the 19th, he fell into a slumber. From that slumber he never awoke, but, like an infant at the breast of its mother, he dozed calmly and beautifully into eternity.

I have said that among the generals of division and brigade in the army, none were more beloved or more respected by the officers and men placed immediately under their command than General Craufurd. In saying this I did but meagre justice either to his merits or to the good sense and correct judgment of the army at large. Of the place which he held in the estimation of the commander-in-chief it will be unnecessary to speak, when

I mention that to Craufurd, though only a brigadier-general, (this is a mistake; Craufurd became a major-general on June 4, 1811), was entrusted the guidance of a division more than all the rest requiring at its head an officer of activity of body and intelligence of mind. Craufurd on every occasion commanded the advance of the army in pursuits, its rear-guard in retreats, its outposts when in position, and its detached corps when such by any chance was needed; nor in any of these situations did he ever fail to earn the decided approbation of Lord Wellington.

This was known throughout the army; and the man himself was in consequence regarded as one of those who, should circumstances ever place him in a situation of distinct responsibility and trust, would unquestionably add to the renown which the British troops had already acquired. Under these circumstances it was to be expected that the deepest sorrow would everywhere be felt, when his premature death came to be known; and it was determined, in order to mark the sense entertained of his extraordinary merits as an officer and a man, that a sort of public funeral should be given to him.

I need not remind you that, when a man dies as poor Craufurd died, nobody dreams of keeping the corpse, for form's sake, any longer than the arrangements deemed necessary for its interment may require. As soon as the fatal issue of his illness became apparent, directions were given to the artificers to prepare his coffin, and he was laid in that, his last bed, on the evening of the same day on which his heroic spirit quitted the body. In the meanwhile, orders were issued directing the forms to be used in committing the sacred burthen to the earth; and it was in obedience to these orders that his own favourite division appeared this morning under arms.

Having advanced to the house where his mortal remains slumbered, the division proceeded on with arms reversed, between a double row of soldiers of the 5th Division, who, with their muskets likewise pointing to the ground, lined the road on each side. This done, so as that the rearmost company of the division should line with the house itself, the troops halted till the coffin, borne by six sergeant-majors, and having six field-officers as supporters, came forth.

The word was given to march, the several bands striking up slow and mournful airs, and the coffin was followed first by

General Stewart and the *aide-de-camp* of the deceased, as chief mourners, and then by Lord Wellington, General Castanos, Marshal Beresford, and a long train of staff and general officers. In this manner we proceeded along the road till we gained the very breach in assaulting which the brave subject of our procession met his fate, where we found that a grave had been dug for him, and that he was destined to sleep, till the last trumpet should rouse him, on the spot where his career of earthly glory had come to a close.

Never have I beheld a more striking or melancholy spectacle. The regiments being formed into close columns of battalions, took post as best they could about the grave, towards which the coffin, headed by a chaplain, advanced. At this moment the military music ceased, and no sound could be heard except the voice of the clergyman, who faltered forth rather than read the solemn declaration, '*I am the resurrection and the life.*' Arrived at the brink of the sepulchre, the procession paused, and the shell was rested upon the ground; and then I could distinctly perceive that, among the six rugged veterans who had borne it, there was not a dry eye, and that even of the privates who looked on there were few who manifested not signs of sorrow such as men are accustomed to exhibit only when they lose a parent or a child.

★★★★★★

Note:—This plain statement of facts observed by Mr. Gleig, together with the ringing cheers with which Craufurd was received on returning to his division at Fuentes d'Onoro, must suffice to confute those who have asserted that he was not loved by the men under his command.

★★★★★★

The few striking sentences having been read which that most affecting of all rituals, the funeral service of the Church of England, requires, the body was lowered into the grave, and dust was committed to dust and ashes to ashes. This part of the ceremony being concluded, there followed that salute, both of artillery and musketry, which the rank of the deceased required; and then the corps, being once more formed into marching order, filed back to their several cantonments. But the scene of deep melancholy which pervaded every breast during the continuance of the ceremony, could not wholly evaporate as soon as the ceremony itself came to a close. Even I, to whom the merits of the deceased were only known by common report, could not all at once shake off the painful impression which a contemplation of the real grief of others had produced; and as I perceived no one to be more light-hearted than myself among all my acquaintances, I found no inducement to follow up the schemes of amusement which I had chalked out for myself during the preceding evening.

It had been determined that several of my friends should initiate me into the mysteries of warfare, by guiding me this day through the town and fortress of Rodrigo; but the business of the morning was of a nature well calculated to strike at the root of all merely pleasurable arrangements; and the appointments into which each and all had, with so much eagerness, entered only a few hours before, were either forgotten or disregarded. Instead of visiting the town, we wandered about in little groups of two and three, during the remainder of the day, some in the immediate vicinity of their quarters, others along the margin of the Agueda; and we retired to our several billets in the evening, as melancholy and dejected as if each were mourning the loss of some much-loved relative.

Here Mr. Gleig's interesting narrative ends. On January 29, 1812, Wellington writes thus concerning Craufurd's death to the Earl of Liverpool, Secretary of State:

Major-General Craufurd died on the 24th instant, of the wounds which he received on the 19th, while leading the Light Division of this army to the assault of Ciudad Rodrigo. Although the conduct of Major-General Craufurd on the occasion on which these wounds were received, and the circumstances which occurred, have excited the admiration of every officer in the army, I cannot report his death to your lordship without expressing my sorrow and regret that His Majesty has been deprived of the services, and I of the assistance, of an officer of tried talents and experience, who was an ornament to his profession, and was calculated to render the most important services to his country.

Craufurd's experience was certainly great, for he entered the army when Wellington was only ten years old.

The following letter concerning Craufurd's death was written by

the adjutant-general, Charles Stewart, afterwards Marquis of Londonderry, to General Charles Craufurd, an elder brother of the leader of
the Light Division.

A.G.O., Gallegos, January 26, 1812.

My Dear Friend,

I have to entreat you to summon to your aid all that resignation
to the will of heaven, and manly fortitude, which I know you
to possess, to bear with composure the sad tidings this letter is
doomed to convey. I think you must have discovered that, from
the first moment, I did not encourage sanguine hopes of your
beloved brother, whose loss we have, alas! now to deplore. But,
my dear friend, as we all must pass through this transitory existence sooner or later, to be translated to a better, surely there is
no mode of terminating life equal to that which Providence
ordained should be his.

Like Nelson, Abercromby, Moore, and inferior to none (if his
sphere had been equally extensive), your much-loved brother
fell; the shouts of victory were the last he heard from the gallant
troops he led; and his last moments were full of anxiety as to the
events of the army, and consideration for his Light Division. If
his friends permit themselves to give way to unbounded grief
under this heavy calamity, they are considering themselves rather than the departed hero. The army and his country have the
most reason to deplore his loss; for, as his military talents were
of the first calibre, so was his spirit of the most intrepid gallantry.
There is but one universal sentiment throughout all ranks of
the profession on this subject; and if you and those who loved
him dearly (amongst whom, God knows,, I pity most his angel
wife and children) could but have witnessed the manner in
which the last duties were paid to his memory by the whole
army, your tears would have been arrested by the contemplation of what his merits must have been to have secured such a
general sensation, and they would have ceased to flow, from the
feelings of envy which such an end irresistibly excited.

As I fervently trust that, by the time you receive this letter, you
may be so far prepared for this afflicting stroke as to derive
consolation even from sad details, and as I really am unequal to
address Mrs. Craufurd at present, I think it best to enter at large
into everything with you, leaving it to your affectionate and

prudent judgment to unfold events by degrees in the manner you deem best.

You will perceive by Staff-Surgeon Gunning's report (Lord Wellington's own surgeon) upon an examination of the wound (which I enclose) that, from the nature of it, it was impossible Robert should have recovered. The direction the ball had taken, the extreme difficulty of breathing, and the blood he brought up, gave great grounds for alarm; but still it was conceived the ball might have dropped lower than the lung; and as there have been instances of recovery from wounds in the same place, we were suffered to entertain a *hope*, but alas! that was all. Staff-Surgeons Robb and Gunning, who were his constant attendants, and from whose anxiety, zeal, and professional ability everything was to be expected, were unremitting in their attentions. His *aides-de-camp*, young Wood and Lieutenant Shaw of the 43rd, showed all that affectionate attention which even his own family could have done to him; the former, I must say, evinced a feeling as honourable to his heart as it must have been gratifying to its object. To these I must add Captain William Campbell, whose long friendship for Robert induced him never to leave him; and he manifested in an extraordinary manner his attachment on this occasion. If my own duties had permitted me, you may believe I never should have absented myself from his bedside; as it was, feeling like a brother towards him my heart led me to act as such to the utmost of my poor abilities.

The three officers I have above named, and his surgeon, alternately watched and attended him from the evening of the 19th until ten o'clock on the morning of the 24th, when he breathed his last. On the 22nd he was considered easier and better; the medicines administered had all the effects desired. He conversed some time with me, principally about the assault, and he was most anxious as to news of the enemy. He was so cheerful that his mind did not revert, as it had done before, to his wife and children; and I was anxious to keep any subject from him that might awaken keen sensations.

I knew well, from many conversations I have had with him, the unbounded influence and affection Mrs. Craufurd's idea was attended with, and his ardent anxiety as to the education and bringing up of his children. These thoughts I was anxious, while a ray of hope existed, not to awaken, it being of the utmost consequence that he should be kept free from agitation; and I trust this will be a sufficient reason to Mrs. Craufurd and yourself for my being unable to give you those last sentiments of his heart which he no doubt would have expressed, had we felt authorised to acquaint him that he was so near his end.

I do not mean to say that he was ignorant of his situation; for when he first sent to me, he said he felt his wound was mortal, and that he was fully prepared for the will of Heaven; but I think subsequently he cherished hopes. At two o'clock in the morning William Campbell wrote me a most cheering account of him. He had been talking of his recovery and every pleasing prospect; and he fell into a comfortable sleep, as those about him imagined; but alas! from that sleep he never woke again. His pulse gradually ceased to beat, his breath grew shorter, and his spirit fled, before those near him were conscious he was no more. So easy was his passport to heaven! If, in detailing so mournful a recital, I can derive the smallest consolation, it arises from knowing his last words united his affection for his wife and his friendship for me in one train of thought, in which he closed his eyes.

Having thus acquainted you, as well as my present feelings enable me, with the last scene, I shall now assure you that no exertion was wanting to prepare everything for the mournful ceremony that was to follow, with the utmost possible regard and respect to his memory. Lord Wellington decided he should be interred by his own division near the breach which he had so gallantly carried. The Light Division assembled before his house, in the suburbs of the San Francisco Convent, at 12 o'clock on the 25th; the 5th Division lined the road from his quarters to the breach; the officers' of the Brigade of Guards, cavalry, 3rd, 4th, and 5th Divisions, together with General Castanos and all his Staff, Marshal Beresford and all the Portuguese, Lord Wellington and the whole of headquarters moved in the mournful procession.

He was borne to his place of rest on the shoulders of the brave lads he had led on; the field officers of the Light Division officiated as pallbearers; and the whole ceremony was conducted in the most gratifying manner, if I may be permitted such an epithet on such a heart-breaking occasion. I assigned to myself the mournful task of being chief mourner; and I was attended by Captain Campbell, Lieutenants Wood and Shaw, and the Staff of the Light Division. Care has been taken that his gallant remains can never be disturbed, and he lies where posterity will commemorate his deeds!

All his worldly affairs here I shall not neglect; his papers, writing-case, books, etc., and everything which I conceive may be in the least gratifying as remembrances, or important, shall be carefully sealed, packed up, and sent by one of his most confidential servants to London as soon as possible. His horses and campaign furniture of every description shall be disposed of by public auction, to the best advantage, as is usual in similar cases. An exact inventory of the whole shall be taken and forwarded; any demands that may be against him shall be liquidated, and his servants paid and discharged; and the paymaster-general's account, and the whole of the above, shall be remitted in proper form without delay to you. Lord Wellington has declared his intention of writing to Mr. Perceval very strongly to do everything possible for Mrs. Craufurd and his children, and to commemorate his memory as he so nobly deserves; and I entertain a perfect confidence that the most gratifying arrangements will be made on this head.

Alas! my dear friend, of our small party of five who were headed by you, and first knew each other in '96, how many are gone, and how cruelly have others suffered, poor Anstruther, and Robert, and yourself who have gone through so much! Proby and myself alone remain; and while we lament over our two invaluable lost friends, the conviction of their merits and the force of their example should never be absent from our thoughts. I hope you know me sufficiently to believe what I must suffer on the present occasion. If I have been silent as to myself, it is because I will not intrude my own affliction on those so heavily borne down. But where shall I find so inestimable a friend again? Excuse me, my dearest friend, I will not now add to this, but will write again shortly, when we shall all be more composed.

Believe me as ever,
Your most affectionate and ever obliged,
Charles Stewart.

I have often heard that Lord Londonderry had many faults; but he was a most gallant soldier, and I think that this letter plainly shows that his heart was a singularly warm one. Later on, he poured forth another eloquent lament over Robert Craufurd in his narrative of the Peninsular War. It seems to me that many of the distinguished soldiers of those days had far keener and warmer affections than most people have in our days, though very probably their language and their morals were less conventionally correct. In almost every age of the world conventionalism has been a foe to friendships of the old heroic sort.

General Charles Craufurd also received the following letter about his brother's death from Captain William Campbell, a most devoted friend, and a man of rare nobleness of character. (For William Napier's estimate of William Campbell's character, see chapter 5 of this volume.)

Gallegos, January 29, 1812.

My Dear Sir,

General Stewart has taken from off me the painful duty of communicating to you the intelligence of the death of your brother and alas! our friend.

But that I received his last words, and that some of them were directed by his tenderness to his wife and children, I should therefore have been silent when my heart breaks to speak. My duty, however, calls upon me to tell to you, in order that they may be conveyed to his wife, his last expressions concerning her. I am quite incapable of doing it myself.

He bid me tell her, for he said that I knew how (not knowing, alas! how incompetent I am to the task), he bid me say that his whole heart and thoughts were of her and of his children. He said most solemnly that, however much he might have neglected the outward forms of religion, that she should believe that he expected to meet her again in heaven.

★★★★★★

Note:—Religion as a system of outward forms or of conventional proprieties is little suited to ardent natures such as those of Robert Craufurd or Charles Napier; but the Christianity of Christ, which is but the eternal consecration of sympathy, is to such an imperious necessity.

★★★★★★

The physicians had desired him not to think in any way calculated to create irritation, and he therefore said no more after the 19th.

General Stewart has related to you the manner of his death, which precluded his entering more into the subject of his wife and children, which I am convinced possessed him wholly during the whole course of his sufferings. Upon them, indeed, was every thought bestowed for which, from his active military duties, he had leisure to give room.

I am thankful that General Stewart's presence insured the communication of our melancholy intelligence in a proper manner. I should have been as incapable of its performance as I am of expressing my misery and the blank which his death has created in my heart. General Stewart has charged me to put up the whole of his papers in a small writing-case which he brought last from England with him. These consist of only a few private letters, as he had destroyed most other papers a few days previous to that on which took place the attack in which he fell.

This case will also contain his watch and some of his accounts, which shall be accompanied by notes in explanation. All the letters must be first seen by you before they are sent to Mrs. Craufurd; for among them there are some of her own which, having arrived after his death, are unopened. In all and every arrangement concerning his effects, his *aide-de-camp* and myself will be governed by General Stewart.

> I am, my dear sir,
> Your affectionate and most unhappy,
> William Campbell.

A monument was erected to General Craufurd in St. Paul's Cathedral by the nation. As General Mackinnon was killed at the same time as Craufurd, one monument served for both these officers. But the most real monument of the leader of the Light Division was Ciudad Rodrigo itself, or perhaps an even better one was the surpassing excellence of his troops, over whom his gifted spirit long continued to exercise a decided sway after his departure from this world. It was in every way most fitting that he should be buried in the breach, and not in St. Paul's or Westminster Abbey. Thus, in death, as in life, he was made one with his own gallant soldiers. Moreover, writing to his wife concerning himself and his career he said truly:

> My whole life has been passed in a kind of storm.

Peace, composure, or tranquillity he never found in this life. And for the bruised storm-warriors in the realms alike of action and of thought, for the leaders of the world's tragical "forlorn hopes," for the half-successful children of glimmering and erratic genius, for distinctly dualistic natures, for such as were never really in harmony with their environment, the serene pomp and finished perfection of an English cathedral seem at times almost a mockery.

★★★★★★

Note:—In the next chapter of this book I think it will appear plainly that Sir William Napier saw deeply into Craufurd's strangely complex nature, when he wrote of him, "If ever the Manichaean doctrine was made manifest in man, it was so in Craufurd." But Napier's words, like some of those of the old Hebrew prophets, had a far wider range and a much profounder significance than he who uttered them was aware of.

★★★★★★

The soldier's simple grave seems better far for such, since war has been their very element. Hollow and unreal indeed, when said over such eager baffled spirits, must ever sound the undiscriminating and almost unmeaning eulogies of sleek commonplace divines. Erected over the graves of storm-tossed heroes, almost all epitaphs seem vain and futile, save only that wise and tender one in which the divine reason expresses at once an effective apologia and a gladdening prophecy:

These are they which came out of great tribulation; therefore, are they before the throne of God.

CHAPTER 8

Anecdotes, and Different Estimates of Craufurd's Character and Abilities

The marked and striking personality of General Craufurd, his love of jokes and keen sense of humour, and also his extraordinary activity, made it quite certain that a great number of amusing anecdotes would be associated with his name during such an exciting period as that of the war waged in the Peninsula. I will now proceed to gather together a few of these. Some of the best have been handed down to us by one of Craufurd's riflemen, Edward Costello, a non-commissioned officer, in his *Adventures of a Soldier*.

One of this writer's most diverting stories about his fiery leader is as follows:

The following laughable incident occurred while we lay at Gallegos, I happened to be acquainted with General Craufurd's private servant, a Frenchman, chiefly through my being em-ployed as orderly to the brigadier. At times, when an oppor-tunity offered, we used to take a glass of wine together on the most convivial terms. One morning, however, when I thought the brigadier had gone out, as was his usual custom, I went to his room, to ask the valet to partake of some wine which I had received from the patron of the house.

On opening the door, I unhesitatingly went in and beheld, as I imagined, the individual I wanted in a morning gown looking out of the window. It entered into my head to surprise my serv-ant friend; so, as he had not been disturbed by my approach, I stepped softly up to his rear and, with a sudden laugh, gave him a smart slap on the back. But my consternation and surprise

178

may be better imagined than described, when the gentleman in the dressing-gown, starting round with a 'Who the devil is that?' disclosed, not the merry phiz of the valet, but the stern features of General Craufurd himself.

I thought I should have sunk through the ground at the moment, had it have opened to swallow me. I could only attempt to explain the mistake I had made, in a very humble way, as I gradually retreated to the door.

'And where did you get the wine from, sir?' said the general, with a good-humoured smile; for he observed the fright I was in.

I informed him.

'Well, well, you may go,' said the general; 'but pray, sir, never again do me the honour to take me for my servant.'

I needed not the permission to vanish in a moment. And many a laugh and jest were created at my expense afterwards among the men, as the circumstance got circulated by the valet.

Strict and stern though Craufurd was as a disciplinarian, his men seem to have thoroughly realised the fact that he had a strong sense of humour; and they acted accordingly. In his *Distinguished Generals during the Peninsular War*, Cole relates the following story:

A rollicking Hibernian of the Light Division was once trudging leisurely along the road with a pig in a string behind him, when, as bad luck would have it, he was overtaken by General Craufurd. The salutation, as may be supposed, was not the most cordial 'Where did you steal that pig, you plundering rascal?' 'What pig, Giniral?' exclaimed the culprit, turning round to him with an air of the most innocent surprise. 'Why, that pig you have got behind you, you villain.' 'Well then I vow and protest, Giniral,' rejoined Paddy, nothing abashed, and turning round to his four-footed companion as if he had never seen him before, 'it is scandalous to think what a wicked world we live in, and how ready folks are to take away an honest boy's character. Some blackguard, wanting to get me into trouble, has tied that *baste* to my cartouch-box.' The general could restrain his risible faculties no longer, and struck spurs to his horse, and rode on.

Two other little stories, though trivial in themselves, may serve to illustrate the appreciation of this side of Craufurd's character by those serving under him. They were communicated to me by the son of a well-known officer who served in the 43rd Light Infantry during the Peninsular War.

The general had given the strictest orders that no soldier should fall out, whilst marching, without a ticket from the medical officer. General Craufurd was fond of poultry and usually carried about a good supply with his division. It so happened that one of his turkeys was injured in the leg. So, one of the men tied the necessary medical ticket to the bird. Craufurd, riding up, saw the bird limping along, and proceeded to mutter some remarks not favourable to the practical joker.

The other little anecdote about Craufurd and his poultry is this: It was Christmas-time, and some people had been round the camp selling a considerable number of geese. Whereupon two choice spirits put their heads together and concocted the following joke. They went from officer's tent to officer's tent, speaking to each occupant in something like the following words: "I say, Brown, have you heard the row? Someone has stolen the general's geese, and been selling them in camp. You have not bought any, have you?"

"Well, yes, I have bought one; but it is not picked; what do you advise me to do?"

"Take it to the general, by all means, and explain to him."

The next officer had just picked his bird, and another had cooked it; but all went, taking their birds in various stages of destruction, and eagerly apologised to their astonished commander. At first General Craufurd thought that all these officers of his had gone mad; but gradually he began to realise the true position of affairs. The story does not inform us what he then said, but in all probability he joined heartily in the harmless joke.

The leader of the Light Division always had the very greatest dislike to punishing any of his men whom he thought fine soldiers; and accordingly, he sometimes went very much out of his way to protect them, as this story, taken from Costello's book, will show: A regiment of Brunswickers being sent to the division, they had to be watched, in order to prevent their deserting to the enemy. Craufurd detested them and was not willing to punish his own men for excessive zeal in watching these traitors.

A sergeant of the Rifles called Fleming, one night being posted in piquet, unluckily came in collision with one of the Brunswick officers, and suspecting his intentions to bolt to the enemy, knocked him down with his rifle and otherwise maltreated him. The result was that Fleming was tried by a brigade court-martial, convicted for the assault, sentenced to be reduced to the ranks, and to receive a corporal punishment of five hundred lashes.

But Craufurd, after saying to Fleming that his crime would be quite inexcusable if it really was exactly of the sort described, took upon himself to remit the corporal punishment on account of the excellent character for gallantry and honourable conduct given of this sergeant by his own officers.

And I here (proceeded the general, turning round to the division) take the opportunity of declaring that if any of these gentlemen (meaning the Brunswickers) have a wish to go over to the enemy, let them express it, and I give my word of honour I will grant them a pass to that effect instantly; for we are better without such.

Fleming was shortly afterwards reinstated, and fell leading on the ladder party in the forlorn hope at Badajoz.

He thus lived long enough to be present at Craufurd's funeral.

This anecdote of Craufurd is very characteristic. No one ever valued a fine soldier more than he did. As his humble follower, "Rifleman Harris," said of him:

He was in everything a soldier, the very picture of a warrior.

I extract from Sir W. Cope's *History of the Rifle Brigade* the following story, as it serves well to illustrate both the unhappy violence of my grandfather's temper and the substantial justice of his anger:

On one occasion during Moore's retreat, Lieutenant Thomas Smith, then a very young officer who had but lately joined, was accompanying ammunition which was in charge of a quartermaster (Ross). On their arrival at Craufurd's headquarters, the wily quartermaster advised Smith to go and report their arrival to the general. The other demurred, saying that he was not in charge of the ammunition, but only accompanying it.

However, the quartermaster urged him, reminding him that he must be hungry; they had not in fact tasted food for twenty-four hours; and that the general would probably ask him to dinner. Thus, counselled by his senior, and impelled by his hunger, he presented himself at the general's quarters, and saw his *aide-*

de-camp, who going upstairs returned with an order to proceed at once a further march of some three leagues. Smith returned to the quartermaster with this woeful order, adding that as *he* was in charge, he might remain with it, for that he should go on and overtake his battalion. The quartermaster declared he should do no such thing; and, after a sharp argument, they both started and joined the battalion.

In the morning, as Smith was sitting down to breakfast, an order came from Craufurd, who had come up, that he and the quartermaster should attend him. On being ushered into the general's presence, they found him warming himself before a comfortable brazier, while breakfast stood on the table. In a voice of great severity, he asked which of the two had received his order the night before.

'I did, sir,' said Smith, 'but—'

'No *but*, sir,' interrupted Craufurd, 'consider yourself under arrest; and, adding a tremendous oath, 'I will smash you.'

Poor Smith—for Craufurd would not hear a word more—returned in dismay to his brother officers, whom he found at breakfast; but hungry as he was, and pressed by them to be of good heart, food had now no charms for him.

Eventually Beckwith represented to Craufurd that the offender was but a boy just joined; and his pleadings, coupled perhaps with the fact that they were just going to fight, when every available officer would be wanted, induced Craufurd, contrary to his wont, to relax his seventy and to release Smith from his arrest.

Long afterwards, as Craufurd was standing talking with the officers of the battalion round a camp fire, he turned to him.

'Smith,' said he, 'did I not once put you under arrest?'

'Yes, sir, you did,'

'And do you know,' he continued, 'what became of the ammunition? I found it steadily going towards the French lines, and had but just time to put spurs to my horse and to turn it back. So that through your default I had nearly lost my ammunition.'

★★★★★★

Note:—Beckwith, afterwards Sir T. Sydney Beckwith, was General Craufurd's favourite of all the colonels who served under him, the two men had much in common, and the general accorded to Beckwith much more freedom and latitude than he granted to any other colonel. Colonel Colborne, afterwards Lord Seaton, of the 52nd, was a still abler man; but he was only a short time under Craufurd. Old Beckwith was probably the best officer that the 95th Rifles ever produced, well described by Napier as "a man capable of rallying an army in flight."

★★★★★★

A large part of General Craufurd's extreme unpopularity with his officers, no doubt, was caused by his firm determination to force them all to do their work thoroughly. That he could genuinely appreciate and value really able and efficient officers is made manifest by the energy with which he successfully resisted Beresford, when that marshal wanted to take George Napier out of the Light Division and make him colonel of one of his own Portuguese regiments. In his *Early Military Life* Sir George Napier thus relates this affair:

I wished at that period very much to be allowed to enter the Portuguese service as a lieutenant-colonel commanding a regiment, and therefore I asked Lord Wellington's permission to make application to Marshal Beresford to appoint me to the command of a Light Infantry regiment, as the Portuguese Army was under the command of the marshal. Lord Wellington granted my request, and accordingly I went to Marshal Beresford, who received me very kindly, and said he would appoint me with pleasure to a Light Infantry regiment which happened to be vacant at that very time.

I was delighted at this and went off to get my things ready, etc., but I found that our General (Craufurd), having heard of my application to enter the Portuguese Army, had gone to Lord Wellington and represented that he had been at great pains to make good field officers in the Light Division, and that, if he was to be deprived of them in this way, the division would be ruined; and as he was pleased to say I was one of his best officers, he positively refused to let me go out of his division. He would have been content if the marshal would appoint me to one of the Portuguese light regiments in his own division, which was commanded by a Portuguese colonel whom Craufurd did not like; but this was out of the question, and Lord Wellington therefore acquiesced in General Craufurd's demand that I should remain where I was.

This was very annoying to me, but from the flattering manner

General Craufurd had spoken of me to the commander-in-chief, I could not be angry; and indeed I think he was right not to permit those officers who had been constantly serving with him, and formed under his own directions in the finest division in the army, to be taken from him just as their long experience had made them more valuable to him.

Lord Wellington sent for me the next day, and told me he was very sorry for my disappointment, but that he hoped it would be made up to me by his informing me I was made Major of the 52nd Regiment, and although I actually belonged to the 2nd battalion, which was in England, I should remain on service with the 1st battalion. This put me in such good spirits that I cared very little about going into the Portuguese service. I went, however, to inform Marshal Beresford, and to thank him for his kindness. He was not very well pleased with General Craufurd, and expressed himself in pretty strong terms on the occasion.

From this narrative it is evident that Wellington was much influenced by Craufurd's judgment in anything that concerned the Light Division. I do not think that General Craufurd ever entertained a very high opinion of Beresford's capacities. I believe that he thought very much as Sir William Napier did about that brave but not conspicuously able leader.

Having now shown how the leader of the Light Division valued a really able officer, I will proceed to illustrate his feelings towards good soldiers amongst his men. Costello, who was an eye-witness of the affair, writes as follows:

The Duke of Wellington attended the funeral of the gallant veteran (Craufurd), who, though most strict in discipline, was averse to punishment, and was beloved by the men for his justice and care for them, as well as for his bravery. The following incident, of which I was an eye-witness, will serve to show his character. I happened to be on guard one day when General Craufurd came riding in from the front with his orderly dragoon, as was his usual custom, when two of our men, one of them a corporal, came running out of a house with some bread which they had stolen from the Spaniards. They were pursued by a Spanish woman crying lustily, '*Ladrone! ladrone!*' (Thief! thief!) They were immediately pursued by the general and his orderly; the bread was given back to the woman, and the men were placed in the guard-house.

The next day they were tried by a brigade court-martial, and brought out to a wood near the town, for punishment. When the brigade was formed, and the brigade-major had finished reading the proceedings of the court-martial, General Craufurd commenced lecturing both men and officers on the nature of their cruelty to the harmless inhabitants, as he called the Spaniards. He laid particular stress on our regiment (the 95th Rifles), who, he said, committed more crimes than the whole of the rest of the British Army. 'Besides, you think,' said he, 'because you are riflemen and more exposed to the enemy's fire than other regiments, that you are to rob the inhabitants with impunity; but while I command you, you shall not.' Then, turning round to the corporal, who stood in the centre of the square, he said with a stern voice, 'Strip, sir.'

The corporal, whose name was Miles, never said a word until tied up to a tree; when, turning his head round as far as his situation would allow, and seeing the general pacing up and down the square, he said, ' General Craufurd, I hope you will forgive me.' The general replied, 'No, sir, your crime is too great.' The poor corporal, whose sentence was to be reduced to the pay and rank of a private soldier, and to receive a punishment of a hundred and fifty lashes, and the other man two hundred, then addressed the general to the following effect: 'Do you recollect, sir, when under the command of General Whitelocke, in Buenos Ayres, we were marched prisoners, with a number of others, to a sort of pound surrounded with a wall? There was a well in the centre, out of which I drew water with my mess-tin, by means of canteen-straps I collected from the men who were prisoners like myself. You sat on my knapsack; I parted my last biscuit with you. You then told me you would never forget my kindness to you. It is now in your power, sir; you know how short we have been of rations for some time.'

These words were spoken by the corporal in a mild and respectful accent, which not only affected the general, but the whole square. The bugler who stood waiting to commence the punishment, close to the corporal, received the usual nod from the bugle-major to begin. The first lash the corporal received, the general started, and turning hurriedly round, said, 'Who taught that bugler to flog? Send him to drill! Send him to drill! He cannot flog! He cannot flog! Stop, stop! Take him down! Take him down! I remember it well, I remember it well,' while he paced up and down the square, muttering to himself words that I could not catch, and at the same time blowing his nose and wiping his face with his handkerchief, trying to hide the emotion that was so evident to the whole square.

A dead silence prevailed for some time, until our gallant general recovered a little his noble feeling, when he uttered, with a broken accent, 'Why does a brave soldier like you commit these crimes?' Then, beckoning to his orderly to bring his horse, he mounted and rode off. It is needless to say that the other man also was pardoned, and in a few days the corporal was restored to his rank.

Scenes such as this must have amply sufficed to convince Craufurd's men that their vehement and passionate leader had a warm heart, and that he keenly appreciated their many fine qualities. But the full pathos of this scene could only be understood by those few such as William Campbell or Charles Stewart who realised the fact that the fiery spirit of Robert Craufurd was in truth quite extraordinarily sensitive and profoundly affectionate, and also that the sore wound inflicted at Buenos Ayres on his aspiring pride remained unhealed to the day of his death. Those few who really knew this stern leader well were quite aware that his heart was ever most eager to respond effectively to all the claims made upon it by gratitude and sympathy. Craufurd was not an amiable man, in the common sense of the term; but his intimate friends considered him a really great man in character as well as attainments.

His wife, who was a woman of the calmest judgment, always thought that his violence of temper was almost entirely caused by his unhappy sensitiveness, which made him feel things far more acutely than ordinary men feel them. And I suppose the fact really is that what the world usually reckons amiability is largely based on obtuseness of feeling; and so, the most affectionate natures are often more liable to stormy gusts of passing anger than colder natures are. In the human heart the sources of tenderness and also of a kind of fierceness are not far apart. The old Hebrew prophets made manifest the truth of this apparent paradox, and in our own military history it was well illustrated by the complex character of Charles Napier. On the other hand, the amiability of some natures is the result of animal selfishness well gratified, and has no more real moral significance than the purring of comfortable cats.

Concerning General Craufurd's abilities strangely opposite opinions have been expressed. Some have even thought that he might have rivalled Wellington, if his sphere had been equally extensive, whilst others have questioned his skill whilst acknowledging his undaunted courage. Charles Lever, in his story, *Charles O'Malley*, very ridiculously represents the leader of the Light Division as:

> Relying on headlong heroism rather than on cool judgment and well-matured plans.

That this estimate is absurd is sufficiently obvious from Sir James Shaw Kennedy's account of the extremely accurate calculations and the great knowledge and skill involved in Craufurd's wonderful outpost work between the Rivers Coa and Agueda. Cole says of Craufurd:

> There have been many opinions expressed as to this brave officer's capability of command. It has been even asserted by his admirers that, with the same opportunities he would have equalled Wellington; but such hyperbolical eulogy is as injurious as detraction. Take him on the whole, he was one of the readiest and most dashing executive officers in the service, and his early death must be considered a national loss.

Lord Wolseley, if I remember rightly, has declared in a magazine article on *Military Genius*, that "with one or two exceptions," Wellington "apparently had the very poorest opinion of his generals of division." Probably Robert Craufurd is included by Lord Wolseley in these extremely few exceptions. But however, this may be, I think I have in this volume made it abundantly manifest that in reality Craufurd's commander-in-chief had a very high opinion indeed of his capacity as well as of his energy and activity.

In the text of Napier's *Peninsular War* there is one well-known passage in which he compares Picton and Craufurd, and is by no means complimentary to either of these renowned leaders. But the place in which this criticism is found explains to a great extent Sir William Napier's apparent depreciation of these generals; and as regards Craufurd, the unfavourable opinion expressed is very much lessened in significance by later utterances of the same judge. Both these generals had given very great offence to Napier by their conduct at the Coa,

Craufurd by righting unnecessarily, and Picton by refusing to come to the assistance of the Light Division in its hour of supreme peril. Consequently, the historian wrote thus concerning them:

Picton and Craufurd were, however, not formed by nature to act cordially together. The stern countenance, robust frame, saturnine complexion, caustic speech, and austere demeanour of the first promised little sympathy with the short thick figure, dark flashing eyes, quick movements, and fiery temper of the second; nor did they often meet without a quarrel. Nevertheless, they had many points of resemblance in their characters and fortunes. Both were inclined to harshness, and rigid in command; both prone to disobedience, yet exacting entire submission from inferiors. They were alike ambitious and craving of glory. Both possessed military talents, were enterprising and intrepid; yet neither was remarkable for skill in handling troops under fire. This also they had in common, that after distinguished services they perished in arms, fighting gallantly; and, being celebrated as generals of division while living, have since their death been injudiciously spoken of as rivalling their great leader in war.

That they were officers of mark and pretension is unquestionable, and Craufurd more so than Picton, because the latter never had a separate command, and his opportunities were necessarily more circumscribed; but to compare either to Wellington displays ignorance of the men and of the art they professed. If they had even comprehended the profound military and political combinations he was then conducting, the one would have carefully avoided fighting on the Coa; the other, far from refusing, would have eagerly proffered his support.

The last sentence in this famous passage seems to me totally unfair to both generals. Napier must either mean that Craufurd and Picton were incapable of comprehending "the profound military and political combinations" which their chief was then conducting, even if they had been in possession of adequate data in the way of full information as to facts, or else merely that they were so incapable with the very scanty and inadequate information which they possessed at that time. In the former case Napier's assertion is quite untrue, and as regards Craufurd it is plainly refuted by the fact that Wellington often discussed his general plans with him, as is made evident in this volume; in the latter case Napier's censure is somewhat meaningless, and applies to his own brother Charles quite as much as to Picton or Craufurd.

Political considerations of a highly complex character often induced Wellington to modify his military operations in a manner otherwise undesirable or even inexplicable. These considerations were thoroughly and exhaustively known only by the commander-in-chief himself; in their fulness he communicated their nature to no one; and consequently, no officer serving under him could be rationally blamed for not completely comprehending the profound combinations which the wisdom of Wellington designed in order to deal with them. Charles Napier did not understand why the commander-in-chief persisted in holding so long the perilous position occupied between the Rivers Coa and Agueda in the summer of the year 1810. In his life, by his brother, Sir William, we find Charles Napier saying at the end of June that the Light Division ought not to stay in its advanced and perilous position; yet Wellington says in a letter to Craufurd on July 16:

It is desirable that we should hold the other side of the Coa a little longer.

From which it appears that even Charles Napier was not always quite omniscient, and did not then "comprehend the profound military and political combinations which Wellington was conducting."

Picton's biographer, Mr. Robinson, not unnaturally found fault with Sir William Napier's remarks as to the abilities of that renowned leader. In reply, Napier says in an appendix to his history:

As to the charge of faintly praising his military talents, a point was forced by me in his favour, when I compared him to General Craufurd, of whose ability there was no question; more could not be done in conscience, even under Mr. Robinson's assurance that he was a Roman hero."

In Cole's *Distinguished Generals during the Peninsular War,* we find another comparison of the rival leaders, Picton and Craufurd. It seems to have been written by Sir Denis le Marchant, from materials furnished by Major-General le Marchant, who served under Wellington. In some respects, this estimate may well be considered more accurate and more fair than the somewhat hostile one written by Napier. It is as follows:

Picton and Craufurd were officers alike distinguished by gal-

lantry and talent, but most opposite in disposition and deport-
ment, and, it may not be uninteresting to add, in person. Picton,
when wrapped in his military cloak, might have been mistaken
for a bronze statue of Cato, and was equally staid, deliberate,
and austere; whilst Craufurd, of a diminutive and not imposing
figure, was characterised by vivacity almost mercurial both in
thought and act; his eager spirit and fertile brain ever hurrying
him into enterprises of difficulty and danger, which he loved
the more because they sometimes left him at liberty to follow
his own views of the crisis of the moment.

Others shunned responsibility, he courted it. He had served on
the staff of the Austrian armies during the revolutionary war,
and was well versed in their tactics, as he had shown by his trans-
lation of one of their best military histories; but this knowledge
was of very questionable benefit to him, for it occasionally led
him to try experiments which were hardly consistent with the
comparative insignificance of his corps. In short, he was too
much disposed to aim at objects which were the province of
the commander rather than of a subordinate general.

Picton had no such ambition; but he was slow to execute orders
of which he disapproved, and the quickness of his perception
was not equal to the soundness of his judgment.

★★★★★★

Picton's biographer says that his hero would not have fought
the action at the Coa, if he had been trusted with the outpost
operations assigned to Craufurd. Probably this is quite true; but
Wellington knew well that Picton had not sufficient rapidity of
perception to carry on successfully for four months the marvellously dangerous work performed by Craufurd and his division.

★★★★★★

Craufurd had the faults incidental to a hasty temper, Picton
those belonging to a morose one. Each was possessed of inde-
fatigable industry and perfect familiarity with all the duties of
his profession; and last, though not least, both were men of the
highest integrity and honour. Next to Lord Wellington, none
stood higher in the estimation of the army. Both these officers
were friends of General le Marchant.

Picton and Craufurd were also singularly different in their feelings and attitude towards the troops forming their respective divisions.

Picton seems to have detested his own men.

On one occasion, while heading a charge, he addressed them with these flattering epithets, 'Come on, you plundering, fighting blackguards.'

And, for some unknown reason, he appears to have especially disliked the gallant 88th, or Connaught Rangers. General Craufurd, on the contrary, "was so vain of the division he commanded that he had persuaded himself that he might safely oppose it to any number of the enemy." Cole, who was very much inclined to prefer Picton to Craufurd, says of Picton:

Although not personally loved by the soldiers, he was respected by them.

Certainly, he was never received by the troops of *his* division with ringing cheers such as were freely given to the leader of the Light Division on his return to the army just before the battle of Fuentes d'Onoro; nor, I imagine, did his heroic death evoke any such pathetic laments as those which Lord Londonderry and William Campbell poured forth over the fiery but warm-hearted Robert Craufurd. In this respect, in the power of attracting the affections of his men, Craufurd certainly was far superior to Picton; and I suppose that there can be no doubt that Lord Wolseley is right in considering such a power a very great one, and an almost necessary attribute of military genius.

Craufurd's efficiency as a leader was greatly lessened by the violence and obstinacy of his temper. These sometimes obscured the clearness of his judgment, and made him determined to hold his ground at all costs, when retreat was decidedly expedient. Thus, genius partially marred by passion characterized his whole career. Sir William Napier expresses this truth, though with some degree of inadvertent unfairness, when he says of his old leader (in the *Life of Sir Charles Napier*):

If ever the Manichaean doctrine was made manifest in man, it was so in Craufurd. At one time he was all fire and intelligence, a master spirit in war; at another, as if possessed by the demon, he would madly rush from blunder to blunder, raging in folly.

Following Napier, a writer in the *Quarterly Review* once spoke of Craufurd as "the good and evil genius of the Light Division."

But to a very great extent such estimates of Craufurd are unintentionally misleading. They suggest that his evil influence was about as extensive and habitual as his good influence, that his errors were about as frequent in their occurrence as his hours of wisdom, vigilant thoughtfulness, and brilliant audacity. And of course, the idea thus inevitably suggested is false. Sir George Napier plainly considered that Craufurd's mistakes were *few* and by no means habitual. He says of him:

> Although in some few instances he got into scrapes, it was more through vanity than anything else.

And of course, it is manifest that his mind must have been well directed in the immense majority of its activities; for otherwise it could never have been truly said of him, as it was by the authority last quoted:

> Every officer in the Light Division must acknowledge that, by his unwearied and active exertions of mind and body, that division was brought to a state of discipline and knowledge of the duties of light troops which never was equalled by any division in the British Army, or surpassed by any division of the French Army.

Certainly, so splendid a service as that was never yet performed by any general whose activities were made up, in about equal proportions, of masterly power and raging folly.

After all, the occasions on which Napier censures Craufurd, in his history of the war, are few some three or four I believe and on other occasions he speaks more highly of him than he ever does of any other general who served under Lord Wellington. He never says of Hill, Beresford, Stapleton Cotton, Sir Brent Spencer, Picton, scarcely even of Thomas Graham Lord Lynedoch, that he was in his better moments "full of fire and intelligence, a master spirit in war."

And it ought to be remembered that, before he praised General Craufurd, William Napier had to emancipate his judgment from a very strong influence which tended to sway it in a contrary direction. Charles Napier very greatly disliked the leader of the Light Division, and lost no opportunity of expressing a bad opinion of him. Charles Macleod of the 43rd, William Napier's dearest friend in the world, absolutely hated Craufurd, as is made extremely evident by a copy of the omniscient young critic's journal—his age was only 25—now to be found amongst the books and manuscripts belonging to the officers of his old regiment. Consequently, one may always feel certain that William Napier's praises of his general are well deserved; especially as to praise Craufurd might sometimes seem to be undervaluing Sir John Moore.

As Colonel Charles Macleod's journal has never been published, it is not necessary that I should take much notice of his remarks about his general. I will content myself with saying that I believe that the temperaments of the two men were so utterly different as to make mutual comprehension almost impossible, Craufurd being of a singularly outspoken nature, and Macleod exceedingly reserved. The fact that the latter was so fervently loved by William Napier is a sufficient proof that he had some remarkably fine qualities; but amongst these intellectual modesty can hardly be numbered. It never seems to have occurred to this virulent critic that his general might possibly know more of war than he knew himself, as Craufurd had been in the army for thirty-three years. And the simple fact that Lord Wellington took great trouble to keep Craufurd in command of a division which more than any other demanded real ability in its leader, might well have caused this juvenile critic to hesitate before pronouncing unmeasured censure on his hated chief.

Craufurd's junior rank amongst the generals often made it difficult for the commander-in-chief to secure to him his command. Macleod might also easily have known that Sir John Moore had a high opinion of General Craufurd. But we all know how self-confident and conceited clever young men frequently are; and the juvenile warrior of the 43rd had evidently some need of a few words of wise warning such as those said to have been addressed to a young student by a famous professor:

We are none of us infallible, *not even the youngest.*

In the *Private Journal of F. S. Larpent, Judge-Advocate-General of the British forces in the Peninsula,* we find the following remarks about the leader of the Light Division:

He was very clever and knowing in his profession, all admit, and led on his division, on the day of his death, in the most gallant style; but Lord Wellington never knew what he would do. . . . Lord Wellington knew his merits, and humoured him; it was surprising what he bore from him at times.

In his *Narrative of the Peninsular War,* Lord Londonderry writes thus of Craufurd:

It is scarcely necessary to add that the loss of so many valuable lives was keenly felt, not only by private friends, but by the army in general; but among them all there fell not one more universally or more justly lamented than Major-General Craufurd. He was an officer of whom the highest expectations had been formed, and who on every occasion found an opportunity to prove that, had his life been spared, the fondest hopes of his country would not have been disappointed; and he was a man to know whom in his profession without admiring was impossible. To me his death occasioned that void which the removal of a sincere friend alone produces.

From the moment of receiving his wound, he knew that all hope of recovery was idle; he lingered on for several hours, and at last submitted to his fate with the magnanimity of a hero and the resignation of a Christian. Poor Craufurd! whilst the memory of the brave and the skilful shall continue to be cherished by British soldiers, thou wilt not be forgotten; and the hand which scrawls this humble tribute to thy worth must be cold as thine own, ere the mind which dictates it shall cease to think of thee with affection and regret.

In *Random Shots from a Rifleman*, Captain Kincaid, of the 95th Rifles, has much to say concerning his old leader. He tells us that:

Craufurd was no common character. He, like a gallant contemporary of his, was not born to be a great general, but he certainly was a distinguished one; the history of his division, and the position which he held beyond the Coa in 1810, attest the fact. He had neither judgment, temper, nor discretion to fit him for a chief, and as a subordinate he required to be held with a tight rein; but his talents as a general of division were nevertheless of the first order. He received the three British regiments under his command finished by the hands of a master in the art, Sir John Moore, and as regiments they were faultless; but to Craufurd belonged the chief merit of making them the war brigade which they became, alike the admiration of their friends and foes.

The assertion that Craufurd "was not born to be a great general," and that he would not have done for a chief, seems a rather rash one to make concerning a leader whom William Napier declared to be in his better hours "a master spirit in war." But Kincaid, though an efficient officer, was in no sense a great one, and his opinion on this point is far from decisive. Lord Londonderry had far better means of estimating Craufurd's capacities, and he thought him quite equal to Sir John Moore in ability, though immensely inferior as regards character. Mr. Gleig also informs us that at the time of Craufurd's death:

The man himself was regarded as one of those who, should circumstances ever place him in a situation of distinct responsibility and trust, would unquestionably add to the renown which the British troops had already acquired.

Mr. Gleig was a shrewd observer, and his testimony as to what was the general opinion in the army as to Craufurd's powers is of considerable value, though this observer's *own* opinion on such a matter could not then be worth much.

Moreover, in the expedition to Buenos Ayres the leader of the Light Division had unquestionably shown that the British Army would never have incurred its greatest disgrace, if he had been commander-in-chief, instead of being a subordinate general. The most serious defect in General Craufurd was his great violence of temper, and Sir George Napier has testified that this was being gradually conquered. Some of his errors also arose, as Sir Denis le Marchant has observed, from his being too apt to aim at objects which were really the province of the commander-in-chief; so that in some respects he might have done better as a chief than as a subordinate. This view is rather confirmed by Wellington when he wrote to Craufurd:

In every event I should have taken care to keep your command distinct, as I am convinced that you will be able to render most service in such a situation.

He was very much wanting in tact, no doubt; but many great generals have certainly been lacking in that quality. That Craufurd had sufficient knowledge and genius to enable him to play the part of a great general is, I think, sufficiently clear; but whether he would ever have conquered his constitutional tendency to perilous rashness, it is impossible to say, though all history, I imagine, teaches us that a position of distinct and grave responsibility very often evokes caution and prudence, to a very remarkable extent, in leaders up to that time characterized by extreme audacity and somewhat reckless obstinacy.

However, it is as a great general of division, as a man of vivid intelligence and extraordinary rapidity of perception, as a master of outpost work, as a leader endowed with unconquerable resolution, as perhaps, in some respects, the greatest disciplinarian that the British army ever produced, that Robert Craufurd will always be remembered. Whatever his failings may have been—and they were many—I suppose that all really impartial students of military history will agree with a recent writer, who says of him:

> Craufurd was an officer who left his mark on the English Army, and was unquestionably the finest commander of light troops who served in the Peninsula. In spite of his faults of temper, he won and retained to the last the devoted love of the soldiers he commanded. (See a sketch of Craufurd's career in the *Dictionary of National Biography*, edited by Mr. Leslie Stephen.)

Captain Kincaid tells us that the men hated Craufurd's extreme strictness at first, but that they afterwards came to understand and appreciate it. He writes thus:

> But Craufurd's cat forced them to take the right road whether they would or no; and the experiment, once made, carried conviction with it that the comfort of every individual in the division materially depended on the rigid exaction of his orders; for he shewed that on every ordinary march he made it a rule to halt for a few minutes every third or fourth mile (dependent on the vicinity of water), that every soldier carried a canteen capable of containing two quarts, and that, if he only took the trouble to fill it before starting, and again, if necessary, at every halt, it contained more than he would or ought to drink in the interim; and that therefore every pause he made in a river for the purpose of drinking was disorderly, because a man stopping to drink delayed the one behind him proportionately longer, and so on progressively to the rear of the column,
> In like manner the filing past dirty or marshy parts of the road, in place of marching boldly through them, or filing over a plank or narrow bridge in place of taking the river with the full front of their column in march, he proved to demonstration, on true mathematical principles, that with the numbers of those obstacles usually encountered on a day's march, it made a difference of several hours in their arrival at their bivouac for the night. He shewed that, in indulging by the way, they were that much longer labouring under their load of arms, ammunition, and necessaries, besides bringing them to their bivouac in darkness and discomfort It very likely, too, got them thoroughly drenched with rain, when the sole cause of their delay had been

to avoid a partial wetting, which would have been long since dried while seated at ease around their camp-fires; and if this does not redeem Craufurd and his cat, I give it up.

The general and his divisional code, as already hinted at, was at first much disliked. Probably he enforced it in the first instance with unnecessary severity, and it was long before those under him could rid themselves of that feeling of oppression which it had inculcated upon their minds. It is due, however, to the memory of the gallant general to say that punishment for those disorders was rarely necessary after the first campaign; for the system, once established, went on like clock-work, and the soldiers latterly became devotedly attached to him; for, while he exacted from them the most rigid obedience, he was, on his own part, keenly alive to everything they had a right to expect from him in return, and woe befell the commissary who failed to give a satisfactory reason for any deficiencies in his issues.

This same author, in *Adventures in the Rifle Brigade*, thus testifies to his old leader's surpassing excellence as a general of division:

General Craufurd fell on the glacis at the head of our division, and was buried at the foot of the breach which they so gallantly carried. His funeral was attended by Lord Wellington and all the officers of the division, by whom he was, ultimately, much liked. He had introduced a system of discipline into the Light Division which made them unrivalled. A very rigid exaction of the duties pointed out in his code of regulations made him very unpopular at its commencement; and it was not until a short time before he was lost to us for ever, that we were capable of appreciating his merits, and fully sensible of the incalculable advantages we derived from the perfection, of his system.

General Craufurd's Standing Orders of the Light Division were justly famous, and have had a great effect on the army. Sir W. Cope informs us that for fully twenty years after the termination of the Peninsular War every officer of the 95th Rifles was required to learn and know these Orders. They were republished in 1844 for the use of the army serving in Ireland; and general and commanding officers were authoritatively requested to enforce the observance of the system therein laid down, on all occasions when circumstances should permit. Again, in the year 1880 they were republished for the use of the

Curragh Brigade by Major-General Charles Fraser, a great-nephew of General Robert Craufurd. Even now, Craufurd's celebrated Orders as to *marches* are much valued in the 43rd Light Infantry.

The most elaborate and careful sketch of the character and capacities of the old leader of the Light Division is given us by General Sir George Napier, who certainly knew him well. It is as follows:

> Indeed, General Craufurd was always kind to me, and ready to do me a service, when in his power. In a day or two he breathed his last, and thus a period was put to his long, faithful, and I may add brilliant services in many instances; for although he was a most unpopular man, every officer in the Light Division must acknowledge that, by his unwearied and active exertions of mind and body, that division was brought to a state of discipline and knowledge of the duties of light troops, which never was equalled by any division in the British Army, or surpassed by any division of the French Army.
>
> I do not mean, or wish to insinuate, that we were better than the others either in physical power or courage (all Englishmen are alike), but most unquestionably we understood our business better, and had a better system of marching and discipline than any other division, the proof of which is the use the Duke of Wellington made of us during the war. In every siege, in every battle, his despatches will bear me out in my estimation of the services and activity of the Light Division.
>
> Again, look at the extraordinary number of privates from our three regiments who were made officers, and who, the moment they joined their new regiments, were almost without exception made adjutants; and the number of field officers and commanding officers promoted from the 43rd, the 52nd, and the Rifle Corps proves the estimation in which his Royal Highness the Duke of York held the division under General Craufurd's command. And at the end of the Peninsular War, nearly all the captains of those three regiments were majors by brevet, having received the rank for their services on the field of battle.

Sir George Napier's exceedingly high estimate of the superior efficiency of the Light Division is confirmed by a passage in his brother's *History of the War in the Peninsula*. Nearly a year after Craufurd's death, Lord Wellington, irritated by the conduct of the army generally, and the many crossings he had experienced during the last campaign, gave

vent to his feelings in a circular letter addressed to the superior officers. In this letter he complained that discipline had deteriorated without the men having suffered any unusual privations, that the officers
had lost all command over their men, and that excesses, outrages of
all kinds, and inexcusable losses had occurred; and he added that this
deplorable state of affairs was to be traced to the habitual neglect of
duty by the regimental officers. Sir William Napier adds:

> Nevertheless this circular was not strictly just, because it ex-
> cepted none from blame, though in conversation Wellington
> admitted the reproach did not apply to the Light Division nor
> to the Guards.

Concerning Craufurd personally Sir George Napier goes on to say:

> To give a sketch of General Craufurd's character is neither an
> easy nor a pleasant task, as truth compels me to acknowledge
> he had many and grave faults. Brilliant as some of the traits of
> his character were, and notwithstanding the good and generous
> feelings which often burst forth like a bright gleam of sunshine
> from behind a dark and heavy cloud, still there was a sullenness
> which seemed to brood in his inmost soul, and generate pas-
> sions which knew no bounds.
>
> As a general commanding a division of light troops of all arms,
> Craufurd certainly excelled. His knowledge of outpost duty
> was never exceeded by any British general, and I much doubt
> if there are many in any other service who know more of that
> particular branch of the profession than he did. He had by long
> experience, unwearied zeal, and constant activity, united to
> practice, founded a system of discipline and marching which
> arrived at such perfection that he could calculate to the min-
> ute the time his whole division, baggage, commissariat, etc.,
> would take to arrive at any given point, no matter how many
> days' march. Every officer and soldier knew his duty in every
> particular, and also knew he must perform it. No excuse would
> save him from the general's rage, if he failed in a single iota. As
> a commissary he was perfect, and if provisions were to be got
> within his possible reach, his division never was without them.

★★★★★★

Note:—This statement is confirmed by the strange exclamation of the Portuguese Caçadores, when they caught sight of
Craufurd at Fuentes d'Onoro, on his return to the army: "Long

live General Craufurd, who takes care of our bellies!"
★★★★★★

His mental activity was only surpassed by his physical powers. The moment his division arrived at its ground for the night, he never moved from his horse till he had made himself master of every part of his post, formed his plan for its defence, if necessary, and explained all his arrangements to the staff-officers and the field-officers of each regiment, so that, if his orders were strictly obeyed, a surprise was impossible. He was seldom deceived in the strength of the enemy's outposts, for he reconnoitred them with the eye of one who knew his business well; and although in some few instances he got into scrapes, it was more through vanity than anything else, as he was so vain of the division he commanded, that he really had persuaded himself he might oppose it to any number of the enemy; and when once in action, he was obstinately bent upon holding his ground at any risk, and in the heat of the battle often let his temper get the better of his judgment. The action with Marshal Ney's corps at the Coa was a proof of this.

I am inclined to think that, had he lived, he would have altered his conduct in many particulars, and conquered in some measure the extraordinary bursts of passion, which knew no bounds, and were the cause of his extreme unpopularity. But, take him altogether, he was an active, clever man, well skilled and experienced in his profession; and when his reason was not obscured by passion, few men possessed more clearness of judgment, or were more inclined to act rightly. I believe the first impulse of General Craufurd's heart was kindness; but as he never made any attempt to control his passions, the least opposition made that kindness vanish, and in its stead, violence, harshness, and hatred ruled his feelings in spite of himself. But he is gone, and as his later life was evidently much improved, and his temper more mild to those under his command, we have a right to conclude he would ere long have mastered his passions. But as a glorious death put a period to his career, let his faults and errors be buried with his earthly remains. His good qualities and his gallantry will ever live in the minds of those who served under him in Spain.

The only important error which I am able to detect in this long and interesting sketch of my grandfather's character is where Sir George Napier says that he "never made any attempt to control his passions." But what Napier really *meant* was that Craufurd never made any *perceptible* attempt of that sort. Sir George was a man endowed with rare justice and nobleness of mind, and he would have been amongst the very first to condemn any attempt to dogmatise concerning the inner depths of his neighbour's heart and soul. Moreover, he distinctly tells us that his general *was* gradually becoming milder in his temper; and such moral improvement always implies considerable effort in natures so fiery and obstinate as that of the leader of the Light Division.

The interior of a great and struggling heart is always interesting, and especially in the case of a famous leader of men. A man's letters to the one person in the whole world who really understands his nature adequately must ever be full of deep moral significance. I propose therefore in some measure to lift the veil which hid the fiery spirit of Robert Craufurd from his fellow-men, and to disclose his true character as he revealed it to his wife. No human being could be more painfully aware of his own besetting infirmities than my grandfather was. Pride often showed itself in his outward bearing; but genuine humility reigned within. Nor was his soul untouched by that profound melancholy which comes to such as have sought God early and have not found Him. Thus, before he was married, writing in the year 1799 to his intended wife, he says:

> The Almighty whose name I would not take in vain knows that I speak the truth when I say that I feel myself unworthy of the blessing He has bestowed upon me in giving me your affection; but I feel, and, with the most religious gratitude to my benevolent Creator, acknowledge in this a proof (if indeed it is true that He notices such insignificant beings as we are, and if it is possible that His bounty should be expressly extended to so imperfect, so little deserving a creature as myself), I acknowledge a proof of His compassion.

★★★★★★

Note:—This terrible "if" inevitably haunts all deep spirits. This and many other similar interesting problems I have carefully considered in a volume of Essays called *Enigmas of the Spiritual Life*, published by David Stott, Oxford Street, London.

★★★★★★

It appears to me as if it was intended that the sort of storm in which, from my own vehement disposition, the acuteness of my feelings, the situations into which I have been thrown, and particularly the misfortunes which have been peculiarly felt by myself as if the sort of storm in which, from these causes, my mind has for many years past been involved, should subside into that state of tranquil happiness, composure, reflection, and confirmed piety which will make me value my existence here, and prepare me for that which is to come. The idea I have always formed to myself of a future state of happiness, the only one my capacity enables me to conceive, and consequently the only one of which I can say without hypocrisy that I have any real hope, is that we shall there meet those with whom we have been united here by the ties of sacred and virtuous affection.

It is evident from this letter that "the eternity of the tabor" would never prove attractive to the vivid nature of Robert Craufurd; but to him, as to all men blessed or cursed with extremely strong affections, a future life seemed absolutely necessary, if human existence was not to be reckoned a tantalising failure.

Writing to his wife in the year 1806, on the death of her parents, my grandfather again discloses a quite pathetic humility and also that feeling of the impossibility or futility of moral self-formation, or righteousness for self, which characterises the ardently affectionate. It is only through the influence of *others* that such can be redeemed or rise to higher things. Speaking of his wife's deceased parents, he says:

Whose absence I hope I shall never cease to lament until the hour comes that I am called to join them there, where, in consideration of their virtues and yours, my own sins will, I trust, be forgiven. Be assured that nothing can exceed my affection for you and my admiration of every part of your character. And although this affection be sometimes obscured by the effects of temper, yet you may be assured that the affection is always there, as warm and immutable in its nature and essence as the sun itself, though sometimes covered by a cloud.

Again, in 1806, we find this strong and resolute man of action imploring his wife, with almost tearful supplication, to exercise an unceasing moral protectorate over the wild anarchical elements of his storm-vexed nature. He says that he should then be happy in every respect except for one thing:

The apprehension lest you should not exert, by all the means which you know you possess, that influence which it is so much for my happiness and pleasure that you should exercise; but my most earnest entreaty to you is that you will do it upon every occasion. Most solemnly I declare to you that, if I was assured that you would do so upon all occasions, I should feel that to be the firmest basis of my happiness, because I am quite sure that nothing can aid so much to make me contented with myself and inoffensive to others, nothing can tend so much to ensure my being on happy terms with my children, as my living constantly under your influence.

Here, as in so many other instances, we find that heroism and genius are in some ways akin to weakness rather than to power, that the incapacity to live upon self or to regulate self is a distinctive mark of many of the noblest and most ardent natures.

I think that the unveiling of Robert Craufurd's real character (so little known to his ordinary acquaintances) will be much assisted if I now put before my readers a letter written by his widow to a most intimate friend concerning her deceased husband's true internal disposition. But I must warn all commonplace people that to them this admirable letter will appear very absurd.

It will be understood and appreciated only by those who know and realise the baffling complexity of human nature, wherein the most opposite elements are ever interpenetrating each other and almost changing characters with each other; so that in man good and evil seem most nearly related to each other, brethren between whom no great gulf is ever fixed in this life. The wise and thoughtful know well that through manifold palpable contradictions lies the way to all valuable truth, that it is only by freely "entertaining" those intellectual "strangers" called paradoxes that we can really "entertain "the veritable "angels" who bring to us a larger revelation of the deep mysteries of man's fathomless heart.

This letter was written more than a year after General Craufurd's death, when the mind of his widow had grown calm and able to estimate things clearly. Mrs. Craufurd was a woman of a singularly serene temperament, in many ways a great contrast to her fiery consort. And, though I hold that nothing could well be of less moral significance than the opinion of a silly woman, I am yet convinced that a really wise woman often sees much deeper into a man's heart and character than any of his fellow-men can see. It should also be borne in mind that the friend to whom this letter was addressed was no conventional or commonplace person, but the heroic and ardently affectionate William Campbell, whose character has been described in this volume. This great soldier had now become a major.

To this sympathising friend Mrs. Craufurd wrote the following letter—

Knightsbridge, February 10, 1813.

My Dear Sir,

You promised me the indulgence of listening to me when I addressed you, and have said that you would answer any questions I might wish to ask concerning my most dearly loved husband. You can hardly know how great a comfort I feel it. The thoughts of him are all that really interest my heart, and after a day of exertion in endeavouring to perform the duties that are, in so peculiar a manner, required from me to my dearest children, and in wearing that cheerful appearance which is due to the kindness of my friends, I feel it an unspeakable consolation, when sitting over my fire in the evening, to express some of the thoughts that engage me, to one who feels so true an interest in the subject of them.

It has occurred to me to endeavour to retrace to you some features of his exalted mind which may have escaped your observation; for though you did admire and value him, you could not be so acquainted with him as I was.

That he was a hero you know that he has proved, too fatally alas! to the whole world; but do you know that to the most exalted heroism he united more than a woman's tenderness? He had a tear for every human woe, a heart of sympathy for every sorrow. As a husband and a father, I dare not speak of him. Such, and so unutterable was his fondness, his devotion, that in mourning his separation from me, I often check a rising spirit of repining, by a conscious sense that I would not exchange my present lot with that of any human being; so much more valuable do I feel to be the remembrance of having been loved as I was loved by him, than the possession of any other blessing my heart could have known.

With all his superiority of talents he had not one particle of arrogance; and who so quick to observe and ready to allow the merit of others? With so high a spirit as his, he could not but take fire at the bare imagination of injustice; but how forgiving he was! and when he found himself in error, how candid in acknowledging it!

During the last few weeks he ever spent with me he gave a memorable instance of forbearance. On his arrival he went, with open arms and full of cordial feelings, to one who *should have been* his friend. He was received by him with a hard-hearted cruelty for which he had not given even the shadow of a provocation; and all that could be done to embitter the few moments he was allowed to devote to his home, was done. You may suppose how indignant *I* felt, and how hurt to see him so wounded. But never shall I forget the benevolent sweetness with which he reproved me, when I expressed myself on the subject. 'My dear Fanny,' he said, 'it is all very true, but he is unfortunate,' and a tear started from his eye.

That the person was unfortunate *from his own misconduct* never appeared to be remembered by Robert; and although persecuted more cruelly than you can imagine, or I am at liberty to tell you, to almost the last hour of his stay, yet this one sentiment, 'he is unfortunate,' so predominated and so blinded him to all resentment, that he kept firm in the resolution to leave no effort to serve him untried, and in fact did make every exertion in his power for this purpose. Oh, how much I could write, and how much I should still have to say!

I do not complain of his having been taken from me. It is a *hard* world, and he had so much feeling to contend with. The bitter strokes that had assaulted him he bore with his own noble fortitude, and with a submission to the will of Providence the most absolute I ever saw; but he felt them with a poignancy proportionate to the ardour of his nature. His sufferings had been great and many, and he was sometimes almost borne down by them. Of his generosity, his complete disinterestedness, and of the social qualities with which nature had endowed him, you must have had proof, and must have observed how, after a day of laborious exertion, and with what peculiar felicity he would receive and diffuse around him amusement from the most trivial circumstances. He was always first to promote the pleasures of others, and to enter into them himself with real zest. Of his children he was the chosen playmate, participating in their little games as if he had been one of them. But here the scene comes too home, and I have not courage to retrace to you the thousand anecdotes, characteristic of his affectionate sympathy in the pleasures of his little ones, which crowd into my mind.

I hasten to the questions I wish to ask you, and which I beg you to answer candidly on reading them, as if to yourself. After his last return to the army how were his spirits? Was he greatly occupied by his military duties, and at other times cheerful? or did the thoughts of home press heavily on him? Do you think, had I gone to Lisbon the last autumn, he could have passed any part of it with me? Did he ever express regret that I was not there? Were you near him when he was wounded? or how soon afterwards did you get to him? I know how unremittingly you watched beside him to the last; but I want to know how soon he had the comfort of your presence, and who took charge of him during the first fatal moments.

Farewell, my dear Sir, and may God protect you. When you write, pray mention your health; for I thought you still looking very ill when I saw you last, and I am anxious to find that you do not suffer from returning to the army so soon after your severe indisposition.

I am ever,

Your very faithful friend,

M. F. Craufurd.

This portrayal of "the stern Craufurd," the rigid disciplinarian, who was prepared to flog any number of his soldiers rather than permit discipline to be relaxed, will seem to some false and unnatural. Doubtless, the picture is here and there touched with the bright hues of the dawning ideal rather than with the glimmering light and changing colours of the fitful and stormy actual. But so, it must ever be with all *adequate* portrayals of vivid natures. In their higher moments rather than in their ordinary days the true meaning of their hearts and the veritable *raisons d'être* of their spirits are best revealed.

Moreover, in the case of General Craufurd it must be distinctly remembered that though hasty and passionate in temper, he certainly was never cruel. Like other generals of that day, he used punishments to the men which we now consider barbarous; but they were not thought so at that time, and one of his own soldiers, Edward Costello, has borne witness that the general was always "averse to punishment." Many a humane judge in those days was *obliged* to sentence men to be hanged for sheep-stealing. In the long run also Craufurd's soldiers derived more benefit and comfort than suffering from his wonderfully vigilant discipline; otherwise they would not have become "devotedly attached to him," as Captain Kincaid has declared that they did become.

Lord Wellington appears to have taken a considerable time in making up his mind as to who should be General Craufurd's successor. During the siege and storming of Badajoz the command of the Light Division had been held by Lieutenant-Colonel Barnard, of the 95th Rifle Corps, who conducted it with great ability through all its arduous work. Later on, the command was given to Major-General Baron Charles Alten, who had served a good deal with Craufurd. (I find this leader sometimes designated Baron Alten and sometimes Count Alten.) He was a very active and efficient officer, more generally popular than Robert Craufurd, but not endowed with such a striking personality or such remarkable abilities. Sir William Napier, for some reason, appears to have disliked Baron Alten; for he refused to subscribe in order to present this general with a sword of honour, at the termination of the war.

And now I have come to the end of my narrative, and with real regret I must take farewell of the glorious old Light Division, consoled in part by the knowledge that in recent times I have formed an intimate friendship with its senior regiment, the 43rd Light Infantry, and also with a large number of the men and some few of the officers of the famous 52nd.

I would fain follow the career of the division after the death of its old leader, even until Lord Wellington took a last look at its collective British regiments near the suburbs of Bordeaux in June, 1814. The great commander departed amidst loud cheers of officers and men, some of whom had followed him in so many successful campaigns. Yet his feelings must have been full of sadness and regret; for then was dispersed and broken up, never to come together again, the very finest division of Light Infantry that the British Army ever produced. The story that when, at Waterloo, some part of the line was terribly pressed, Wellington exclaimed, "Send the 43rd there," seems well authenticated; but the forgetfulness implied in this order is so unlike the great commander that I hesitate to believe it, though he, like Robert Craufurd, held habitually the very highest opinion of that splendid regiment, which then, alas! was far away from the battlefield of Waterloo. However, the Riflemen were there, bold and enterprising as in the days of old, and the 52nd added to, though they could never surpass, their heroic achievements in earlier years.

To me personally it must ever be a source of profoundest gratification to feel persuaded, as I do feel, that the assertion of Cole, in his *Distinguished Peninsular Generals*, remains a solid truth:

> While memorials of the war in the Peninsula exist, the name of Robert Craufurd will be for ever identified with this noble body of troops, (*i.e.* 43rd, 52nd, and the 95th Rifles. In helping to look after the men now serving in the 43rd and 52nd.)

★★★★★★

> Note:—Owing to the present arrangement of linked battalions, many of the 43rd soldiers whom I knew best are now serving in the 52nd. The present system is hated by the men, is exceedingly uncomfortable, and almost fatal to *esprit de corps.*

★★★★★★

I have always felt a peculiar affection for them, as if it were my natural and inherited privilege to help them in a really fraternal way, as though they were the descendants of the soldiers who served under my grandfather, and so in a spiritual sense bound to me by strongest ties of kinship and unfading memories of the grandest heroism. And, being naturally interested in the men, I greatly rejoice to know that the hearts of many of these soldiers have been opened to me, that I have done all I could to help, console, and cheer them, and that I have gained the affection of many of them.

I have often wished that General Craufurd had lived to see the splendid services of his division at Badajoz, even though he should have died directly afterwards. His *aide-de-camp* "the intrepid Shaw" was there, and, as Napier tells us, displayed "inexpressible coolness." Napier is never so graphic and so enthusiastic as in describing the glories of Badajoz. Great were the achievements and sad the losses of the Light Division on that occasion. The historian says:

> And how deadly the breach strife was may be gathered from this; the 43rd and 52nd Regiments lost more men than the seven regiments of the 3rd Division engaged at the Castle."
> Who shall do justice to the bravery of the British soldiers, the noble emulation of the officers! Who shall measure out the glory of Ridge, of Macleod, of Nicholas, of O'Hare of the 95th, who perished on the breach at the head of the stormers, and with him nearly all the volunteers for that desperate service!

Who shall describe the springing valour of that Portuguese grenadier who was killed the foremost man at the Santa Maria? or the martial fury of that desperate rifleman who, in his resolution to win, thrust himself beneath the chained sword-blades, and there suffered the enemy to dash his head to pieces with the ends of their muskets! Who can sufficiently honour the intrepidity of Walker, of Shaw, of Canch, or the hardiness of Ferguson of the 43rd, who, having in former assaults received two deep wounds, was here, his former wounds still open, leading the stormers of his regiment, the third time a volunteer, the third time wounded!

But the fiery spirit of Robert Craufurd had then gone to its rest. The Light Division went on its conquering way under another leader; but the genius and the methods of its old leader were with it even unto the end. The division produced many other famous officers, conspicuous amongst whom was Colborne, Lord Seaton. Still, I think all careful and candid students of military history must agree in holding that Craufurd never really had any perfectly adequate successor. Amidst a crowd of heroes associated with the undying glories of the Light Division, three brilliant personalities must ever appear most dominant and most characteristic.

Amongst many illustrious names connected with that famous corps, three names must always remain the greatest and most distinctive of all, the names of John Moore, Robert Craufurd, and William Napier. The first of these trained the division with far-seeing sagacity and wisest methods principally in days of peace; the second trained it in time of war, and communicated to it much of his own boundless activity and wonderful rapidity both of perception and of movement; the third served it with admirable power, and then wrote its splendid annals with a fire, an energy, a fulness of knowledge, and a picturesqueness of language unsurpassed by any military historian throughout the long ages of the world.

Appendix

ADDITIONAL LETTERS, ANECDOTES, ETC

The following letter was addressed by Sir Morton Eden (the first Lord Henley), the diplomatist, to Robert Craufurd in the year 1795, when he was serving with his brother Charles on a military mission to the Austrian armies. Then, as on so many other occasions, the well-known slowness of the Austrian military authorities was acting in a very prejudicial manner for the interests of Europe.

Vienna, Monday, September 7, 1795.

My Dear Sir,

I avail myself of an opportunity offered by the return to the army of Count Dietrichstein to acknowledge the receipt of your letter of the 29th past, by express, which reached me last night.

I feel most sensibly all the mischiefs that arise to the common cause from the inaction of the Austrian Army, which I am convinced has, moreover, done more prejudice to the interests of this Court in the Empire than the loss of a battle. My representations, consequently, to bring them to act offensively *on any point and in any manner* that they may deem to be the most likely to produce success, are unremitting. That they intend immediately to commence offensive operations, the appointment of a man of General Wurmser's decided character to so great a separate command (which has given very particular satisfaction to the king's ministers), and the opinions which I know he has expressed since his arrival at Fribourg, with the preparations making for the passage of the Rhine, furnish, independently of the most solemn assurances to that effect, just grounds to expect.

The passage through the territory of Basil may militarily be a very wise measure, though exclusively of all political considerations, it would in its execution become a very hazardous one, if there be in that part of the country any denies where a handful of men might stop the progress of an army. I will take a very early opportunity of insinuating it here, but with that delicacy which you must feel is necessary as well towards this Ministry as the commander-in-chief; and be assured that I shall at all times be happy to receive from you any suggestions that you think can promote our common views.

We understand here that the troops, magazines, artillery, etc., are all drawing to a centre for the purpose of attempting the passage. Of this you are able to give Lord Grenville more accurate information than I can do.

I have the honour to be, with great and unfeigned regard,

> Ever, my dear Sir,
>> Your most faithful humble servant,
>>> Morton Eden.

General Robert Craufurd, as well as his brother, General Sir Charles, seems to have been favoured with the steadfast friendship of His Royal Highness the Duke of Kent. For at the end of January, 1820, just after the death of the Duke of Kent, the Duchess of Newcastle (wife of Sir Charles Craufurd) makes the following remarks in a letter addressed to her sister-in-law, the widow of General Robert Craufurd, who also seems to have known His Royal Highness very well:

We thank you for so kindly complying with our anxious wish to have the earliest and most authentic details of the poor Duke of Kent, but fear the last you sent must have been very distressing to you. His invariable friendship for the general, and his having been quite like a father to my poor Pelham, when he was for two years in his family at Gibraltar, can now be remembered by us but with the greatest gratitude, and gave us an interest in his illness beyond that of most people, though he is so much and generally regretted. . . . You gratified us beyond expression, my dear Fanny, by the account of the Christian manner in which the Duke of Kent's last hours were past.

There were persons before who cast reflections on him in some respects; but who shall say now that he was not a good man, and one who, had he lived, would have set the best example? He, so suddenly called to appear before our great Judge, was perfectly prepared. Did you know that the regent had written the most affectionate and most anxious of letters to his brother, to whom it was of the most essential comfort, as assuring him that the regent was in brotherly affection towards him (though some disagreeable things had passed previously), and that his widow and child would find from the regent the kindest protection? Poor souls, they need it.

I will now give a few more extracts from *The Adventures of a Soldier*, by Edward Costello, a non-commissioned officer of the 95th Rifles, and afterwards a captain in the British Legion.

He writes thus favourably of one of his own officers:

The Honourable Captain Pakenham was a brother-in-law of the Duke of Wellington. This gentleman, who belonged to my regiment, was very much beloved by us all. On every occasion, when the fresh arrival of necessaries, meat, wine, etc., brought the men in crowds about the stores, he invariably would abide his turn, and, as though he were one of ourselves, oblige every newcomer, whatever his rank, to submit to the same. This, though mere justice, for its rare occurrence with the other officers, was never forgotten by the men.

Costello confirms the truth of the stories so often told as to the way in which French and English soldiers fraternised, when not engaged in actual fighting.

All this time, and for a great part of that in which we were quartered here, a, very friendly intercourse was carried on between the French and ourselves. We frequently met them bathing in the Rio Mayor, and would as often have swimming and even jumping matches. In these games, however, we mostly beat them; but that was attributed perhaps to their half-starved, distressed condition. This our stolen intercourses soon made us awake to, until at length, touched with pity, our men went so far as to share with them the ration biscuits which we were regularly supplied with from England by our shipping. Indeed, we buried all national hostility in our anxiety to assist and relieve them.

Tobacco was in great request; we used to carry some of ours to them, while they in return would bring us a little brandy. Their reveille was our summons as well as theirs; and although our old captain seldom troubled us to fall in at the reveille, it was not unusual to find the rear of our army under arms and, perhaps, expecting an attack. But the captain knew his customers; for, though playful as lambs, we were watchful as leopards.

Even immediately after the fierce fighting at Fuentes d'Onoro, this strange habit of fraternising appears to have been kept up by the French and English soldiers. For at the termination of that battle Costello writes as follows:

> The opposing lines of sentries were very close to each other, the French being divided from us only by a narrow plank thrown across the mill-dam, which was occupied on one side by our company, who were now on piquet.
> A blacksmith of ours, of the name of Tidy, who had erected his forge in the old mill, was at work close by, shoeing the officers' horses. The French sentry had crossed the plank to light his pipe, and was standing carelessly chatting with me, when who should I see approaching but General Craufurd, inquiring if Tidy had shod his horse. The Frenchman's red wings soon attracted the general's notice, and he suddenly, with his well-known stern glance, inquired, "Who the d——l's that you're talking with, rifleman?" I informed him the French sentry, who had come over for a light for his pipe.
> "Indeed," replied Craufurd, "let him go about his business; he has no right here; nor we either," said he in a low whisper to his *aide-de-camp*; and away he walked.

Costello's dislike of the Portuguese troops has already been shown in this work; but the following passages make it still more manifest:

> The sanguinary nature of the Portuguese during the whole period of the war was notorious. When crossed or excited, nothing but the shedding of blood could allay their passion. It was always with the greatest difficulty that we could preserve our French prisoners from being butchered by them, even in cold blood. They would hang upon the rear of a detachment with prisoners, like so many carrion birds, waiting every opportunity to satiate their love of vengeance, and it required all the firmness and vigilance of our troops to keep them in check. It was well known that even our men fell in stepping between them and the French whom they had marked out as victims. Indeed, it was not infrequent for our men to suffer from the

consequences of their ferocity, and I myself, while at Vallee, had a narrow escape. I had crossed the hills to purchase some necessaries at the quarters of the 52nd Regiment, and on my return fell in with several of the soldiers of the 3rd Caçadores.

One of them, a fierce-looking scoundrel, evinced a great inclination to quarrel, the more particularly as he perceived that I was unarmed and alone. Having replied rather sharply to some abuse they had cast upon the English, by reflecting on their countrymen in return, he flew into a rage, drew his bayonet, and made a rush at me, which I avoided by stepping aside, and tripping him head foremost on the ground. I was in the act of seizing his bayonet, when a number of his comrades came up, to whom he related, in exaggerated terms, the cause of our disagreement. Before he had half concluded, a general cry arose of "Kill the English dog;" and the whole, drawing their bayonets, were advancing upon me when a party of the 52nd came up, the tables were turned, and the *Caçadores* fled in all directions.

Writing concerning another occasion, this same writer says:

The same evening Colonel Colborne, with less than two hundred men of the 43rd, 52nd, and the Rifles, carried in the most gallant manner a strong fort of the enemy. Prior to its being stormed, a number of *Caçadores* had been ordered to take blankets to convey away the wounded French as well as the British. But most of those employed in this duty took advantage of it to strip the prisoners, whom, to the number of fifty, they left almost as naked as they were born, and exposed to all the rigours of the inclement month of January. I was present near the tent of General Craufurd when a talkative, smart little Frenchman, whom I guessed to be an officer, was brought before him. The poor fellow had nothing on but his trousers, and bled profusely from the nose and mouth, through the blows he had received. The general was very chagrined at the sight, and lamented his inability to give him clothes, his own baggage being so distant. Tom Crawley (a private), however, who had been actively employed in hunting the Portuguese from them, immediately stepped forward, and touching his hat after his own inimitable manner, 'Yer hornier,' said Tom, his eyes sparkling at being able to assist, 'I'll lend him my great-coat, if ye'll allow me.'

Craufurd, much pleased at his frank offer, instantly answered,

'You are very good, rifleman, let him have it;' and Tom proceeded to strip. Meanwhile more of the Frenchmen were marched in, many worse off than their officer. One of them, a sergeant and a smart-looking fellow, as soon as he perceived the officer, ran to embrace him, and leaning his head on his shoulder, burst into tears over their mutual misery. Captain Smith, the general's *aide-de-camp*, being present, generously pulled forth his pocket-handkerchief, and wrapped it round the sergeant's totally naked person, till further covering could be obtained.

Writing about the storming of Ciudad Rodrigo, Costello says:

Regardless of the enemy's fire and every other impediment, the men dashed in over the breach, carrying everything before them. I had got up among the first, and was struggling with a crowd of our fellows to push over the splintered and broken wall that formed the breach, when Major (George) Napier, who was by my side encouraging on the men, received a shot, and staggering back, would in all probability have fallen into the trench, had I not caught him. To my brief inquiry if he were badly hurt, he squeezed my hand, whilst his other arm hung shattered by his side, saying, 'Never mind me, push on, my lads, the town is ours.'

This anecdote is thoroughly characteristic of that brave, noble-minded and unselfish officer, Sir George Napier, in whom General Robert Craufurd always placed such firm trust.

Costello says further,

There is no doubt but Wilkie, Major Napier, and indeed several others in advance, fell by the fire of the Portuguese, who, being panic-struck by the first volley they received from the town, instantly lay down on the glacis, and commenced firing on the breach; a random shot through the embrasure deprived my friend (Wilkie) of life.

I fancy that this writer has a little exaggerated the demerits of the Portuguese, though General Craufurd also appears at first to have thought very little of them; for Wellington says in a letter to him:

I hope you will find the Portuguese Caçadores better than you expect.

Speaking of a later period—about the time of the siege of San Se-

215

bastian—Costello gives us a very curious bit of information.

It was about this time that those men of the 52nd who were fortunate enough to have survived the 'forlorn hope' of Rodrigo and Badajoz, were distinguished with a badge of laurel on the right arm. It was given by their commanding officer as a testimonial of their gallant conduct, which was expressed by the two letters V. S. or valiant stormer, placed beneath: the wreath. Why the men of our battalion (of the 95th Rifles) and those of the 43rd, who had equally distinguished themselves on those occasions, were not similarly honoured, I know not.

This information is very interesting as well as strange. It shows in a marked way the intense sympathy and pride which that great soldier John Colborne, Colonel of the 52nd (afterwards Lord Seaton), always felt for the men of his glorious regiment. But I know well that General Craufurd always considered his Riflemen—who had been with him in so many hours of marvellous peril and adventure—and the men of the old 43rd quite on an equality with the heroes of the 52nd. Colonel Macleod, of the 43rd, very greatly disliked Robert Craufurd; yet he testifies that the general always liked the regiment.

I will conclude my almost unending extracts from the work of my grandfather's gallant Rifleman—to whom I am so greatly indebted in compiling this record—with one truly pathetic and tragical story. It was told to Costello by a Corporal Henley, of the 14th Light Dragoons, a regiment which Craufurd very highly valued, and which our Rifleman designates as "that gallant and highly distinguished regiment." Henley continued, with deep emotion:

I must here relate an event which at the time filled all who were present with a sorrow which indeed I shall never forget. General Slade, observing the numerous cavalry against which his brigade had to contend, advised the officer in command not to allow their ranks to be weakened by conducting prisoners to the rear, but, after disarming them, to let them proceed of their own accord. It was not uncommon, therefore, to observe groups of French dragoons riding quietly to the rear, looking for anyone to take them in charge. It happened that a hussar of the 3rd Germans, having taken a prisoner, ordered him to fall back also. The latter, having ridden some little distance as directed, suddenly applied both spurs to his horse, making a detour to his regiment. The German, observing this, as quickly pursued, and, upon closing with him, fired his pistol, and the dragoon fell dead from his horse.

The hussar, having secured the Frenchman's rein, conveyed him some little distance to the rear, and proceeded to take off his valise, when, overhauling the contents, he discovered a letter from his father, on reading which, he found that it was his own brother who had fallen by his hands. Stupefied with horror, he sat motionless and speechless on his horse for some minutes, when he exclaimed, the big tears rolling down his veteran cheek, 'The king has commanded, and my God will forgive me,' at the same time applying his spurs, he rushed headlong into the battle.

A few days after, meeting a patrol of the same regiment near Gallegos, inquiry was made respecting our unfortunate hussar, when we were informed that he too had that day been numbered with the dead, not far from the corpse of his brother.

Poor soldier! Kingly commands and even divine forgiveness could not really avail to heal the grievous wounds of self-reproach and sorrowing affection. To noble natures led into transient errors quite alien to their true character, the most difficult thing of all is *self*-forgiveness.

Consequently, though the first duty of a *soldier* is unquestionably obedience, it cannot be so in civilian life. *There* the individual conscience must be our highest guide, and must often lead to apparent rebellion against authority. This is well illustrated by a story told of one of General Craufurd's ancestors, a certain Kennedy of Drummellane, an Ayrshire laird in the old days. He was called upon to assist Claverhouse and his party in hunting down the Covenanters. But, though opposed to the Covenanters, he refused to join in persecuting them. As the story tells us:

The laird proudly replied, that he would serve his king in the field, but would not be his executioner.

The tragical misfortune of the German hussar happened at Fuentes d'Onoro, where Lord Wellington was so badly off for cavalry.

In a work called *A Narrative" of Events in the South of France*, by Captain Cooke of the 43rd Light Infantry, who served in the Peninsular War from the year 1811, we find some apparent corroboration of Lord Wolseley's statement that Wellington never gained the affection of his soldiers.

I know that it has been said that Wellington was unpopular with the army. The question now is, with what part of the army, those actually carrying arms or the absentees? Now I can assert with respect to the Light Division that the troops rather liked Wellington than otherwise. The soldiers would exclaim in the ranks, 'Oh, here he comes.'

Although Wellington was not what may be called popular, still the troops possessed great confidence in him, nor did I ever hear a single individual express an opinion to the contrary. And yet, singular as it may appear, although the troops were glad to see him, and when ordered on to the attack, threw on their knapsacks with intrepid alacrity, yet I never for a moment heard his absence regretted, or a single soldier express the least anxiety at the want of his presence in any onset that I ever saw made, from the storming of a field-work to the assault of a breach, or even on the eve of a great battle.

I do not think that these somewhat depreciatory reflections of Captain Cooke have much real significance. The commander-in-chief would, in the nature of things, seem to the soldiers at the time being of less importance *to them* than the officers more immediately in command of them. The average private would naturally look for guidance to the subordinate officers whom he knew well personally, and not to the comparatively far-oft superintendence of the presiding genius. That the *officers*, on very many occasions, sorely missed the direct instructions of the great chief is abundantly manifest.

This Captain Cooke goes on to say:

Let it be clearly understood that when I assume to talk upon the popularity of the Duke of Wellington with the army at large, I do so with the military pen, well knowing that popularity has nothing to do with military discipline, nor indeed is needful for one of His Majesty's lieutenants or generals to possess in the command of an army; his soldiers being only living instruments placed at his disposal by a superior power, to be employed in whatever manner may be most conducive to the honour and welfare of the country.

Lord Wolseley would, no doubt, very greatly disagree with the views expressed by Captain Cooke in this last passage, and in so disagreeing he would have the whole teaching of military history on his side. The career of Sir John Moore was a living and striking refutation of Cooke's ridiculous assertion that "popularity has nothing to do with military discipline;" and I think it is also manifest that the "popularity" which Robert Craufurd obtained amongst the men, owing to his unceasing care for their wants, made his soldiers far more willing to submit to his extraordinarily rigid discipline than they would otherwise have been.

It seems to me that all really thoughtful and intelligent people must agree with Lord Wolseley in holding that the capacity for gaining the affection of the soldiers is one great attribute of military genius. And yet I am perfectly convinced that Lord Wolseley is wrong in denying to Wellington the possession of great military genius, on the ground that he was never loved by his men. I believe that the truth really is that Wellington had not *the usual temperament* of genius, and that he was lacking in some of its most attractive and brilliant attributes, whilst yet possessing substantially those high and very rare capacities for war which may certainly claim to be called genius. Wellington had not the *fervour* of nature which usually characterises *inspired* men in almost every department of intellectual and moral greatness. His personality was unquestionably a far less striking one than that of Napoleon or Hannibal.

His temperament was not suited to evoke enthusiastic attachment. It was more in harmony with the spirit of the eighteenth century philosophy, which shunned enthusiasm as a vice, than with our modern thought, which regards it as the very source and fountain of all true goodness and of all true religion. The highest and grandest of all mental faculties is that imperial one called imagination, and this was in Wellington extremely fettered and restricted in its range. That he had that kind of imagination which is necessary in order to guess at or divine the intentions of a subtle enemy in war, cannot be reasonably doubted; but he never displayed the faintest traces of any other sort of imaginative power.

Yet, on the other hand, the very fact which Lord Wolseley adduces as fatal to Wellington's pretensions to high military genius, is in some ways calculated to *enhance* our sense of his vast capacity for war. The very fact that this great commander was able to accomplish such splendid results in the face of almost overwhelming difficulties, *without that great advantage* which arises from the power of attracting the enthusiastic affection of the soldiers, does but show the more plainly his genuine intellectual greatness. He was able to do without a kind of help which is commonly deemed essentially necessary to success in war.

Emerson said of the greatest of all German writers, "Goethe can never be dear to mankind;" and doubtless the remark is true. And we might say the same of the greatest of all British generals. A certain coldness of temperament marred to some extent the splendid qualities of these two widely different kings of men. Yet in *both cases alike*, the very fact that the intellect had, to a considerable extent, to *do the work of the heart* as well as its own proper work, tended to *develop* certain phases of mental power, and thus to vindicate and assert the possession of true genius, even whilst limiting its influence. Fervour of nature is a glorious power, but genius sometimes exists without it. The intellect sometimes appears to grow all the stronger because it eats up the rations of the heart as well as its own.

General Craufurd had, of course, a far more intimate knowledge of Wellington in war than Lord Wolseley can have. And I know for certain that the leader of the Light Division always had the very highest admiration of the military genius of his great chief, though I know equally well that to "the fiery Robert Craufurd" Wellington often seemed somewhat cold-hearted and deficient in geniality and other attractive qualities of human nature.

The following description of the different qualities of the regiments composing the Light Division was written by Captain Cooke, of the 43rd Light Infantry, and is very interesting:

> This was the last of the Light Division. The separation now came. Though amongst the regiments which composed it there existed an unanimity which was almost without a parallel in war, yet there was a shade of difference between them, a something peculiar to each corps, distinguishing it from all the others; which was the more remarkable as amongst them there was a sort of fraternal compact, and it has occurred that three brothers held commissions at the same time in the 43rd, 52nd, and the Rifle Corps.
>
> The 43rd were a gay set, the dandies of the army, the great encouragers of dramatic performances, dinner parties, and balls, of which their headquarters was the pivot.
>
> The 52nd were highly gentlemanly men, of a steady aspect; they mixed little with other corps, but attended the theatricals of the 43rd with circumspect good-humour, and now and then relaxed, but were soon again the 52nd.
>
> The Rifle Corps were skirmishers in every sense of the word, a

sort of wild, sportsmen, and up to every description of fun and good-humour; nought came amiss; the very trees responded to their merriment, and scraps of their sarcastic rhymes passed current through all the camps and bivouacs.

In this way the brothers of the three regiments met together, each being the very type of the corps to which he belonged. Amongst them are to be enumerated the Napiers, the Maddens, the Booths, the Rowans, the Whichcotes, the Maynes, the Dobbs, the Patricksons, the Harvests, and others. And before we take our farewell, I may affirm that, although these troops were bound together by an iron code of discipline, no Roman tribune could ever boast of more camp orators, nor was there any fraternity that ever lived in happier independence when off duty.

It may interest some of my readers to be reminded that these famous regiments have never entirely parted from each other, but remain permanently honorary members of each others' messes. Perhaps, also, I may be permitted to remark that the 52nd is still supposed to be characterised by its old gentlemanly sedateness.

Captain Cooke of the 43rd also tells us, in his work just quoted, that:

The eight British Divisions, during the war in the south of Europe, were known by the names of the generals who usually commanded them, such as 'Graham's Division,' 'Hill's Division,' 'Picton's Division,' 'Cole's Division,' and 'Craufurd's Division.'

It may gratify some of my readers to know that an appreciative, though brief, sketch of the career of the heroic Sir T. Sydney Beckwith is to be found in the *Dictionary of National Biography*, edited by Mr. Leslie Stephen. The writer of Beckwith's life in this work justly says concerning him:

He, with Craufurd, shares the honour of being one of the finest leaders of light troops ever known.

Craufurd and Beckwith were staunch friends. In my grandfather's last letter to his wife written a week before he was fatally wounded, he says that Beckwith had managed to procure some greyhounds for him. As I have before observed, the leader of the Light Division trusted this famous soldier more than any other colonel serving under him. And there is no doubt that Beckwith was the greatest officer that the 95th

Rifles ever produced, an ideal hero, of whom the Rifle Brigade ought for ever to be proud. He was simply adored by the soldiers serving under him.

Though very many of our most valiant soldiers in the Peninsular War were Irish, Sir James Shaw Kennedy tells us in his diary of General Craufurd's outpost operations in 1810 that a considerable number of Irishmen served against our country systematically in the ranks of the French. This writer says that at the beginning of July, 1810, "a sergeant who deserted from the enemy's Irish Brigade" gave information that the Irish Brigade was then in Junot's corps, that it was commanded by General Torny, and that the brigade had two battalions with about three hundred and fifty men in each, and that the 70th (French) Regiment was brigaded with it.

General Sir James Shaw Kennedy evidently thought that his old leader (Craufurd) was, to say the very least, fully equal to Marshal Soult in his knowledge of outpost work. In a long letter addressed to Lord Frederick Fitzclarence in the year 1850, this experienced veteran says:

> Your Lordship mentions having been with the French army three years ago, and having found their instruction very perfect in all that regards outpost duty. I suppose that at the time you allude to (three years ago) they were regulated in this respect by what is ordered in the paragraphs from 81 to 97 inclusive of the Ordonnance of 1832, "*Sur le service des Armées en campagne*," issued by Marshal Soult; which regulation seems to be very good, and yet not to contain even all that was adopted by General Craufurd in the Light Division, and not much that was not adopted by him.

Even the experience gained in many years subsequent to Robert Craufurd's death seems to have scarcely enabled Marshal Soult to surpass that wonderful knowledge of outpost work which, together with their matchless discipline, made the soldiers of the Light Division, in its palmy days, superior, as regards some of the most hazardous operations of war, to any troops produced by any other nation throughout the world's long history of brilliant and heroic contests.

Almeida June 12th 1810

My dear General

The state of the Insurrection in Ciudad Rodrigo is not so bad as to render it necessary that you should incur the risk of any loss, in order to throw in an additional quantity. It is what they are most deficient in; & it would have been better if their wants had been fully supplied in time. Such they are

Lt General Crawfurd

for the purpose of this interchange.

With an Army one fourth inferior in Numbers, a part of it being of a doubtful description, & at all events but just made, & not more than one third of the numbers of the enemys' Cavalry, it would be an operation of some risk to Repass our Mountains, & bring on a general action in the Plains; & would most probably accelerate the Period of our Evacuation of the Peninsula.

However I shan't give over all
thoughts of attempting their ships,
at least by throwing in supplies;
which probably might be done
without a general action. This
will depend upon the position
which Mahon continues to hold
with the fleet of the enemy.

You will be concerned to hear of the
illness of Mr. Windham. I hear
Mr. Shelbury Liverpool writes to
be of him on the 25th Wednesday
&c

on the 30th he was still very ill.

Ever yours most faithfully

Washington

My dear Crawford

I return the Paper you left with me.
I have added, upon a separate Paper,
such observations as occurred to me.
The fault of the proposed arrange-
-ment is that it is complicated.
I own I cannot bring my mind to
approve of the limited service. The
more I reflect on it, the more I dread
its effects — I doubt if a single man
will be induced, by it, to come into
the Army, who would not have
enlisted at any rate — and I wish
that, for the present, Mr Wyndham
had been satisfied with the
                   raising

raising the Pay of the Non Commd Officers,
bettering the Chelsea Pensions, &
giving the Soldier a right, at the
expiration of 21 years, to his dis
charge & to a shilling pension
& even to more, in cases where
the general strength is requisite
so that the old Soldier, who
could not work, should never
be seen but in a comfortable
situation.

       I remain your faithfully

          John Thorne

Major-General Robert Craufurd
By John William Cole

There is a tear for all that die,
A mourner o'er the humblest grave;
But nations swell the funeral cry.
And triumph weeps above the brave.

Byron.

Born 1764—Killed at Ciudad Rodrigo, 1812.

Robert Craufurd, descended from an old Scottish family, was the third son of Alexander Craufurd, Esq., of Newark, in Ayrshire. His father, a collateral branch of the ancient line of the Craufurds of Kilbirney, was created a baronet in 1781. The nephew of the deceased general, and son of his elder brother James, is the present inheritor of the title and estate. The gallant subject of this memoir entered the army in the year 1779, at the early age of fifteen, and served four years as ensign and lieutenant in the 25th Foot. His first colonel was Sir Charles Stewart, an officer of great ability, whose name would have stood higher on the roll of fame, if favourable opportunity had seconded his pretensions.

★★★★★★

Sir Charles Stewart commanded in the Mediterranean in 1799-1800; he conceived and submitted to the war minister a most able plan for offensive operations in that quarter, which required the employment of fifteen thousand effective men, and had every prospect of a great result. The force was promised, but dwindled first to ten thousand, and then to five. The general, who was of a hot temper, thought he had been ill used, and threw up his command in disgust. His services were thenceforward lost to the country, and he died in the following year. The men withheld from him, were frittered away in expeditions which ended in failure, and reflected no credit either on the government, or their chosen instruments.

★★★★★★

We have spoken of him elsewhere as having originated the idea which suggested to a greater military genius the lines of Torres Vedras. He perceived the enthusiastic devotion with which his young subaltern gave himself up to the study of his profession, discovered his daring spirit and perseverance, and extended to him the ready hand of patronage, without which the most exalted merit often languishes in obscurity. Young Craufurd was so fortunate as to be promoted to a company at the early age of nineteen, shortly after which he had an opportunity of attending the reviews at Potsdam, and passed some time on the continent, principally employed in military studies. The leading nations of Europe were then at peace, but his regiment, the 75th, being ordered to India, he served throughout the first war against Tippoo Saib, under Lord Cornwallis, and on more than one occasion was distinguished by special mention.

It so happened that for a period he commanded his battalion as senior captain. Returning to England in 1794, his elder brother, Colonel Charles Craufurd, who was attached by the British Government to the Austrian headquarters in a military capacity, expressed a wish that he should join him. He did so, and they saw together the campaigns of 1795, 1796, and 1797, during which they were present at several of the most important battles and sieges in Italy and Germany.

In 1798, Craufurd having reached the rank of lieutenant-colonel, was appointed deputy quartermaster-general in Ireland. Between the invasion by Humbert (which was suffered to obtain a momentary success, little creditable to the tactics of the British commander), and the domestic rebellion, that year proved a very busy one in the sister kingdom. After much bungling on our side, ("The races of Castlebar," on the 28th of August, 1798, have obtained unenviable notoriety), Humbert was forced to lay down his arms, having marched with a contemptible detachment of a thousand men into the very "bowels of the land," and causing at least some twenty thousand to be set in motion to surround and exterminate him. The insurgents fought several desperate actions, and were crushed by hard fighting.

Throughout these "untoward events" Colonel Craufurd had his hands full of employment, and in the discharge of very complicated duties, received repeated marks of approbation from his former commander, Lord Cornwallis, then Lord-Lieutenant of Ireland, and General Lake, who directed the military operations. In 1799, he was a second time employed on a military mission to the Austrian armies in Switzerland, and remained there until the expedition to North Holland under the Duke of York, required his services in another quarter. Here again he was attached to one of the staff departments, and displayed his usual energy and activity.

The campaign was short and disastrous, conveying a salutary though expensive lesson that we had yet much to learn before we could compete with our strong enemy in continental warfare. In 1807, the ministry of the day determined to make another attack on Buenos Ayres, which had been won and lost in the preceding year. The first expedition was a sort of wild crusade, a buccaneering adventure, undertaken without sanction from the superior authorities, successful at first from its prompt boldness, but finally rendered abortive, owing to the inadequacy of the forces employed, who were lost and swallowed up in the extent of their own conquest. On this second attempt the means employed were sufficient to ensure success, and the proceedings opened with great *éclat* by the storming of Monte Video, under Sir Samuel Auchmuty on the 3rd of February.

But all future prospects were marred and rendered hopeless by the selection of General Whitelocke for the chief command; a man of most unpopular character, unrecommended by previous services, and void of all claim or pretension beyond powerful interest. The future heroes of the Peninsula stood ready and panting for opportunity; yet they were set aside for one who seemed specially chosen to earn undying infamy for himself, and to stamp a foul blot on the military glory of his country. The subsequent court-martial and disgrace of the miserable individual came on in the ordinary course; but the penalty should with more justice have fallen on the heads of those who gave him such a fatal opportunity of proving his incompetence. The whole affair is in truth an *infandum dolorem*, which makes the heart sicken as often as memory reverts to the painful particulars. The Secretary of State for the department of war and colonies said:

> As it was advisable, that an officer of high rank, as well as talents and judgment, should be sent to take the command of such of His Majesty's forces as were at that time employed, or likely soon to be employed, in the southern provinces of South America, His Majesty's government had made choice, for that purpose, of General Whitelocke.

In this ill-fated undertaking, Craufurd, now a brigadier-general, commanded the 95th and light companies, formed into a select division, which constituted the advanced guard of the army. On the 26th of June, the whole force, directed by Whitelocke, with Major-General Leveson Gower for his second, arrived off Ensenada da Barragon, a port on the Rio-de-la-Plata, about thirty-two miles distant from Buenos Ayres, and disembarked on the 28th without firing a shot The Spaniards were commanded by the same Liniers who had re-captured their city from Beresford, and in whom they placed the most implicit confidence. An opposition to the landing formed no part of his arrangements.

On the 29th, the British troops moved forward. The light brigade took the lead, supported by the 36th and 88th regiments under Brigadier Lumley, and followed by the other corps in succession. On the 1st of July the army was concentrated near the village of Reduction, about seven miles from the capital, from whence it again advanced on the following day, forded the Chuelo, a small stream scarcely deserving the name of a river, and traversed the low ground on the opposite side, at the extremity of which Buenos Ayres is situated.

The invading army numbered 7822 rank and file, including 150 mounted dragoons. It was provided with eighteen field pieces of small calibre, and 206 horses and mules for their conveyance. There had been large quantities of ordnance stores embarked, with heavy guns, mortars, and howitzers, but all these were left in the ships, with the intrenching tools and pontoons, as it would appear, because the time had arrived when it would become necessary to use them.

The enemy suffered the British to advance beyond the Chuelo without showing himself in force, and offering only a feeble resistance, which a few rounds from our artillery were sufficient to overcome. But when the right column, commanded by Major-General Gower, arrived near the Coral de Miserere, the Spaniards displayed a formidable body of infantry and cavalry, supported by a brigade of guns with others in reserve. Brigadier-General Craufurd, placing himself at the head of his light troops, made a vigorous charge, drove the enemy back in confusion, and captured nine guns and a howitzer. Profiting by the panic which had seized his opponents, he gave them no time to rally, but pressed them with a hot pursuit to the very suburbs of the city. Had he been supported promptly by the main body, he would have carried the town on that day, with very little further resistance. Such was his own strongly expressed opinion, backed by that of many other officers, and borne out by intelligence afterwards received.

But the opportunity was suffered to pass by, and such minutes once lost are not to be recalled. General Gower checked this career of victory, and having first ordered a halt, finally withdrew about a mile to the rear, and took up a position, for the night, close to the principal slaughtering place of the city. The troops remained under arms exposed to heavy and incessant torrents of rain. In the morning General Whitelocke summoned the governor to surrender, who derided the invitation and replied by an attack on the outposts. It was then determined to carry the place by assault on the morning of the 5th. The delay was most unfortunate, as it gave the enemy additional time for preparation, and cooled the ardour of the assailants, who desired to be led to instant conflict.

Whitelocke was well aware that the inhabitants were hostile, and determined to defend their houses individually; yet he divided his force into small detachments, and sent them in unloaded and unprovided with anything like proper and sufficient means for forcing barricades or other impediments in the streets. The following anecdote which Craufurd related in the course of his evidence on the trial, renders this part of Whitelocke's conduct more than unaccountable. The day after the brigadier's arrival at Monte Video, the commander-in-chief proposed to him to walk round the works. In returning through the town, he desired him to notice the peculiar construction of the houses, their flat roofs surrounded by parapet walls, and other circumstances, which, as he observed, rendered them peculiarly favourable for defence, and added, that he certainly would not expose his troops to such a contest as that in which they would be engaged if led into so large a town as Buenos Ayres, all the inhabitants of which were prepared for its defence, and with houses similarly constructed to those he then pointed out to him. In the obvious propriety of General Whitelocke's intentions, Craufurd most heartily acquiesced.

There is no occasion to heap, even on Whitelocke, more obloquy than he justly merits. The plan of attack on Buenos Ayres was, after all, none of his own contrivance, but one proposed to him by General Leveson Gower. This fact was distinctly admitted on the trial. Amongst other deficiencies for command, Whitelocke was ever wavering and undecided, without confidence in his own judgment, reposing on the counsel of the last speaker, and ready to give ear to a legion of advisers. Let us now look at this notable plan itself, which presented not a shadow of hope, and was weak to the point of ludicrous absurdity. It must be recollected that Buenos Ayres at that time contained about fifty thousand inhabitants, was a regularly built town, the streets running at right angles, and divided into squares of one hundred and forty yards on each side.

Brigadier-General Auchmuty was directed to take possession with one regiment of the Plaza de Toros and the adjacent strong ground, and there to maintain himself. Four other regiments, divided into wings, were to penetrate into the streets directly in their front. The light battalion divided into wings, and each followed by a wing of the 95th and a three-pounder, was ordered to proceed down the two streets on the right of the central one, and the 25th regiment down the two adjoining; and after clearing the streets of the enemy, this latter regiment was to take post at the Residencia.

Two six-pounders were ordered along the central street, covered by the *carabineers* and three troops of the 9th Light Dragoons, the remainder of which regiment was placed as a reserve in the centre. Each division was to proceed along the street directly before it, till it arrived at the last square of the houses next the river, of which square it was to take possession, forming on the flat roofs, and there to wait for further orders. *Two corporals with tools were ordered to march at the head of each column for the purpose of breaking open the doors.* All were unloaded, and no firing was to be permitted until the columns had reached their final points and formed. Beyond this no orders were given, everything rested here at a dead-lock; and supposing this arrangement had been carried out, there these columns must have stood, for nothing seemed to be determined beyond.

An erroneous report became prevalent in England, that the troops engaged in the assault on Buenos Ayres were ordered not only to advance unloaded, but actually to take the flints out of their muskets. Two companies of the 88th only were thus deprived of every means of offence or defence except their bayonets. They had been on a picket the night before at "White's House," and consequently joined their corps at daybreak with loaded arms. The order to draw their charges occasioned some delay; General Gower, who was present, became impatient, and directed those who had not drawn to take their flints out. The consequence was, that several of these men were killed in the streets whilst in the act of screwing in new flints.

At half-past six, on the morning of the 5th of July, the attack commenced. The troops of the different divisions, as soon as the word was given, advanced at a rapid pace in columns of sections; no sound was heard except their measured tread, the ranks were closed up, and a death-like silence seemed to breathe throughout the town, which resembled a city without inhabitants. Not a single human being was encountered, no advanced posts were dispersed, and the surrounding solitude bewildered the assailants. At length a few detached shots appeared to announce a prearranged signal, at which the entire population were to burst from concealment, and in an instant after the flat roofs of the houses swarmed with a living mass of well-armed defenders, who poured a deadly and almost unerring fire upon the British soldiers. Under any circumstances, the combat between men exposed in an open street, and adversaries ensconced behind the parapets of houses on each side, must have been a very unequal one; but the British were for a time utterly unable to retort or defend themselves, having been ordered to advance with uncharged muskets.

The doors of the houses were barricaded with such strength that it was impossible to force them. The streets were intersected by deep ditches dug across, and heavy cannon planted on the inside of these, poured volleys of grape shot on our advancing columns. There were also flanking batteries at the corners of many streets. Every householder, with his negroes, defended his own dwelling, which was in itself a fortress. Yet, despite this overwhelming opposition, Sir Samuel Auchmuty, with the 37th and 87th regiments, possessed himself of the strong posts of the Retiro and Plaza de Toros, and with heavy loss on his own part, captured thirty-two pieces of cannon, an immense quantity of ammunition, and six hundred prisoners. The 5th regiment took possession of the church and convent of St. Catalina.

The 36th and 88th, under Brigadier-General Lumley, nearly reached their point of destination; but the 88th were overpowered, and after many had fallen, the survivors were compelled to surrender. The 36th and 5th, unable to maintain themselves when their flanks were uncovered, retired upon Sir Samuel Auchmuty's post of the Plaza de Toros, which he continued to hold against every repeated effort of the enemy. But the British divisions were separated; no one could tell what was next to be done, and the commander-in-chief was not to be found at the critical point and moment to issue orders, even if it was still possible to obey them.

The left of General Craufurd's brigade, under Colonel Pack, had approached the great square, with the view of taking possession of the Jesuits' College, but from the deadly effect of the enemy's fire, this was found impracticable. After much slaughter, one portion threw itself into a house, which, being found untenable, nothing remained but to surrender, while the remaining part, after enduring a hot fire, which they were unable to return with effect, and by which Colonel Pack was wounded, retired upon the right division, commanded by Brigadier-General Craufurd himself. On ascertaining the fate of his left, General Craufurd thought it advisable to take possession of the convent of St Domingo. But the Spaniards surrounded the convent on all sides, and attempting to take a three-pounder which lay in the street. Major Trotter, of the 37th, charged them with a few light infantry.

In an instant the greater part of the company and Major Trotter were killed, but the gun was saved. The Brigadier-General was now obliged to confine himself to the defence of the convent, but the quantity of round shot, grape, and musketry, to which they were exposed, at last obliged them to quit the top of the building; and the surrounding enemy, to the number of six thousand, bringing up cannon to force the wooden gates, Craufurd, judging from the cessation of firing, that those next. him had not been successful, with a bitter pang of heart, surrendered at four o'clock in the afternoon.

The result of the action left Whitelocke in possession of the Plaza de Toros, a strong post on the enemy's right; the Residencia, another strong post on his left, and an advanced position in the centre. But these advantages had cost 2500 men in killed, wounded, and prisoners (about one-third of his entire force), while the enemy had suffered little in proportion. He had still 5000 effective soldiers, and his communication with the fleet was uninterrupted. But to convert such a check into a victory required a spirit, and a ready, commanding genius fertile in resource, of which he was utterly destitute. On the following morning, July the 6th, Liniers, who had shown himself as able as his adversary was incompetent, addressed a letter to Whitelocke, offering to give up all his prisoners captured on the day preceding, together with the 71st Regiment and others taken with General Beresford, if he desisted from any further attack on Buenos Ayres, surrendered Monte Video at the end of two months, and withdrew His Majesty's forces from the River Plata.

He intimated at the same time, that such was the exasperated state of the populace, he could not answer for the safety of the prisoners, if offensive measures were persisted in. The defeated commander says in his despatch:

Influenced by this consideration, which I knew to be founded in fact, and reflecting of how little advantage would be the possession of a country the inhabitants of which were so absolutely hostile, I resolved to forego the advantages which the bravery of the troops had obtained, and acceded to a treaty, which I trust will meet the approbation of His Majesty.

The country, as might be expected, was outrageous at this unexpected failure: the army returned home; the general who had betrayed their hopes was tried by a court-martial, and cashiered with infamy,—and so ended the attempt to obtain a footing by conquest on the Spanish continent of South America. Far better would it have been for that vast province had it then passed under the permanent and improving rule of England, instead of enduring the many internal wars and revolutions of which it has since been the theatre. But the Power that governs the universe had otherwise decreed.

Liniers was very kind and complimentary to the British officers during the short time they remained his prisoners. He spoke of General Beresford in the highest terms, and said he had derived from his excellent defence the plan and idea of his own proceedings. But without wishing in the least to detract from the merit of an able enemy, he was seconded by the inhabitants with such cordial co-operation, that his resources were infinitely multiplied, and his difficulties diminished.

In October, 1808, Craufurd accompanied the expedition, which sailed from Falmouth, under Sir David Baird, destined to reinforce and co-operate with Sir John Moore in the north of Spain. He was now a major-general, and commanded the second light brigade. The British army united at Mayorga on the 20th of December. Their numbers actually amounted to only 23,580 men, infantry and cavalry included, with sixty pieces of artillery. The whole were organised in three divisions, a reserve, two light brigades of infantry, and a single division of cavalry. They were at that time unbroken in discipline, full of strength and ardour, and equal to an encounter with any enemy likely to be opposed to them. Superior numbers they little heeded, unless, as it happened, they poured on with such overwhelming masses that to face them would have been rashness rather than valour.

The inevitable march to the rear began, and with the despondency of all retiring movements, came also the straggling, drunkenness, murmurs, hardships, privations, losses, and relaxed discipline, which convert the most imposing army into a host of tattered brigands, and stamp the vicissitudes of war with such repulsive features. It is needless to dwell on a fact so often stated and proved, as the impatience with which an English Army endures the mortification of a retreat. Sir John Moore seized the moment which yet remained to escape from the danger into which he had been nearly entrapped by false intelligence, and little rest or pause remained for him until he traversed the long and dreary space which lay between his army and the western coast.

During the retreat, it became important to hold the bridge of Castro-Gonzalo, over the Esla, until the cavalry and stragglers had passed the river. General Craufurd was posted there, with orders to check the advance of the enemy as long as possible, and when the time desired was gained, to destroy the bridge and bring off his brigade. During the night of the 28th of December, and amidst torrents of rain and snow, while the enemy were gathering closely round him, he contrived to destroy two arches of the bridge (an ancient edifice constructed of solid masonry) and to blow up the connecting buttress. Napier says:

> The troops then descended the heights on the left bank, and passing with the greatest silence by single files over planks laid across the broken arches, gained the other side without loss; an instance of singular good fortune, for the night was dark and tempestuous; the river rising rapidly with a roaring noise, was threatening to burst over the planks, and the enemy was close at hand. To have resisted an attack in such an awkward situation would have been impossible, but happily the retreat of the troops was undiscovered, and the mine being sprung with good effect, Craufurd marched to Benevente, where the cavalry and the reserve still remained.

It was a bold feat, and deserved success, while it marked the spirit of the man by whom it was directed. Dangerous audacity often opens the road to great advantages. Craufurd seems often to have acted on this principle, and thus conveyed an impression that he was more rash than prudent, and that constitutional impetuosity sometimes superseded his more sober judgment On the 31st of December, the light brigades were separated from the main body, and marched by cross roads to Orense and Vigo. There was then no intention on the part of the English general to fight a general action, and this detachment was made with the double object of lightening the commissariat supplies, and protecting the flanks of the army. On the 1st of January, 1809, eighty thousand French troops, with two hundred pieces of artillery, commanded by the Emperor Napoleon in person, took possession of

Astorga.

Sir John Moore, with his small army, had slipped away from the grasp of the giant, but he had also drawn this large force from more important objects to a remote corner of the Peninsula, and at great hazard to himself had gained breathing time for Spain, if Spain could have seen the passing opportunity, and sprung up with energy to take advantage of it. It was Sir John Moore's intention to embark his army at the most convenient port, and carry it round to Cadiz, which point he could reach in a few days' sailing, while miles of toilsome marches would be required to bring the enemy from Galicia to that neighbourhood. He had his choice between Vigo, Corunna, and Ferrol, but was compelled to hesitate and change his course from day to day until the reports of the engineers could reach him as to which of the three harbours was the most eligible for his purpose.

On the 8th of January, Sir John Moore, being hard pressed by Soult, departed from his original plan, and drew up his army at Lugo, offering the battle which the enemy declined to accept. The discipline of the troops was at once restored, and there can be no doubt of what the result would have been, had the French marshal accepted the challenge. The English general, in the absence of the light brigade, which he now regretted, had still nineteen thousand men in line opposed to twenty-one thousand, and a respectable proportion of artillery. General Craufurd was not present at Lugo or at the Battle of Corunna; it is, therefore, needless to repeat here the further incidents of the retreat to the winding-up of that well-fought day.

During the winter the war languished; the English ministers were paralysed by the result of Sir John Moore's campaign, notwithstanding the barren laurels of the closing battle. The nation began to despond, and the objects for which we were so lavishly expending our blood and treasure appeared to be dissolving into vapour in the troubled horizon. But, with the approach of summer, hope and energy returned, and Sir Arthur Wellesley once more appeared in Portugal at the head of an English Army. The passage of the Douro, the expulsion of Soult, and the Battle of Talavera, followed in rapid succession; and occupied something less than three months. We do not find General Craufurd again in action until the day after the great battle just named, when he arrived with three splendid regiments—the 43rd, 52nd, and 95th, and immediately took charge of the outposts.

These battalions formed the pith of the far-famed "light division." They had been trained in the camp at Shorncliffe, under the eye and on the plan of Sir John Moore: in all that constitutes the character of the soldier they were perfect; in every narrative of war they may be quoted as models; and it may be said without exaggeration, that they never met their match in a fair field, when opposed to anything like equal numbers. While memorials of the war in the Peninsula exist, the name of Robert Craufurd will be for ever identified with this noble body of troops. Their advance to Talavera has been justly commemorated as an instance of practical discipline and endurance, to which it would be difficult to produce a parallel They were in bivouac at Malpartida de Placencia, which place they had reached after a march of twenty miles, and had only been allowed a few hours to rest and cook their rations, when flying rumours reached them to the effect that the British Army was defeated, and the enemy close at hand.

Craufurd hastened on, determined not to halt until he verified the state of affairs with his own eyes. In twenty-six hours, he crossed the field of battle, moving in perfect order as if on parade, having during that time passed over sixty-two English miles, under the burning rays of a Spanish sun in July, each man carrying from fifty to sixty pounds weight, and of the entire division only seventeen stragglers were left behind. Napier, who was with them, has recorded the fact in these words, and adds, with just exultation:

> Had the historian Gibbon known of such an effort, he would have spared his sneer about the delicacy of modern soldiers.

The Battle of Talavera, although glorious to the British Army and their commander, produced no favourable effect on the progress of the war. The conduct of the Spanish generals rendered it impossible to help them to any good purpose. Lord Wellington retired into Portugal, and the tide rolled rapidly towards the invasion of that kingdom on the northern frontier. Offensive operations on our part were ended for a time. For four months General Craufurd occupied an advanced and dangerous post with the light division only, and continued to keep the whole French Army on the alert. Time was of the greatest importance to the English commander, both for political and military reasons; and to achieve his object, more peril was incurred than sound judgment might have sanctioned under ordinary circumstances.

Craufurd was strictly instructed to keep his ground as long as he could with safety, but on no account to risk an action on the French side of the Coa. His force consisted of the light division, two regiments of cavalry, and six pieces of horse artillery, opposed to an army in his immediate front numbering not less than thirty thousand men. He engaged in several skirmishes with varied success, and fought a serious action on the right bank of the Coa, with a deep ravine in his rear, between him and the river, and only one narrow bridge for a retreat.

Much as we admire the hardihood and dauntless valour of the soldier, it is impossible, in this instance, to accord praise to the dispositions of the general. The action ought not to have been fought, and the lives there lost might have been preserved until a more indispensable occasion called for their sacrifice. The particulars of the action are so vividly described by Napier, that it is unnecessary to repeat them. After fighting at great disadvantage for several hours, Craufurd brought off his division to the English side of the Coa, and during the ensuing night retired unmolested behind the Pinhel River. His loss amounted to twenty-eight officers, and three hundred and sixteen men killed, wounded, and missing; while the French suffered to the amount of at least one thousand.

There can be no doubt that Lord Wellington was highly vexed at the imprudence of his lieutenant, although he said less of it at the time than might have been expected. Craufurd, in a short despatch to his superior, treated it lightly, as a matter of course, occurring in the ordinary routine of business. When he presented himself at headquarters after this perilous escapade, Lord Wellington said, rather drily, "I am glad to see you safe, Craufurd."

The latter replied, "Oh! I was in no danger, I can assure your Lordship."

"But I was, from your proceedings," said Lord Wellington.

Upon which Craufurd whispered aside, "He is d—d crusty today." (See Larpent's *Private Journal* vol. 1.)

Lord Wellington knew his merits, and bore with his humours more than with those of any officer in his army. The principal peril to be apprehended from a man of such restless activity and ambition, was that he would exceed his orders, and endeavour to do something beyond what was either expected or practicable. In this he was the very reverse of Sir Rowland Hill and Sir Lowry Cole, who were so constitutionally impressed with the value of subordination, that no incidental occurrence could ever lead them to depart from the strict letter of their instructions. Craufurd was specially adapted for a partisan leader, or the conduct of a detached, flying corps; and the singular acuteness of Lord Wellington was as admirably displayed as that of Napoleon, in selecting the right men for the particular work they were destined to perform.

Marshal Massena, in his official report, indulged in some statements which were contrary to the fact, while they reflected discredit on the conduct of the light division at the Coa. Their fiery leader took up his pen with indignation, and published a reply in the *Times* newspaper. The letter has an additional value, as containing his own version of what really occurred, together with a defence of his arrangements, and cannot fail to be read with interest. It was highly characteristic, and ran thus:—

Marshal Massena, not content with the gross misrepresentations which were contained in his first official account of the action of the 24th of July, near Almeida, has, in a subsequent despatch, reverted to it in a tone of boasting wholly unjustified by the circumstances; assuring the war minister that his whole army is burning with impatience to teach the English army what they taught the division of Craufurd in the affair of the Coa.

Brigadier-General Craufurd has therefore determined to give this public contradiction to the false assertions contained in Marshal Massena's report of an action, which was not only highly honourable to the light division, but which positively terminated in its favour, notwithstanding the extraordinary disparity of numbers. A corps of five thousand men remained during the whole day in presence of an army amounting to twenty-four thousand. It performed, in the presence of so superior a force, one of the most difficult operations of war; namely, a retreat from a very broken and extensive position over one narrow defile. It defended, during the whole of the day, the first defensible position that was to be found in the neighbourhood of the place where the action commenced; and in the course of the affair, this corps of four thousand men inflicted upon this army of twenty-four thousand, a loss equal to the double of that which it sustained.

Such were the circumstances of the action in which Brigadier-General Craufurd's corps was opposed to the army commanded by Marshals Massena and Ney, on the 24th of July; and it is, therefore, indisputable that they had the best of it. From Marshal Massena's official despatch, containing a statement of the force to which we were opposed, it appears that the cavalry consisted of the 3rd Hussars, 50th Chasseurs, 10th,

15th, and 25th Dragoons, and that the whole of the infantry of Ney's corps was present, except one regiment of the division of Marchand. The infantry of Ney's corps, according to the intercepted official returns, amounted at that time to upwards of twenty-two thousand effectives; and the cavalry regiments were certainly between six hundred and seven hundred each. It therefore appears that the force with which Marshals Massena and Ney advanced to attack the light division on the morning of the 24th of July, consisted of twenty thousand infantry, and between three and four thousand cavalry; to which were opposed three English battalions (43rd, 52nd, and 95th), two Portuguese battalions (1st and 3rd Chasseurs), and eight squadrons of cavalry, making in the whole a force of about three thousand two hundred British, and eleven hundred Portuguese troops.

Almeida is a small fortress situated at the edge of the declivity forming a right bank of the valley of the Coa, which river runs from the south to the north, and the bridge over which is nearly an English mile west of the town. From the 21st to the 24th of July, the chain of our cavalry outposts formed a semi-circle in front of Almeida, the right flank being *appuyé* to the Coa, near As-Naves, which is about three miles above the place; and the left flank rested on the river near Cinco-Villa, which is about three miles below the fortress. The centre of this line was covered by a small stream, and looked towards the principal roads by which it was expected the enemy would advance, namely, on the right and centre of the position. The cavalry posts were supported by piquets of infantry.

The only road which our artillery and the body of our cavalry could make use of to retreat across the Coa, was that which leads from Almeida to the bridge. The nature of the ground made it difficult for the enemy to approach this road on our left, that is to say, on the north side of the town; and the infantry of the division was therefore placed in a position to cover it on the right or south side, having its right flank *appuyé* to the corps above the bridge, its front covered by a deep and rocky ravine, and its left in some enclosures near a windmill which is on the plain, about eight hundred yards south of the fortress. The governor had intended to mount a gun upon the windmill; and one was actually in it, but quite useless, as it was not mounted. Another gun (also dismounted) was lying near the mill. These are the guns which Marshal Massena says he took in the action. On the morning of the 24th, the centre of our line of piquets was attacked; namely, that which occupied the road leading from Almeida to Val de la Mula, which village is about four English miles east of the fortress. These piquets were supported by the 14th Light Dragoons, and two guns; but when the head of a considerable column with artillery presented itself, and began to form on the other side of the rivulet, the piquets were withdrawn. The enemy then passed the rivulet, a cannonade took place, and they formed a line of fifteen squadrons of cavalry, at the distance of about a mile from the above-mentioned windmill, with artillery in its front, and a division of about seven thousand infantry on its right. Other troops were seen, though not so distinctly, advancing upon our right.

It being now evident that we were opposed to such a force as to render it impossible for Brigadier-General Craufurd to prevent the investment of the place, he determined to cross the Coa. He ordered the artillery and cavalry to move off by the road leading from the town to the bridge, and the infantry to follow, retiring across the vineyard in the same direction.

The infantry were directed to move in *échellon* from the left, it being necessary to hold the right to the last, in order to prevent the enemy approaching the bridge by a road coming from Junca, and which runs along the bottom of the valley close to the river. Some companies which formed the left of our line, were in a vineyard so completely enclosed by a high stone wall, that it was quite impossible for cavalry to get into it; but the preceding night had been excessively severe, and some of the troops stationed in the vineyard had unfortunately pulled down the wall in many places to make use of the stones to form a shelter against the violent rain.

This wall, which Brigadier-General Craufurd had considered as a complete defence, was therefore no longer such; and after our artillery and cavalry had moved off, the enemy's horse broke into the enclosure and took several prisoners. Our total loss in prisoners and missing amounted to about sixty, after all those who were at first returned as such had contrived to rejoin their regiments. The 43rd Light Infantry having been on the left of the line, was the first that arrived near the bridge. The brigadier-general ordered some companies of this corps to occupy a height in fronts and the remainder to pass on and form on the heights on the other side of the river. Part of the 95th Rifles, and the 3rd battalion of Chasseurs, who arrived next, were formed on the right of those companies of the 43rd regiment that were in front of the bridge. This position was maintained until everything was over, and until one of the horse artillery ammunition waggons, which had been overturned in a very bad situation, was got up and dragged to the other side by the men.

During the remainder of the day, the bridge was most gallantly defended by the 43rd and part of the 95th regiments; and after it was dusk, we retreated from the Coa. To retire in tactical order over such ground, so broken, rocky, and intersected with walls, as that which separated the first position from the second, would have been impossible, even if not under the fire of the enemy; and the ground on the other side of the river was equally unfavourable for reforming the regiments. Whoever knows anything of war, knows that in such an operation, and upon such ground, some derangement of regular order is inevitable; but the retreat was made in a military, soldierlike manner, and without the slightest precipitation. In the course of it the enemy, when he pressed, was attacked in different places, by the 43rd, 52nd, and 95th regiments, and driven before them.

With respect to the enemy's loss, it is of course difficult to say what it was, because we know that from the commencement of the revolutionary war, no French official report has ever contained true statements on this point. Upon this occasion. Marshal Massena says, 'We have taken one stand of colours, four hundred men and two pieces of cannon; our own loss amounted to nearly three hundred killed and wounded.' He took no colours, the cannon were the two dismounted guns belonging to the fortress which were lying in and near the windmill; and instead of four hundred prisoners, he took only about sixty, supposing every one of those we returned as missing, to have fallen alive into the enemy's hands.

Now, if in the same paragraph in which he states his own loss at three hundred, he calls sixty prisoners four hundred, we may fairly infer that he is not more accurate in the one statement than in the other; and this circumstance, as well as the usual practice of their service, and the probability of the thing from what we could observe, folly justify us in assuming it to have been from six to seven hundred. Ours amounted, in killed, wounded, and prisoners, to three hundred and thirty.

Such is the true account of this affair, upon which the Marshal prides himself so much, but in which it is certain that the advantage was on our side. We could not pretend to prevent the investment of the place; but in our retreat we did not lose a gun, a trophy, or a single article of field equipage; and we inflicted on the enemy a loss certainly double that which we sustained. The account, contained in the commencement of the Marshal's despatch, of what had passed on the 21st of July is equally contrary to the truth. He talks of having forced the passage of the little rivulet that runs between Almeida and Val de la Mula on the 2lst; whereas our piquets remained there, and not a single Frenchman passed it until the morning of the 24th. He says that many of our sharpshooters fell into their hands on the 21st; the truth is, they did not take a single man. The retreat of the 14th Dragoons from Val de la Mula was conducted in the most slow and regular manner, and all our intentions with respect to Fort Conception were completely fulfilled.

(Signed)   Robert Craufurd, Brigadier-General.

Four months after the affair of the Coa, Lord Wellington fought and won a defensive battle on the ridge of Busaco. This took place on the 27th of September. Craufurd here displayed the skill of an adroit commander in addition to the impetuous valour by which he was always characterised. The light division, admirably posted, received the attack of Ney's corps, led by General Simon; and when they had nearly gained the crest of the hill on which the English stood, the 43rd and 52nd charged with the bayonet, and sent them rolling back in scattered confusion. Simon was wounded and taken prisoner, and this prompt movement decided the action in that quarter. Craufurd and his division were warmly commended in Lord Wellington's despatch. On the night of the 23rd of September, four days before the battle, a singular circumstance took place, which has been thus related:

The light division, falling back only a league, encamped in a pine wood, where happened one of those extraordinary panics that, in ancient times, was attributed to the influence of a hostile god. No enemy was near, no alarm was given; yet suddenly the troops, as if seized with a frenzy, started from sleep, and dispersed in every direction; nor was there any possibility of allaying this strange terror until some persons called out that the enemy's cavalry were amongst them, when the soldiers mechanically ran together in masses, and the illusion was instantly dissipated. (Napier, vol. 3.)

A simultaneous terror possessed the whole of the Spanish infantry at Talavera. During the night which divided the two days of combat, they started up, fired two or three tremendous volleys at nothing, and ran furiously to the rear. But there they remained; and there was this distinction between them and the gallant light division, that no remonstrance could induce the Spaniards to shake off their alarm, or look the enemy in the face, when he actually advanced in the morning.

During the winter of 1810, while the British Army occupied the lines of Torres Vedras, and Massena watched them from Santarem, General Craufurd obtained leave to go to England on his private affairs. During his absence the command of the light division devolved upon Sir William Erskine. Craufurd returned in time for the Battle of Fuentes d'Onoro, fought on the 5th of May, 1811, and was received with a shout of welcome when he galloped unexpectedly up to the fronts just as the action was about to commence. In this battle, it has been observed by sound military authority that there was less skill than error on both sides. Massena, had he been as active and enterprising as he had shown himself in earlier campaigns, might have turned the advantages he gained at the onset to better account Lord Wellington himself admitted subsequently, in conversation at his own table, (see Larpent's *Private Journal*, vol. 1), that he committed a fault in extending his right too much to Poço Velho; and that if the French had profited by it, as they could have done, there might have been bad consequences; but that they let him recover himself and change his front before their faces.

The British position was, in fact, too much spread out for their numbers, and was strengthened by giving up the ground on the right, and concentrating with the right flank thrown back on the Turones, as the army stood when the fighting ceased. The light division throughout the day performed a distinguished part. They had first to cover the passage of the seventh division over the Turones, and then to retire across a plain at least three miles in extent, in presence of a body of five thousand of the enemy's cavalry, supported by the entire infantry of the eighth corps. They moved slowly and deliberately in squares, while Montbrun with his horsemen crowded round their flanks, and appeared to be gathering in a mass for a concentrated charge.

But they, threatened without attempting to execute; and the dangerous crisis of the battle passed over innocuously. Craufurd cleared the plain, with very little loss, presenting such a close and determined front wherever the enemy pressed too eagerly, that they held back, and suffered the retiring divisions of the British Army to take up their new ground in regular order. If Massena, as was expected, had renewed the attack on the following day, there seems little reason to doubt that the result would have been decisively against him. But he drew off his army without any further effort, leaving Almeida, which he sought to relieve, to its fate, and resigned the command of the army of Portugal to Marmont, who was destined to sustain a more signal overthrow in the following year. Let all who read of the Battle of Fuentes d'Onoro bear in mind that Massena outnumbered the English Army by more than two to one, and that he had an overpowering preponderance in cavalry.

During the remainder of 1811, General Craufurd and the light division were actively employed in various field movements; but no other general action took place under the immediate command of Lord Wellington. The renewed siege of Badajos was abandoned after the Battle of Albuera, in consequence of the junction of Soult and Marmont, whose forces, when united, so materially exceeded the British, that it is marvellous how they suffered such a favourable crisis to pass without striking a blow which, if successful, might there and then have terminated the war in their favour. The genius of the English general was never more triumphantly displayed than during this period, which seemed portentous of decisive events; but the lowering clouds which gathered round him, he contrived to baffle and dissipate, and even to wrest from the enemy an important fortress, watched by eighty thousand men, while he had little more than half that number to oppose to them. The campaign, too, was carried on in winter, in the face of every incidental impediment which the season seemed likely to supply.

The siege and capture of Ciudad Rodrigo was a very rapid operation; necessarily so, for Lord Wellington fought against time, and unless he could carry the place by a given date, there was every probability of its being relieved. On the 8th of January, 1812, the trenches were opened, and on the same night an important outwork, the redoubt of Francisco, was stormed by select companies of the light division, under the command of Colonel Colborne (now Lord Seaton). On the 14th the batteries opened; and on the 19th two breaches were reported practicable. Lord Wellington examined them in person, and issued the order for attack, concluding with these memorable words:

Ciudad Rodrigo must he stormed this evening.

The larger breach was to be assailed by the third, and the lesser by the light division. At seven in the evening, the town clock struck, the signal was given by a rocket, and the columns rushed forward. The garrison were prepared for a desperate resistance: a mine was sprung in the principal breach, by which many brave men perished; but in less than an hour the place was won. The stormers of the light division consisted of three hundred volunteers, led by Major George Napier (afterwards Lieutenant General Sir G. Napier), with a forlorn hope under Lieutenant Gurwood. General Craufurd accompanied them, and fell, pierced through the body by one of the first shots fired.

It is neither usual nor requisite that generals of division should thus perform the duties of young colonels and regimental officers; but throughout the Peninsular War, many valuable lives were lost in this manner, from the conviction that an animating example would inflame the courage of the men, and insure success. Still, the principle is a mistake. The head of the general to superintend, is of greater importance than his arm to execute. If he marches up to a breach, he is no more than the grenadier who accompanies him, and even less, if, as is likely, his physical strength is inferior, or his arms are not so well adapted for personal conflict.

Craufurd's last address to his division, a moment before they moved on, was short and clear, in his usually decisive manner:

Soldiers! The eyes of your country are upon you. Be steady— be cool—be firm in the assault. The town must be yours this night. Once masters of the wall, let your first duty be to clear the ramparts; and in doing this keep well together.

There have been many opinions expressed as to this brave officer's capability of command. It has been even asserted, by his admirers, that with the same opportunities he would have equalled Wellington; but such hyperbolical eulogy is as injurious as detraction. Take him on the whole, he was one of the readiest and most dashing executive officers in the service; and his early death must be considered a national loss. It cannot be said that Napier is lavish of praise either to Picton or Craufurd, when in a memorable passage he compares these two renowned leaders.

Picton and Craufurd were not permitted by nature to agree. The stern countenance, robust frame, saturnine complexion, caustic speech, and austere demeanour of the first, promised little sympathy with the short thick figure, dark flashing eyes, quick movements, and fiery temper of the second; nor did they often meet without a quarrel. Nevertheless, they had many points of resemblance in their characters and fortunes. Both were harsh and rigid in command; both prone to disobedience, yet exacting entire submission from inferiors. Alike ambitious and craving of glory, they were enterprising, yet neither was expert in handling troops under fire.

After distinguished services, both perished in arms, and being celebrated as generals of division while living, have been, since their death, injudiciously spoken of as rivalling their great leader in war. That they were officers of mark and pretension is unquestionable, and Craufurd more so than Picton, because the latter never had a separate command, and his opportunities were necessarily more circumscribed; but to compare either to the Duke of Wellington, displays ignorance of the men and of the art they professed.

★★★★★★

When we remember and enumerate the many general actions and important operations in which Picton was prominently engaged after the premature death of Craufurd, we can scarcely admit the conclusion in the last sentence.

★★★★★★

General Craufurd lingered for five days; and it was at first hoped that his wounds although reported dangerous, would not prove mortal. Lord Wellington's despatch to Lord Liverpool, dated Galegos, January 29th, 1812, thus records his death, and the estimation in which he was held by his illustrious commander:—

Major-General Craufurd died on the 24th inst. of the wounds which he received on the 19th, whilst leading the light division of this army to. the assault of Ciudad Rodrigo. Although the conduct of Major-General Craufurd on the occasion on which these wounds were received, and the circumstances which occurred, have excited the admiration of every officer in the army, I cannot report his death to your lordship without expressing my sorrow and regret that His Majesty has been deprived of the services, and I of the assistance, of an officer of tried talents and experience, who was an ornament to his profession, and was calculated to render most important services to his country.

Craufurd was buried on the ramparts of Ciudad Rodrigo, close to the breach which his division had so gallantly carried. Lord Wellington attended the funeral, in tribute of his respect for the departed general. The nation erected a monument to his memory in St. Paul's Cathedral. The following most interesting letter, containing an account of his last hours, first appeared, by permission, in *Stocqueler's Life of the Duke of Wellington*, from whence we have extracted it. The writer is the late Marquess of Londonderry; the person addressed. Sir Charles Craufurd, the elder brother of the deceased, and himself a general:—

Galegos, Jan. 26th, 1812.

My dear Friend,—I have to entreat you to summon to your aid all that resignation to the will of Heaven, and manly fortitude, which I know you to possess, to bear with composure the sad tidings this letter is doomed to convey. I think you must have discovered that, from the first moment, I did not encourage sanguine hopes of your beloved brother, whose loss we have, alas! now to deplore. But, my dear friend, as we all must pass through this transitory existence sooner or later, to be translated to a better, surely there is no mode of terminating life equal to that which Providence ordained should be *his*.

Like Nelson, Abercromby, Moore, and inferior to none (had his sphere been equally extensive), your much loved brother fell; the shouts of victory were the last he heard from the gallant troops he led; and his last moments were full of anxiety as to the events of the army, and consideration for his Light Division. If his friends permit themselves to give way to unbounded grief under this heavy calamity, they are considering themselves rather than the departed hero. The army and his country have the most reason to deplore his loss; for, as his military talents were of the first calibre, so was his spirit of the most intrepid gallantry. There is but one universal sentiment throughout all ranks of the profession on this subject; and if you, and those who loved him dearly (amongst whom, God knows I pity most his angel wife and children), could but have witnessed the manner in which the last duties were paid to his memory by the whole army, your tears would have been arrested by the contemplation of what his merits must have been to have secured such a general sensation, and they would have ceased to flow, from the feelings of envy which such an end irresistibly excited.

As I fervently trust that, by the time you receive this letter, you may be so far prepared for this afflicting stroke as to derive consolation even from sad details, and as I really am unequal to address Mrs. Craufurd at present, I think it best to enter at large into everything with you, leaving it to your affectionate and prudent judgment to unfold events by degrees in the manner you deem best. You will perceive by Staff-surgeon Gunning's report (Lord Wellington's own surgeon), upon an examination of the wound (which I enclose), that, from the nature of it, it was impossible Robert should have recovered. The direction the ball had taken, the extreme difficulty of breathing, and the blood he brought up, gave great grounds of alarm; but still it was conceived the ball might have dropped lower than the lungs; and as there have been instances of recovery from wounds in the same place, we were suffered to entertain a *hope*, but alas! that was all.

Staff-surgeons Robb and Gunning, who were his constant attendants, and from whose anxiety, zeal, and professional ability everything was to be expected, were unremitting in their exertions; his *aide-de-camp*, young Wood, and Lieutenant Shawe, of the 43rd, showed all that affectionate attention which even his own family could have done to him; the former, I must say, evinced a feeling as honourable to his heart as it must have been gratifying to its object To these I must add Captain William Campbell, whose long friendship for Robert induced him never to leave him; and he manifested in an extraordinary manner his attachment on this occasion.

If my own duties had permitted me, you may believe I never should have absented myself from his bedside; as it was, feeling like a brother towards him, my heart led me to act as such to the utmost of my poor abilities. The three officers I have above named, and his surgeon, alternately watched and attended him from the evening of the 19th until ten o'clock on the morning of the 24th, when he breathed his last.

On the 22nd, he was considered easier and better; the medicines administered had all the effects desired. He conversed some time with me, principally about the assault; and he was most anxious as to news of the enemy. He was so cheerful, that his mind did not revert, as it had done before, to his wife and children; and I was anxious to keep any subject from him that might awaken keen sensations. I knew well, from many conversations I have had with him, the unbounded influence and affection Mrs. Craufurd's idea was attended with, and his ardent anxiety as to the education and bringing up of his children. These thoughts, I was anxious, while a ray of hope existed, not to awaken, it being of the utmost consequence he should be kept free from agitation; and I trust this will be a sufficient reason to Mrs. Craufurd and yourself, for my being unable to give you those last sentiments of his heart which he no doubt would have expressed, had we felt authorised to acquaint him that he was so near his end.

I do not mean to say he was ignorant of his situation; for when he first sent to me, he said he felt his wound was mortal, and that he was fully prepared for the will of Heaven; but I think subsequently he cherished hopes. He obtained some sleep on the night of the 22nd; and on the 23rd he was, to all appearance, better. At two o'clock in the morning, William Campbell wrote me a most cheering account of him. He had been talking of his recovery, and every pleasing prospect; and he fell into a comfortable sleep, as those about him imagined; but, alas! from that sleep he never awoke again. His pulse gradually ceased to beat, his breath grew shorter, and his spirit fled before those near him were conscious he was no more. So easy was his passport to heaven!

If, in detailing so mournful a recital, I can derive the smallest consolation, it arises from knowing his last words united his affection for his wife, and his friendship for me in one train of thought, in which he closed his eyes. Having thus acquainted you, as well as my present feelings enable me, with the last scene, I shall now assure you that no exertion was wanting to prepare everything for the mournful ceremony that was to follow, with the utmost possible regard and respect to his memory. Lord Wellington decided he should be interred by his own division, near the breach which he had so gallantly carried. The light division assembled before his house in the suburbs of the San Francisco Convent, at twelve o'clock on the 25th; the 5th division lined the road from his quarters to the breach; the officers of the brigade of guards, cavalry, 3rd, 4th, and 5th divisions, together with General Castanos and all his staff.

Marshal Beresford and all the Portuguese, Lord Wellington and the whole of headquarters, moved in the mournful procession. He was borne to his place of rest on the shoulders of the brave lads he had led on, the field officers of the light division as pall-bearers, and the whole ceremony was conducted in the most gratifying manner; if I may be permitted such an epithet on such a heart-breaking occasion. I assigned to myself the mournful task of being chief mourner, and I was attended by Captain Campbell, Lieutenants Wood and Shawe, and the staff of the light division. Care has been taken that his gallant remains can never be disturbed; and he lies where posterity will commemorate his deeds.

> Believe me, as ever,
> Your most affectionate and ever obliged,
> Charles Stewart.

Craufurd was stern and strict, and being impetuous in manner, and not very ceremonious in language when excited, many of his subordinate officers disliked him; but with the private soldiers he was universally popular, as he always looked to their comforts, and treated them justly, while he maintained rigid discipline. Punishment parades were a source of great annoyance to him; and the necessity of superintending one ruffled his temper for the whole day. The following characteristic anecdote is related in Costello's entertaining *Adventures*. There can be no doubt of its authenticity, as the retailer was an eye-witness. He says:—

I happened to be on guard one day, when General Craufurd came riding in from the front with his orderly dragoon, as was his Visual custom; when two of our men (Rifles), one of them a corporal, came running out of a house with some bread which they had stolen from the Spaniards; they were pursued by a Spanish woman, crying lustily, '*Ladrone! Ladrone!*' 'Thief! Thief!' They were immediately pursued by the general and his orderly; the bread was given back to the woman, and the men were placed in the guard-house. The next day they were tried by a brigade court-martial, and brought out to a wood near the town for punishment.

When the brigade was formed, and the brigade-major had

finished reading the proceedings of the court-martial, General Craufurd commenced lecturing both men and officers on the nature of their cruelty to the harmless inhabitants, as he called the Spaniards. He laid particular stress on our regiment, who, he said, committed more crimes than the whole of the British Army. 'Besides, you think,' said he, 'because you are riflemen, and more exposed to the enemy's fire than other regiments that you are to rob the inhabitants with impunity; but while I command you, you shall not.' Then, turning round to the corporal, who stood in the centre of the square, he said, with a stern voice,—'Strip, sir!'

The corporal, whose name was Miles, never uttered a word until tied up to a tree, when, turning his head round as far as his situation would allow, and seeing the general pacing up and down the square, he said, 'General Craufurd, I hope you will forgive me.' The general replied, 'No, sir, your crime is too great.' The poor corporal, whose sentence was to be reduced to the pay and rank of a private soldier, and to receive a punishment of one hundred and fifty lashes, and the other man two hundred, then addressed the general to the following effect: — 'Do you recollect, sir, when you and I were taken prisoners, when under the command of General Whitelocke, at Buenos Ayres? We were marched with a number of others to a sort of pound, surrounded by a wall. There was a well in the centre, out of which I drew water with my mess-tin, by means of canteen straps I collected from the men who were prisoners like myself. You sat on my knapsack; I parted my last biscuit with you. You then told me you would never forget my kindness to you. It is now in your power, sir. You know how short we have been of rations for some time?' These words were spoken by the corporal in a mild and respectful accent, which not only affected the general, but the whole square. The bugler, who stood waiting to commence the punishment close to the corporal, received the usual nod from the bugle-major to begin.

The first lash the corporal received, the general started and, turning himself round, said, 'What's that—what's that?—who taught that bugler to flog? Send him to drill—send him to drill! He cannot flog—he cannot flog! Stop! stop! Take him down! Take him down! I remember it well—I remember it well!' while he paced up and down the square, muttering to himself words that I could not catch, at the same time blowing his nose and wiping his face with his handkerchief, trying to hide the emotion that was evident to the whole battalion. While untying the corporal, a dead silence prevailed for some time, until our gallant general recovered a little his noble feeling, when he uttered, with a broken accent, 'Why does a brave soldier like you commit these crimes?' Then beckoning to his orderly to bring his horse, he mounted and rode off. It is needless to say that the other man also was pardoned, and in a few days the corporal was restored to his rank.

According to our dates. General Craufurd, when he fell, was in the forty-eighth year of his age, and the thirty-second of his service. He married Bridget, daughter of Henry Holland, Esq., and left a family of three sons and a daughter. We do not recollect to have seen any engraved likeness of General Craufurd, and we believe his portrait was never taken.

In stature, he was below the middle size; but his air was commanding, and the animated expression of his countenance denoted the energetic qualities of his mind. In all the relative capacities of husband, parent, brother, friend, companion, and enlightened officer, he discharged the noblest duties of humanity with affection, rectitude, and honourable consistency. His general acquirements not only rendered his society agreeable, but instructive, and won the esteem of all who had the privilege of his intimate acquaintance.

He was devoted to his profession, and the predominant object of his life was military distinction. He loved his country as a true patriot, and acknowledged all the advantages of her laws, religion, and government. The diligence and regularity which he always exhibited in the performance of his duties, made him desirous of producing the like qualities in those under his command; and he proved himself the soldier's true friend in strictly enforcing discipline, in protecting the rights and promoting the claims of his veteran associates, and in administering to their personal comforts.

Such a leader was deeply and unanimously mourned by the faithful band to whom his actions while living had so frequently furnished the theme of praise. In the nave of St. Paul's Cathedral, a monument (by J. Bacon, junr.) has been erected to commemorate jointly the services and deaths of Craufurd and Mackinnon, who fell together. They were both North Britons, for which reason, we suppose, a Highlander is selected as an appropriate mourner over the tomb of the two gallant officers. The monument is tabular, and the inscription runs as follows:

Erected by the nation to Major-General Robert Craufurd, and Major-General Henry Mackinnon, who fell at Ciudad Rodrigo, January 18th, 1812.